GOD'S
Restoration Shop

GOD'S Restoration Shop

WHERE BROKEN PIECES BECOME MASTERPIECES

Keith McEntire

EQUIP PRESS

Colorado Springs

God's Restoration Shop, Where Broken Pieces Become Masterpieces
Copyright © 2022 Keith McEntire

All rights reserved. No part of this publication may be reproduced, distributed, or transmitted in any form or by any means, without prior written permission.

Scripture quotations marked (ESV) are taken from The ESV® Bible (The Holy Bible, English Standard Version®) copyright © 2001 by Crossway, a publishing ministry of Good News Publishers. ESV® Text Edition: 2011. The ESV® text has been reproduced in cooperation with and by permission of Good News Publishers.

Unauthorized reproduction of this publication is prohibited.
Used by permission. All rights reserved.

Scripture quotations marked (KJV) are taken from the King James Bible.
Accessed on Bible Gateway at www.BibleGateway.com.

Scripture quotations marked (NASB) are taken from the New American Standard Bible® (NASB), copyright © 1960, 1962, 1963, 1968, 1971, 1972, 1973, 1975, 1977, 1995 by The Lockman Foundation, www.Lockman.org. Used by permission.

Scripture quotations marked (NIV) are taken from the Holy Bible, New International Version. Copyright © 1973, 1978, 1984, 2011 by Biblica, Inc.® Used by permission. All rights reserved worldwide.

Scripture quotations marked (NKJV) are taken from the New King James Version®. Copyright © 1982 by Thomas Nelson, Inc. Used by permission. All rights reserved.

Scripture quotations marked (NLT) are taken from the Holy Bible, New Living Translation, copyright © 1996, 2004, 2015 by Tyndale House Foundation. Used by permission of Tyndale House Publishers, Inc., Carol Stream, Illinois 60188. All rights reserved.

Scripture quotations marked (NRSV) are taken from the New Revised Standard Version Bible, copyright © 1989 the Division of Christian Education of the National Scripture quotations taken from the Amplified® Bible (AMP), Copyright © 2015 by The Lockman Foundation Used by permission. www.Lockman.org

First Edition: 2022
God's Restoration Shop / Keith McEntire
Paperback ISBN: 978-1-951304-50-8
eBook ISBN: 978-1-951304-51-5

In Others' Words

Immerse yourself in this book! Keith makes it easy with short chapters and vivid writing. Here are deep truths for the mind. Warm thoughts for the heart. Courage for the discouraged. Best of all, restoration for the broken, the weary, the troubled, the anxious. These pages tell you where to find hope, no matter how hopeless you feel.

    Steve Sorensen
    Outdoor writer, field contributor to *Deer & Deer Hunting Magazine*, and popular sportsman's dinner speaker
    www.EverydayHunter.com

If "despairing, disoriented, all-done, dried-out, a little (to a lot) dead inside" describes you or someone you love, *God's Restoration Shop* will hydrate your hope and bring fresh wind and new perspective to the worn and weary places of your life. Through relatable stories, engaging humor, keen insight, practical application, and sound biblical teaching, Keith invites dry-boned valley dwellers to encounter the only One with a proven track record in restoring life and making all things new!

    Dr. Dwight Robertson, CEO of Forge
    International Speaker and Author of *You Are God's Plan A* and *Forged by Fire*
    www.ForgeForward.org

One of the best books of the year! It offers hope, biblical perspective, and divine wisdom to anyone who may find themselves in a space of unclarity and uncertainty. This book will reassure you that you're not alone in your journey of rediscovering God's timing, God's presence, and most of all, God's validation.

    Dr. Jeffrey Francis
    Foundations Counseling Center of Hampton Roads
    Virginia Beach, VA
    www.fcchr.org

God is in the restoration business! Keith shares God's desire and capability to work in our life situations to bring about His masterpiece work, which is restoring us to Himself, and restoring our self-worth. To read *God's Restoration Shop* is to find hope and help in seemingly hopeless and helpless circumstances. It's a ray of sunshine on a gray and bleak day.
    "Coach" Bill Carr
    Retired District Superintendent
    Church of the Nazarene

Countless people question their worth when circumstances seem hopeless. Keith comes alongside as a helper who has been there and reminds us we are valuable to the One who is bigger than our circumstances. He says, "Broken now doesn't mean broken forever." Seeking God's direction for your next step? Keith says, "Sometimes all He asks of us is to stay." Those are comfort-inducing words when we think we have to produce in order to be productive.

Keith uses Bible retelling to help us see practical applications and provides personal illustrations and coping skills for dark days. Keith's frankness is lightened with a fun sense of humor as he tackles a tough subject. *God's Restoration Shop* bolstered my faith and I know it will do the same for you.
    Sally Ferguson
    Author, *How to Plan a Women's Retreat* and *The Helper Series*
    www.sallyferguson.net

Sure to encourage anyone going through a season of doubt and brokenness. Keith helps us see how such times are actually the norm in the life of God's people, gives us hope that there's light at the end of the tunnel, and shows how to proceed through those difficult times in ways that result in unanticipated growth and purpose.
    TS John
    President, South Asia Access
    www.southasiaaccess.org

I thought it was average.
    Joe Schmo

A book for all who have, are, or will someday journey through a barren wilderness or dark night of the soul. Launched from the context of Ezekiel 37 in the Bible, McEntire invites us to travel with him on the road from dry bones and broken pieces to hope, worth, and purpose. His titles hook readers. He's imaginative and uses personal stories and illustrations that are relatable and seamlessly interwoven with the biblical narrative.

Old and New Testament heroes come to life not only at the height of their success, but in the depth of their failure. This is not only to be read but lived. It's not a warm and fuzzy read or self-help book but is filled with promise and hope. The Sovereign Lord is the active initiator and by grace, we are the active responders. It is *God's* Restoration Shop. He's the *Restorer;* we're the *broken pieces*. And the *Craftsman's* heart is that of transforming us into His *masterpieces*.

    Pastor Thom Daubenspeck
    Clymer, NY

Whether listening to Keith teach at a conference in Uganda, or absorbing his discernment shared with pastors gathered to pray in Jamestown, NY, I am invariably blessed and edified by what God has put into Keith's heart, mind, and mouth. This book is no exception. It's filled with fresh and welcome revelation to this septuagenarian. No doubt, anyone reading this will find themselves on these pages and be positively moved.

    Dr. Roy L. Miller
    Director, The Better Place
    Author, *My Gospel*
    www.TheBetterPlace.org

This is an excellent book. You will be challenged and encouraged. My biggest endorsement is not just for words on a page. This author is the real deal. Keith is a friend, and his life and years of experience are poured into this. You are not just reading a bunch of theories that someone wrote down. Rather, this book is written out of a genuine life that has seen the goodness of God. Enjoy the read and let God impact your life.

    Rick Rohlin
    President, International Sports Academy
    Russell, PA
    www.ISAsports.org

Who is this Keith guy anyway?
John and Jane Doe

Keith hasn't just given us some pointers on how to find restoration in the midst of brokenness but has allowed us to enter into his heart to see how that work is happening in his life. I've known Keith over twenty years, and one of the things I appreciate about him is his transparency. This book allows the reader to discover for themselves the reality of God's presence, who desires to bring us refreshment, especially when we're in a personal desert.

In a year when both of my parents died and I've been leading a congregation through a global pandemic, Keith's words reminded me of the hope Jesus brings regardless of the challenges we face. So grab a lemonade, imagine yourself on a beach with the soothing sound of waves lapping in the distance, and allow God's restoration to bring peace amid your storm.
Pastor Roy Ferguson
Busti Church of God
Jamestown, NY
www.busticog.org

God created us in His own image. When one loses that vision, and the purpose God created them for, they fall into the depths of hopelessness and despair. This incredible book that my friend has written is truly for anyone caught in such a quagmire. It brings hope, restoration, and renewal in unpretentious terms anyone can understand and embrace. This is a manual for those feeling hopeless and lost, and for those trying to help them. A much-needed, thought-provoking, and timely gift that hurting humanity needs today.
Dr. Sam Stevens
President, India Gospel League
www.iglworld.org

This book addresses that dreadful secret so many hide—the feeling of being a failure, disqualified, no longer useful to God. We find this difficult to talk about, and it eats at our soul, making us spiritually lifeless. How grateful I am for a book which speaks openly about this. It's refreshed me and given me hope.

Most significant for me was to see that my sense of failure and uselessness was not unique to myself, but something shared by the heroes of the Bible: Moses, Elijah, Peter. See how God in His compassion met them all—to restore them, affirm them, and breathe new life into their weary souls. For all who seek restoration and a breath of new life from God, this book will be a cherished blessing.

    Tim Kangas
    Church Planter in Cambodia
    OMF International
    www.omf.org

Keith, in this refreshing book, threads together examples of famous greats in the Bible who fell on hard times, to illustrate that dry seasons can be restored. Our experiences are not unique, and our restoration is not impossible. His wide-ranging examples make this book relevant to those longing for hope and encouragement in times of difficulty. A rich resource for pastors and readers going through valley experiences.

    Rev. Cosmos Mutowa
    Africa Regional Coordinator
    Nazarene Compassionate Ministries
    www.ncm.org

Dedication

It's my honor to dedicate this
to The Restorer—Jesus Christ!
You found me in the valley
and gently put me back together.
I'm forever grateful.
This book exists because You
met me at my dead-end,
and helped me rise again.
I know there are many more
You long to restore.
I humbly offer this as a tool
for Your use.

I also dedicate this
to my wife Melissa and daughter Rachel.
You consistently loved me when I was a hollow shell.
Your joy, encouragement, and life
sustained me until I could breathe again.
I'm forever grateful.
This book is only possible because of you.
I love you!

WELCOME TO GOD'S RESTORATION SHOP!

Where Broken Pieces Become Masterpieces

Glad you're here! Please make yourself at home!

A Note from Keith 1
Foreword 4
Introduction: *Moses* was Here?! 6
The Vision Behind the Book 11

PART 1: THE RESTORER *SPIES ON* BROKEN PIECES IN *UNDESIRABLE PLACES*. HE'S NOT DONE WITH THEM 13
   1: The Waste Place 15
   2: Valley Living (or Dying) 20
   3: Getting Whys 25
   4: The "Wait a While" Tree 29
   5: The Story of the Captain 33
   6: (Gasp!) 35
   7: Desperados 38
   8: Graveyard Walker 42
   9: The Q&A 46

PART 2: THE RESTORER *SPROUTS HOPE* IN BROKEN PIECES WHO FEEL *UNRAVELED* 49
   10: There's Good News and Bad News 51
   11: I Fly Solo 54
   12: Death Threat 57
   13: Five More Minutes 61
   14: Everyone Needs a White Bench 63
   15: I Have My Sources 68

PART 3: THE RESTORER *SPEAKS GREATNESS* OVER BROKEN PIECES WHO FEEL *UNWORTHY*. 73
- 16: Just Look at You! 75
- 17: The (Embellished) Autobiography of Moses 78
- 18: Detour - Next 40 Years 81
- 19: Who Am I? (And Other Gnawing Questions) 84
- 20: Back-Country Wisdom 87
- 21: The Story of G. Lee the First 90
- 22: Bible Study at the Devil's House 92
- 23: God Is Not Made in Our Image 96
- 24: My Dad, the Abolitionist 101
- 25: Hi, I'm Your Image Consultant 105

PART 4: THE RESTORER *SPENDS TIME* PUTTING BROKEN PIECES TOGETHER. HIS CRAFTSMANSHIP IS *UNPARALLELED AND UNCOMPROMISING*. *111*
- 26: Shoddy Work Sucks 113
- 27: My, What Strong Sinews You Have! 117

PART 5: THE RESTORER *SPURS PURPOSES* IN BROKEN PIECES WHO FEEL *UNQUALIFIED*. **123**
- 28: El Diablo vs. Quickdraw Pete - The Throwdown 125
- 29: El Diablo vs. Quickdraw Pete - The Showdown 129
- 30: Collecting Firewood 133
- 31: Breakfast on the Beach 137
- 32: Good Morning, Mr. Failure! 140
- 33: Jesus' Death Wish 145
- 34: Grab *That* 148
- 35: Defying Gravity 153
- 36: Bad Credit? No Problem! 156
- 37: What Was This Chapter About? I Forgot 160
- 38: Fruitless in a Fruitful Land 164
- 39: The Story of J. Mark, Author 169

PART 6: THE RESTORER *SPREADS GRACE* OVER BROKEN PIECES WHO FEEL *UNCLEAN* OR *UNACCEPTABLE*. **175**
- 40: One Great Big Dysfunctional Family 177
- 41: A Big Fat "F" 181
- 42: Where are You Going on Your Guilt Trip? 185
- 43: I Hear Footsteps Approaching 189
- 44: The Sting Means It's Working 193

45: Clothes by Jehovah......197
46: All Hail the Dirtfighter!......201
47: Graces Supremas......205

PART 7: THE RESTORER *SPARKS LIFE* IN BROKEN PIECES WHO FEEL *UNINFLATED* OR *UNSPIRITUAL*.......211
    48: Well, Light a Match and Call Me a Doldrum......213
    49: Highly Combustible......217
    50: God's Got Fresh Breath......220
    51: *Who's* Moving In?......224
    52: The "Son of Thunder" Saga
        Episode 1 - #1......227
    53: The "Son of Thunder" Saga
        Episode 2 - He Didn't Smell Like Us......229
    54: The "Son of Thunder" Saga
        Episode 3 - Pyromaniacs for Jesus......235
    55: The "Son of Thunder" Saga
        Episode 4 - Feelin' the Love......237
    56: The Parable of the Pallet......242

PART 8: THE RESTORER *SPRINGS FAITH* UNDER BROKEN PIECES ONCE *UNABLE* TO STAND......243
    57: Blueprints, Part 1 - Untangling Fish......245
    58: Blueprints, Part 2 - Well Done Stakes......248
    59: Blueprints, Part 3 - It'll Make a Mime Talk......252
    60: Blueprints, Part 4 - Hard Rock......254

PART 9: THE RESTORER *SPEARHEADS KINGDOM MOVEMENTS* THROUGH ONCE-BROKEN PIECES NOW MADE *USEFUL*......257
    61: Special Forces......259
    62: The Shepherd Wears Flannel......262
    63: Marching Orders......266

PART 10: THE RESTORER *SPECIALIZES IN REWARDING* BROKEN PIECES WHO ENTRUSTED THEMSELVES TO HIM *UNASHAMEDLY*......269
    64: Bullheaded Blessings......271
    65: Restored to Greater......274
    66: Saving the Best for Last......278

BONUS FEATURES **281**
    BIBLICAL PROPORTIONS 283
    HOPE'S LIST 285
    THE FATHER'S BLESSING 286
    HIS-STORY LESSON 288
    EXPERIENCES! 291

A Note from Keith

I boldly announced, "I'm going to right a book!" Imagine my amused horror after realizing I wrote *the wrong write!* A great start into the world of authorship. Actually, plenty of *righting* has occurred after *writing*! Early on, a friend asked how much of the book's content I already gathered. I estimated 85%—and overshot by about 75%! It's been a grander process than assumed since writing that first paragraph, but I'm excited to share this message with *you*. It's embedded deep in my soul.

I've cherished this assignment. It's been a walk with God, of regularly looking up for wisdom, help, and stamina. I wish I could do this every day. It's made many settings extra special, especially those involving picnic tables amid God's creation. I've met great people. I've typed through tears because a lot of this is raw. I've raised my hands in thanksgiving because a lot of this is powerful. I'm humbled to simply be God's messenger. Many pages challenge me, resembling aspiration more than expertise.

I've occasionally loathed this assignment. It's taxed me and affected my family. I've wanted to never look at it again. I've been stuck too many times to count, but God has enabled me to endure, reminding me someone needs The Restorer. Now I have too many answered prayers to count! This wouldn't exist without praying, supportive friends. It has *slowly* come together. It's sat dormant for months while God focused on the writer. It's suffered extensive dismantling and been painstakingly reworked, I'm confident better than before. As such, it serves a living example of the message it tells.

It's not created for its own glory. God meant it for you. You are its purpose. He is its grand subject.

This Book, That Book

I was born near a Bible. I began reading it in third grade. By sixth grade, I read the last word. The next day I opened to *Genesis* and started over. Sometimes it's felt like a bunch of words or religious duty, but many times it's refreshed my soul and brightened my darkness. I've discovered bedrock truth, heartfelt prayers, stirring stories, timeless wisdom, and a hundred other blessings. The Bible has been a constant companion in the writing of *God's Restoration Shop* and has seeped into its pages. It's given me something to say. *This* book wouldn't exist without *that* book.

If you're unfamiliar with the Bible, *please* don't consider yourself disqualified or alienated, and *please* don't stop reading this book for that reason. I've diligently tried to incorporate it in a way anyone will find relatable. If these pages introduce you to the Bible, I hope you find it intriguing, inspiring, and insightful. Maybe you'll even fall in love with it. If these pages reacquaint you, I hope you enjoy catching up. If you're already familiar with the Bible, I hope you find something to glean. If any of this happens, I'll consider the years spent on these words a success. New to the Bible? Or interested in my use of it? Read "Biblical Proportions" in the *Bonus Features*.

Chapter Features

I'll never know why God has allowed me to meet so many great people across the globe. In my desire to honor some, each chapter is dedicated to an individual, group, or organization, found in a footnote at the last word of each chapter.[1]

Chapters also include a six-fold "breather" for additional thought, prayer, or action:

Point. Related to the main points.

Ponder. For further study or reflection.

Prayer. Chat with God.

Practical. *Do* something.

Playlist. Music is powerful. These selections helped me or others along the way. You likely won't love them all, but you might discover one you can't live without! If the genre isn't your style, simply read the lyrics, or play another song that comes to mind. These range from the '70s (1870s!) to 2021. I smile at the thought of someone reading this book decades from now, saying, "Listen to these *oldies!*"

Pocket. *Your* biggest takeaway. This will be blank.

This format makes the book versatile. Think of these as frequent rest areas along a highway. Stop when you need to; keep going when you don't. Read a chapter or two a day like a devotional. Use as an individual or group study guide. Sometimes I read a book straight through, "dot" the margin next to meaningful points (in pencil), then reread and ponder. Adopt or adapt for *your* benefit.

---

[1] If your name isn't found, maybe you should've been nicer to me! (Just kidding, of course!)

Want pictures? www.keithmc.org offers pictures and videos coinciding with the book's chapters! Use as a companion.

High Hopes

I hope this book facilitates encounters with the God of restoration. I hope it's an oasis for weary wilderness wanderers to catch their breath at the end of another rough day. I hope it's a tree whose trunk gives a place to lean and whose branches provide shade. I use stories and lessons and attempt occasional humor. Stay as long as you want; restoration is sometimes quick, sometimes it's a long process.[2]

While the book's bulls-eye target is for broken people in bewildering seasons, it's not confined to such. If you've wrestled with worth, purpose, or guilt, you'll relate. Maybe you don't need a Restorer, but a Savior, Shepherd, Transformer, Encourager, Healer, Cleanser, Equipper. God is unlimited! He can meet *you* in these pages, or help you encourage a struggling loved one. Whenever you experience a wilderness season, know you're always welcome back.

Dear friend, I've prayed often for you. I hope these pages entertain. I hope a story hits close to home. I hope a point makes you think. I'll be disappointed if at some point you don't chuckle.

Even more, I hope these pages encourage. I hope God's presence hits close to home. I hope a point makes you free. I'll be disappointed if at some point you don't close the book and pray.

Thank you for coming to *God's Restoration Shop*!

- Keith

---

[2] As you read, record special moments in "Experiences!" in *Bonus Features*!

Foreword

Keith and I have known each other over 20 years, and I've enjoyed watching him grow with God. We first met as colleagues in western New York while navigating the joys and challenges of pastoring small churches. We laughed frequently—some might have said too much—but our occasions of fellowship provided mutual moments of refreshment and renewal.

In my present position as chaplain with *Operation Heal Our Patriots*, a ministry of Samaritan's Purse, I deal extensively with injured veterans. When meeting veteran couples for the first time, I commonly ask their credentials. They immediately give information about rank, medals, or degrees. I quickly explain that I'm inquiring about their *God-given* credentials. I want to know what experiences God has allowed in their lives which could be used to bring about change in the life of someone else. Suddenly, injuries are viewed through a different lens and recognized as potential assets as individuals seek answers to the "Why?" questions.

God has given me the privilege in all my professions—funeral director, professor, pastor, chaplain—to walk alongside broken lives. I've encountered broken people in all stages of life who have expressed the desire to be made whole. So many are searching for meaning and purpose. The book you hold is an excellent place to start for anyone seeking such answers. Readers will find that God has given Keith many valuable "credentials." Through his application of God's Word and wide range of life experiences, Keith masterfully walks through God's plan for all of us to be made whole for our good and for use in His ultimate purpose.

This is not to be read in a couple of evenings. Each morsel should be taken in slowly to allow God to challenge and encourage you. Keith's vulnerability is refreshing, and alongside the truth of the Bible, a new light emerges on one's own past—you'll discover true worth and value there. The six-fold format at the end of each chapter provides an opportunity to spend time with God and discover new perspectives concerning how special God has made you.

I wish I could ask each one, "What are *your* credentials?" before you begin page one of this excellent text, so that after you have completed it, I could see how your answers have changed. My prayer is that you find a sense of renewed hope and spiritual growth as you savor each encouraging and challenging thought. May God bless you immensely on your journey to wholeness in Him!

> Patrick Fleming
> Titles in order of importance: Child of God, Husband, Father, Grandpa, Brother, Friend, Pastor, and Chaplain.
> *Operation Heal Our Patriots*
> *samaritanspurse.org*

Introduction:
Moses was Here?!

I don't even know where to go.
I hate this!
Get in, get out.

This was a sampling of the chatter in my head while consulting the directory on the wall. I hoped to find my destination without conversation.

Maybe no one is here morphed from wishful thinking to honest prayer as I ascended the stairs to the second floor. No such luck. Noisy chitchat consumed the atmosphere behind the tall door on the right. Names spoken without emotion beckoned the packed audience. My dread intensified.

I hope nobody knows me.

The room's chaos resembled my inner strife. I located a chair furthest from anyone and hung my head. Self-talk raged like wildfire.

Don't make eye contact.
What a failure.
Not where I thought I'd be at forty.
Bet all my high school classmates are doing better than me.

I sat alone in the crowded health department, hoping my family qualified for insurance. I soon humbly admitted to being unemployed and living at my mom's house. The rep happily enrolled us. Good thing. Two weeks later, my ankle broke from a volleyball injury.

Can anything else go wrong?
I guess life isn't meant to include fun.

I increasingly felt broken beyond repair. I needed someone to put me back together.

A Most Unusual Scene

The Bible tells a dramatic story about human bones scattered across a valley floor. They represented people in deep despair, living hopeless, dried-out lives, which they despised. Physically alive but inwardly dead, they hated their "place" in life, and their address. Their conversations, and the self-talk in the barren confines of their minds, echoed, "We have become old, dry bones—all hope is gone" (Ezekiel 37:11).

That described me. The inside of me died somewhere along the way, relegating me to a hollow shell. The long-range forecast showed little hope. As I write, the once-living flames in the fireplace have dwindled to ash and coals. Within a minute, it rekindled. What about the cold, ashen fireplace whose fire disappeared months or years ago? Can it burn again? God asked something similar: "Can these bones become living people again" (Ezekiel 37:3)?

For you who carry the dead weight of a deadened soul, and for you who are painfully watching a loved one internally "die," hear God's message to the dry bones: "Look, I am going to put breath into you and make you live again" (Ezekiel 37:5)! May these fourteen words saturate desert souls and spark embers of hope. God can make you or your loved one live again! He has done it countless times; many have been this way before. **He still walks the valley where the bones are dry.**

I know. Some of those dry bones were mine.

The Guestbook

Guestbooks instigate my curiosity. *Who's been here? What did they say?* One of my favorites greets diners in a very ordinary restaurant far off the beaten trail in West Virginia. Signatures and hometowns written with pride hail from Texas to Michigan. It's surreal to read page after page and realize—all these people from all these places stood in *this exact spot*. It made me feel connected.

Millions throughout the centuries have visited the valley of dry bones. Some are there now. If there was a guestbook, it would record dates from every era and places from every corner of the globe. Names of the famous and acclaimed take their place with the ordinary and unknown. Some are likely from your family and hometown. You'd be surprised who has perused these waste places! Many "greats" came here. Ironically, many became great *because* they came here.

Let's meet some.

Moses. His name exudes *greatness*. He garnered rockstar status as a young man in that time's foremost empire. One historian described him as "powerful in both speech and action" (Acts 7:22). Moses possessed a distinguished education and a divine calling. No future looked brighter, until one choice shattered his world, catapulting him into an extensive season of difficulty and mediocrity. His once-glorious life evaporated in a desert.

Was powerful. A testament of the past, but not the present. Moses *used to be* strong, influential, articulate. Now, isolated from anything significant, he wastes his life at a monotonous, entry-level job. He's babysitting sheep when he should be leading a nation. He's the ultimate example of wasted potential, and time no longer ticks in his favor. Sound familiar? Maybe not the sheep part, but the wasted-potential part? The used-to-be part? The blown-off-course part? The *I thought I'd be better than this by now* part?

God wasn't done with Moses, never forgot where he lived or worked, nor His[3] purposes for him. One day God met the old man at a burning bush in the back of a desert. When it looked like his final chapter, God's best chapters lay ahead. **What if Moses never encountered The Restorer?** He gained a nation's independence, authored books, walked through a seabed, mentored leaders, and spent forty days face-to-face with God!

Elijah. His name exudes *faith*. This fearless man of God boldly preached and performed miracles. At a national gathering, Elijah prayed, "O LORD…prove today that you are God. Answer me so these people will know that You are God and that You have brought them back to Yourself" (1 Kings 18:36-37). The story highlights one of the greatest recorded answers to prayer. That evening, he prayed for rain to end a three-year drought, and the *Amen* culminated with a cloudburst.

A few days later he prayed to die.

Prayers often change in the wilderness. Have you hit bottom? Lost all fight? Perhaps your work or ministry took more than you had, and you secretly wish things would end.

I'm not strong enough for this.

What good am I doing anyway?

Oxygen fills your lungs, but your soul remains empty. Elijah became a knotted mess of anxiety and fear. On the heels of life-is-good experiences, he's reduced to a shell. Tired out, bummed out, burned out, he wants to tap out and walk out. Some label him severely depressed, others suicidal. But something unexpected happened. Something more powerful than an earthquake or tornado.

The Almighty whispered.

There's nothing like the voice of God to restore and revive a weary wanderer. Perfectly chosen words seeped like fresh oil into Elijah's corroded heart, causing it to beat again. Stirred to the core, he rises with a new spring in his step and new purpose in his veins. **What if Elijah**

---

3   Capitalized pronouns at the middle or end of a sentence refer to God/Jesus.

never encountered The Restorer? He went on to help three young men discover their God-ordained destinies. Two became kings and the other his protégé. When God wanted to confront evil kings and queens, Elijah remained a chosen spokesman. **God's greats are rarely giants who never fell, but common people made stronger in the rising.**

Peter. His name exudes *all-in*! He's the kind who makes you feel insignificant. Sure, he can be brash and thoughtless, but who can fault his faith as he steps onto tumultuous waters? Or his discerning spirit as he confidently professes Jesus as the Messiah? Or his vow to die for Christ?[4] He was the hero, the super-saint, better than everyone. When others left because it got hard, Peter remained in it to win it. He had the Most Valuable Disciple trophy all but clinched. "Even if everyone else fails, You can count on me, Jesus!"

It's easy to talk large in the locker room. On game day he struck out by a nobody and a couple girls. He wasn't as strong or loyal as assumed. When Jesus looked his way, Peter was too ashamed to look back. He crumbled. Let Jesus down. Let himself down. *Just like everybody else.* His mind surely raced with lines like:

I'm disqualified.

There's no place in God's kingdom for losers like me.

Jesus isn't deterred by self-proclaimed disqualifications, for His calling doesn't originate or terminate by us. Instead, He sought Peter. A robust conversation became a means of restoration, signaling the past had passed and a new dawn had begun. **What if Peter never encountered The Restorer?** He would've missed his best days! Preaching to thousands, working miracles, providing irreplaceable leadership to the early church movement. His impact is still reaching around the world. Many never recover from humiliating failure, but many rise into a new day.

Their stories are unique, but each endured a wilderness and rose again. What about you? You might be face down in the muck. Hope *seems* lost. Purpose sounds like fantasy. Worthlessness has set in. Regardless of these and a hundred other burdens, I ask: **What if *you* are never restored?** Your reaction may echo what mine would have been. *So? Big deal.*

But what if it *is* a big deal?

What if your restoration affects not only your own soul, but your

---

4   *Christ:* a title, referring to the one Savior whom God promised to send—Jesus!

family? What if it affects your community, friends, church, work, the next generation, a nation, the kingdom, eternity? While the *extent* is unknown, the *reality* of impact is certain. I began with these stories to illustrate that dry seasons are common. You are not alone; your experience is not wildly unusual, and your restoration is not impossible. Restoration has far greater potential than you can see right now. It's a critical matter—one of life and death.

The significance of these three restorations is epic. When you consider how much would have been left undone if they remained undone, the loss is staggering. **The restoration of broken people is imperative—crucial—to the things God wants to do around the world.** We've spoken about three. What about the multitudes in similar desert places?[5]

> **Point:** Can you identify with:
> —Moses wasting away in mediocrity; not where he "should be" in life?
> —Elijah burned out, fearful, depressed, hopeless?
> —Peter disqualified, defeated by sin or failure?
> Your best chapters may lie ahead!
> **Ponder:** Read about Moses: Exodus 1-4; Acts 7:17-38; Hebrews 11:23-27.
> Read about Elijah: 1 Kings 17-19.
> Read about Peter's restoration: John 21.
> **Prayer:** God said, "I am going to put breath into you and make you live again." Repeat several times. When ready, respond back.
> **Practical:** Note your internal chatter and prayers lately.
> **Playlist:** *Haven't Seen it Yet* by Danny Gokey
> *Something Beautiful* by Gaither Vocal Band
> **Pocket:** (What will you take with you? Most helpful?)

---

5   Dedicated to Melissa McEntire, my favorite human, my steady rock, the one I'm honored to do life with. Hopefully, other readers will "want to run around the block and eat cake!"

The Vision Behind the Book

2600 years ago God gave a man named Ezekiel a message for a specific group of people. An enemy obliterated their nation and killed scores of their countrymen, then trafficked them 500 miles away. They couldn't descend lower. Though broken beyond repair, God wanted them to know He wasn't done. He would put them and their nation back together![6]

> *The LORD took hold of me, and I was carried away by the Spirit of the LORD to a valley filled with bones. He led me all around among the bones that covered the valley floor. They were scattered everywhere across the ground and were completely dried out. Then he asked me, "Can these bones become living people again?"*
>
> *"O Sovereign LORD," I replied, "you alone know the answer to that."*
>
> *Then he said to me, "Speak a prophetic message to these bones and say, 'Dry bones, listen to the word of the LORD! This is what the Sovereign LORD says: Look! I am going to put breath into you and make you live again! I will put flesh and muscles on you and cover you with skin. I will put breath into you, and you will come to life. Then you will know that I am the LORD.'"*
>
> *So I spoke this message, just as he told me. Suddenly as I spoke, there was a rattling noise all across the valley. The bones of each body came together and attached themselves as complete skeletons. Then as I watched, muscles and flesh formed over the bones. Then skin formed to cover their bodies, but they still had no breath in them.*
>
> *Then he said to me, "Speak a prophetic message to the winds. Speak a prophetic message and say, 'This is what the Sovereign LORD says: Come, O breath, from the four winds! Breathe into these dead bodies so they may live again.'"*

---

6   Check out "His-Story Lesson" in *Bonus Features* for a short historical account.

> *So I spoke the message as he commanded me, and breath came into their bodies. They all came to life and stood up on their feet—a great army.*
>
> *Then he said to me, "These bones represent the people of Israel. They are saying, 'We have become old, dry bones—all hope is gone. Our nation is finished.' Therefore, prophesy to them and say, 'This is what the Sovereign LORD says: O my people, I will open your graves of exile and cause you to rise again. Then I will bring you back to the land of Israel. When this happens, O my people, you will know that I am the LORD.*
>
> *I will put my Spirit in you, and you will live again and return home to your own land. Then you will know that I, the LORD, have spoken, and I have done what I said. Yes, the LORD has spoken!'"*
>
> ~ ***EZEKIEL 37:1-14***

This remarkable message of hope serves as the basis for this book.

But this isn't old history. God is still restoring broken lives today!

PART 1:
The Restorer *spies on* broken pieces in *undesirable places.* He's not done with them.

> *He led me all around among the bones that covered the valley floor. (Ezekiel 37:2).*

Sometimes we experience
a dark season of life
— a bewildering state of the soul—
characterized by hardship, trial, or loss.

This season often:
—damages our "self,"
making us feel unworthy.

—devastates our sense of significance,
making us feel unqualified.

—disgraces our soul,
making us feel unclean.

—settles despair over our situation,
making us feel utterly hopeless.

Spying sounds mean or inappropriate,
but The Restorer is ever looking for broken pieces,
desiring to put them back together!

1: The Waste Place

> ...*to **a valley** filled with bones (Ezekiel 37:1).*

It was the quintessential spring evening as my friend Keith and I neared our destination—a charming little town in southern West Virginia. The hills exclaimed color, the sun still bright and warm. With spirit soaring, I confidently threw the bait, "Know what we should do?"

"What's that?"

"Let's get settled into the cabin, then ride into town for a steak dinner!"

Easy sell. What a perfect way to start our four-wheeling expedition. Within minutes, we walked past vintage gas pumps to the small general store.

"Can I help y'all?" the lady asked in her southern drawl.

"Good evening. We're staying in one of your cabins."

"Cabins? We ain't got no cabins!"

"Ummm. What do you mean you don't have cabins?"

Our mood dampened when she asked the name of our lodging. "Paradise" was in the over-worded title.

She barked, "Paradise! You're headed *straight to hell!*" Apparently, she didn't think highly of that area or lodging! The confirming groans of circling customers red-flushed my face and sent my stomach into a tailspin. Somehow I booked with Paradise, or "hell," but printed directions to this place. They estimated two hours to get there and offered some muddled directions involving down-home landmarks.

There goes our steak dinner.

We opted for a second opinion from our GPS. The route looked like a two-year-old's maiden voyage with a marker and estimated one hour, forty-seven minutes. *That can't be right.* I stowed the device next to the 4wd shifter. Some locals offered, "We could take you there by trails, but have no idea how to get there by road. Sorry! Good luck!" We finally pieced together some directions and headed out, looking for a bizarre town name and a long bridge. With little effort, we found our road, pleasantly surprised by its asphalt base. The owner of our lodge instructed us to stay straight until reaching an intersection with a telephone pole.

Asphalt gave way to dirt as quickly as daylight conceded to dusk. Moments later, we approached a three-pronged fork in the road. The sharp left was easily eliminated. The curve to the right looked like the main road. Straight ahead looked narrow and foreboding. I pointed my headlights at some weathered signs and got out for a closer look when a truck approached. "Where ya headin'?" came the friendly concern of the ol' Mountaineer. I gave him the name and he told us to go straight to Barrittstown, and something about a small bridge and bearing to the right. Then his tone sobered. "Oh…and…be careful." With that, he sped away.

My senses flared. *What's that supposed to mean?*

We proceeded down the primitive, dark grade, determined to find the intersection with a telephone pole. The lonesome road turned blindly to the left around hilly terrain, straightened briefly, then swept wide to the right around a gully. Another blind left curve. Wide right. Now left. Sharp right this time. The curves clinging to the mountainside fixed my speed at twenty mph, making us question if we were repeating the same road every two minutes. We saw no lights, houses, trucks, or signs. The darkness made us weary. The desolation made us slightly insane. This continued for an hour.

The mood felt serious until Keith remarked, "I'm waiting to see knuckle-fisted children crossing the road on all fours!" I had no idea what that meant, but we shared a good hearty laugh. Without admitting it, I was thankful I wasn't alone. His comment proved madness was gaining dominion over our unstimulated, exhausted minds. Then, in the distance—a light! That little illumination made its way into our souls and reignited hope. Then it was gone. Eventually it reappeared, and we faced a decision. One road went up to the left, while another veered downward toward the right. Drawn by the little light, we chose the right and soon crossed a little bridge. *That must be the bridge!*

We passed three homes and started climbing a hill that made my tires seek all the traction they could find. The narrowing route soon became an ominous bowl of mud soup. We were on a logging trail with no way to turn around. Our bloodshot eyes stared at the impasse. Would we ever find paradise? Keith tried guiding me backward, but we gave up after twenty minutes. We unhooked the trailer and swung it around, which surprisingly went easier than expected.

I backed the truck a quarter mile, turned around, then reversed to my courageous friend in the darkness. Once loaded, we descended the hill, passed the houses, crossed the little bridge, and rejoined the "main" road. Good riddance, deceitful light. Back to blind left-turns and endless right curves. Eventually, we beheld a strange cause of hope: a telephone pole! Hadn't seen one in years! Then a house, a community building, a bridge, the road to the right, and soon our cabin. It didn't resemble the biblical imagery of paradise, but we were glad to be there—*three hours* after the gas station with no cabins.

Sunshine poured through the forested hills as a new day greeted our steak-deprived stomachs. Finding a quaint little restaurant, the diners asked where we were from and which way we came. They couldn't believe we pulled a trailer up Crumpler Road at night. During our conversation we learned *Barrittstown* was really *Beartown!* The old guy added a syllable. Our eyes opened wide and Keith volunteered some news: while waiting in the dark, a crashing sound crossed the trail and down the other side, then came back up but veered in a different direction. Most likely a bear.

Oh...and...be careful!

Wild and Wonderful!

The setting of Ezekiel's vision was a barren, expansive *valley*. I employ several synonyms throughout the book—wilderness, waste place, wasteland, desert, dry spell, dry season, dark night, winter. It's also known as a funk or pit. *Wild and Wonderful* is West Virginia's famous claim. My experience certainly included both! What about a motto for life's valleys and wildernesses? *Monotonous and Mediocre? Wearying and Wasteful?* Moses dubbed it *Great and Terrifying* (Deuteronomy 1:19). The Merriam-Webster dictionary defines *wilderness:*
- "an empty or pathless area"
- "characterized by bewildering vastness, perilousness"
- "a state of neglect, powerlessness or disfavor"

The Bible describes it as a lonely, dangerous, or abandoned place, where demoniacs or bandits loiter, where people of faith wander. It figuratively refers to a bewildering state of the soul or trying season of life. **Such seasons often appear to be a waste of time, waste of space, and a waste of life.** Take Noah for example. After the floodwaters receded and the ark rested, they were eager to disembark the floating zoo that served as home for nearly a year. Yet they had to stay two more *months*! Would Noah emerge anyway, or trust God's timing? God knew it wasn't dry enough. The "wasted" time waiting kept them from having to rescue massive land animals stuck in mud. It would have jeopardized the lives of humans and creatures.

Ironically, the wilderness can also be a good place—of refuge, pause, or even ministry. "For Jesus, the 'place without inhabitants' is one where nothing separates Him from God and which He, therefore, seeks when he wants to escape the crowds or when He tries to find a place of quiet for His disciples."[7] God sometimes implements it as a venue to re-engage wandering people, "I will win her back once again. I will lead her *into the desert* and speak tenderly to her *there*." (Hosea 2:14 italics mine).

Desert Starts With "D"

I share my West Virginia story because it describes some typical "feels" of the valley:
- **Dangerous**. Uncharted, inhospitable, fearsome.
- **Dark**. Hard to see.
- **Disorienting**. Uncertainty, loneliness. Directions offer little help.
- **Discouraging**. Monotonous. Every road feels like a dead-end.
- **Disappointing**. It's not meant to be this way. You didn't sign up for *this*.
- **Despairing**. Increasing apathy. Giving up feels logical.
- **Draining**. Weariness. Even small things look daunting.

This story includes lessons too!
- **Laugh!** When it felt like a breaking point, humor lightened the mood. It was a welcome aspect of coping. My personality bends toward melancholy, so this is unnatural for me. Intentionally seek laughter and lightness. If laughter is medicine, find some good "humor doctors." I consult Tim Hawkins, Ken Davis, and Matt Fore, who send my meds via video, radio, or email. Some media can lighten a heavy mood; just be discerning and watch in moderation.
- **Don't go alone.** I can't imagine doing that solo. Contact a friend, pastor, organization, or counselor. Find a Christian forum or online group. Get on *somebody's* radar.
- **God is writing a story**—*even here*, which may inspire others.
- **A device for guidance** sat next to me, but I never consulted it again, even though I'd never been this way before. Truthfully, I forgot about it. I relied on my understanding, any old sign, and anyone's advice. Some instruments are available to you, especially the Bible.[8]

---

7 *Theological Dictionary of the New Testament, Vol. II*. Gerhard Kittel. Wm. B. Eerdmans. 1974. (657)

8 Dedication: Keith Campbell and Todd Crocker. Always an adventure with y'all!

Point: What motto would you use for "the valley"? Any "D"s resonate?
Ponder Noah's story (Genesis 6-8).
Can you identify with wasted time, space, or life? What if it's *not* a waste?
Prayer: Throw your "D"s on God (I Peter 5:7). He's tough.
Practical: Search "Wilderness of Judah" to see where David wrote Psalm 63 (one of my "valley lifelines"). What's your favorite Psalm in the Bible? With 150 flavors, there's one for every occasion!
Practice one of the lessons.
Playlist: *The Story I'll Tell* by Maverick City
Pocket:

2: Valley Living (or Dying)

> *I have faced **dangers...in the deserts** (2 Corinthians 11:26).*

I knelt bedside and prayed for the unnamed masses of God's people struggling in wilderness valleys. My heart agonized during this short but intense time. Warm tears fell as my stomach heaved with gut-wrenching heaviness. The dangers of the desert are all too real, and I thought of God's precious ones being beat down by life, perhaps to rise no more. "Nooo!" I groaned, "what if they don't make it?" The desert blinds, breaks, kills. I didn't pray for anyone specific. Perhaps my prayer was for you. Two realities fueled my prayer:

The desert is dangerous.
The Lord intently watches those in the desert.

The book of Isaiah mentions some desert dangers, "They travel through the wilderness, a place of lionesses and lions, a place where vipers and poisonous snakes live" (Isaiah 30:6). These creatures caricature our great adversary, the devil—a lion targeting his victim, a viper poised to strike. Both excel at surprise and possess tools to kill. **The lion intimidates.** "Stay alert! Watch out for your great enemy, the devil. He prowls around like a roaring lion, looking for someone to devour" (1 Peter 5:8-9). **The serpent tricks.** "I'm afraid that exactly as the Snake seduced Eve with his smooth patter, you are being lured away..." (2 Corinthians 11:3 MSG). The lion boldly roars in your face, freezing your heart in fear. The snake whispers smoothly in your ear, deceiving with every carefully selected word. The lion is a formidable foe. The constrictor masquerades as a friend. (Metaphorically. I've yet to bond with a snake.)

Jungle Friends and Enemies

In Kipling's classic *The Jungle Book*,[9] young Mowgli is raised by wolves, but because of imminent danger, must relocate to the man-village. He faces many perils during the arduous trek—falling trees, trampling elephants, pesky monkeys, and King Louie, the orangutan who

---

9   *The Jungle Book*. Rudyard Kipling. Macmillan. 1894.

desperately wants Mowgli's secret. But the biggest threat is Shere-Khan, the tiger whose roar dispenses fear into everyone. He crouches in the grass, waiting for Mowgli, who narrowly escapes with the help of friends.

But something pivotal happens in Mowgli after a season of despair. He learns the big cat has a hidden fear—*man's red fire*. This knowledge transforms the boy from defenseless prey to bold action. Though Mowgli proved no match for the muscular titan, Shere-Khan was no match for what the man-cub possessed. Fire made him stronger. When Mowgli tied a flaming stick to the tiger's tail, his panicked flight aroused a jungle celebration like no other. We may be no match for our enemy, but he can't compete with The One whose eyes blaze with heavenly fire, who lives in us. Every enemy is terrified of Jesus, the triumphant Lion![10]

Something else scared the tiger—Mowgli growing up. That's why he wanted to terminate him before he got older, wiser, stronger. **The enemy is afraid of God's children growing up.** You are not defenseless. You possess great weapons. May a holy shot of God's fire rise inside us and grow us up. "Greater is He who is in us than he who is in the world" (I John 4:4). We belong to Jesus, from whom the enemy flees in terror!

Don't forget about Kaa, the sssslithering sssnake sssseeking to lure Mowgli to do one little thing—look him in the eye. The lad knows it's a trick, but Kaa's persistence wears him down. In a moment of weakness, the boy looks into the snake's hypnotic eyes. Bedazzled, a great succumbing intoxicates him with the mental venom of *whatever happens is fine, why fight?* He puts himself at the mercy of a merciless one hoping to devour him. **That's desert life—wears you down, wears you out, dismantles your defenses.** The wilderness is dangerous, and the serpent would love for you to see the way he sees, indulge his whispers, and curl up in his ever-tightening grip. That's not a hug, my friend, that's a stranglehold.

Jesus warned, "Look out! Satan has asked to sift you like wheat" (Luke 22:31 HCSB). While the dangers are real, we are given weapons for victory. God's presence is foremost.

> *Those who live in the shelter of the Most High will find rest in the shadow of the Almighty. You will trample upon lions and cobras; you will crush fierce lions and*

---

10 Revelation 5:5; 19:12.

> serpents under your feet! The LORD says, "I will rescue those who love me. I will protect those who trust in my name. When they call on me, I will answer; I will be with them in trouble. I will rescue and honor them. I will reward them with a long life and give them my salvation" (Psalm 91:1, 13-16).

Learning to Live

In 2014 we moved to Uganda, where Melissa taught first grade. Though not our first trip to Africa, this one didn't include return tickets. We were flying over the Atlantic when that reality jolted my slumber. I stared ahead, frozen. *What have we done? Are we ready for this?* Thankfully, we had a strong support group on the ground and back home. Most expats told us the same thing—expect two to six months before you feel you can make it.

So reassuring.

One day I met a missionary named Jeff at The Bean Café, a quaint shop that served a great chicken salad sandwich under a pleasant canopy. I gleaned a lot, but what I remember most was, "Keith, before you do anything in Africa, you have to learn how to live here." Missionaries dream of changing people and communities. They expect challenges with finances and food. But one crucial, underestimated element is learning to live in a land vastly different from home. We literally re-learned groceries and getting around; things done with ease now caused tremendous frustration and fatigue.

Another advised, "Don't hit the ground running. Hit the ground sitting!" Learn how life works. Adapt. Reflect. You're here for the long haul. We feel the urgency to do something great, yet if we don't learn to survive, the results could be dampened, even deadly. And all potential productivity forfeited. You may be living in a figurative wasteland. It's a foreign place that needs to be taken seriously. Learn how to live here. **Jesus not only battled Satan's insidious temptations in the wilderness, He faced the wilderness itself.**

#1 Killer

The Bible tells a unique war story. King David's men are in an unwanted skirmish with his son and his rebel forces, which is unusual. But the most unusual aspect was the battle's biggest champion. It wasn't David the legendary giant slayer, a valiant captain, or his son. The title goes to—
the forest!
Yep, the terrain.

> *There was a great slaughter that day, and 20,000 men laid down their lives. The battle raged all across the countryside, and more men died because of the forest than were killed by the sword (2 Samuel 18:7-8).*

Many parts of the world are inherently challenging, if not dangerous, due to isolation, cliffs, unrelenting sun, unforgiving cold, incessant wind, annual flooding, wild animals, dreadful monotony. I wonder how people survive. Many godly, courageous, mature people win battles against fear, addiction, disease, or wicked people, only to be consumed by some difficult landscape of life. No one volunteers to peruse the wasteland. It's a battle we don't want or expect. Often, we don't realize it is a battle, so we slumber in despair, sulk in disappointment, or fight those we love.

Shortly after our arrival in Africa, a newfound friend prayed for us, then asked what would help us cope practically. Our phones didn't work, our pillows were worthless, and we needed fans to drown the noise. "OK, we'll pick you up at 4:00 to get your essentials. And some great food." Allison and her incredible family became a tremendous lifeline. Those items didn't cure every struggle or magically make everything better; they simply made it more doable.

The wilderness is tough, so let me conclude with a positive, almost unbelievable, perspective: "Spiritual experience is nourished best in the wilderness."[11] God works in the wilderness! If you want to grow, you're surprisingly in a good place.[12]

---

11 *Where Is God When It Hurts?* Philip Yancey. Zondervan. 1996. (53)
12 Dedication: Wayne & Allison Costley (*www.Estherschool.org* in Zambia), Jeff & Charlotte Connally, Tommy & Marcia Hopson. So grateful for great companions along life's journey!

Point: Don't underestimate the wasteland. Learn to live here. Expect battles here.
What strategy of the enemy could most likely destroy you right now?
If you're experiencing the roaring lion, don't fear. *Stand!*
If you're experiencing the cunning snake, don't listen. *Run!*
What "weapons" are at your disposal?
Ponder: The enemy wants to wear you down, devour you and your family. He also fears your growth. How does this affect you?
Prayer: Acknowledge your answer to the strategy question above. Prayer is a powerful resource.
Jesus conquered temptation *and* the wilderness. He can help you too (Hebrews 2:16-18)!
Practical: What can better your situation practically?
Playlist: *Weary Traveler* by Jordan St. Cyr
Pocket:

3: Getting Whys

> ***Why** have you tossed me aside?*
> ***Why** must I wander around in grief (Psalm 43:2)?*

The fireplace at our pastor's house is delightful and welcoming, which is a great reflection of its occupants. One evening, Melissa and Sally chatted in the kitchen, talking about whatever women talk about. Pastor Roy and I struck up our own conversation in the living room's comfortable environment of gently-dancing flames. I don't recall how our dialogue began, but I remember where it went. He asked if I'd consider being a pastor again. Not really. It never seemed the right fit; it daily felt like David wearing Saul's cumbersome armor. I habitually rallied that analogy to confirm my lack of usefulness in ministry.

"OK, but that doesn't mean you don't have a place in the battle," he said. I never thought of that. True, Saul's armor wasn't the right gear for David, but a slingshot was. As our exchange continued, in the safety of that warm atmosphere, I unmasked my thoughts, which had matured into a belief.

"I feel like a forty-year-old failure."

Destructive venom had infected me. Roy's pastoral heart twinged from my confession, and he immediately sought to encourage me. *Dangerous ideas* exist in the wilderness, threatening to undo our faith, all we've worked for, and even our soul. Many arise from our thirst for answers, especially to the question *why*.

*The **What** and **Who** About **Why***

***Why* is a natural reaction.** Kids speak it fluently, don't they? *Why is a hippolomatus called that? Why do we burp? Why do fingers get shrivelly during bath time?* We do the same during struggles. I questioned why I was in this dark time, hoping Roy would just know. When everything goes wrong and prayers clunk to the floor, we wonder why. *Why is this happening? Why me? Why doesn't God answer?*

Ask *why* without guilt. You're simply being human.

***Why* wants to know the reason.** Sometimes the answer is obvious. We're reaping the consequences our actions have sown. We fell in the hole our shovel dug. Why are we losing the house? *We gambled it away.* Why am I getting fired? *Umm, you don't show up.* It's not always negative though. Why did I get in that accident? *The doctor found a potentially fatal heart issue.* When unknown, our dogmatic bents quickly declare such-and-such, but the Bible doesn't favor a one-size-fits-all approach. There's the sovereignty of God, the activity of the Spirit, the work of Satan, the choices of humans, the development of character, and plenty others. The most common assumption?

Divine punishment.

An ancient man named Job suffered the darkest season ever. His heartbreaking story reveals a tendency: **In dark seasons we incline to blame.** His wife blamed God, so she told Job to curse Him. His friends accused him, so they fished for his sin that caused the predicament. They knew it was classic divine punishment because bad things only happen due to someone's fault. *Why* can inadvertently be asking *who's to blame? Who* incurred this trouble? My *why* was rooted in self-blame. *I* somehow caused or perpetuated this, so justice demanded I go behind the barn and beat myself some more.

Philip Yancey, tackling our engrained thirst to know *why*, addresses the belief that suffering is *always* punishment:

> *There is a huge difference between the suffering most of us encounter—a skiing injury, a rare form of cancer, the bus accident—and the suffering-as-punishment described in the Old Testament. There, punishment follows repeated warnings against specific behavior. To be effective... punishment requires a clear tie to behavior. Think of a parent who punishes a young child. It would do little good...to sneak up at odd times during a day and whack the child with no explanation. The people of Israel knew why they were being punished. I believe that unless God distinctly reveals otherwise, we would do better to look to other biblical models.*[13]

Don't we assume if we are "right with God" and "do the right things," there shouldn't be trouble or dry spells? Some may experience

---

13 Yancey, 81-82.

life like this; I haven't. **Sometimes a "pruning season" can feel like a wilderness.** Jesus said, "My Father is the gardener...He prunes the branches that do bear fruit so they will produce even more" (John 15:1-2). Every autumn my neighbor mows beautiful bushes to the ground. Looks pitiful and unnecessary, if not cruel. Until spring, when they rise again, healthy and bountiful. God may intentionally withhold good feelings, answers, and results in order to accomplish something deeper. He may remove props or strip away our cherished grounds for pride. We may be enduring the difficult process of *growth*. **Don't lose heart, don't let go, don't give up, dear one. He's maturing you.**

Ask *why* cautiously. The answer may not be so obvious.

Why **is rarely satisfied,** either by simplistic cliché or professional explanation. Often, there's no plausible answer. Ask kids why they misbehaved, and chances are one will shrug their shoulders and say *'cause*. While the boys point fingers and the girls roll eyes, there's the youngster who offers no good reason, clever alibi, or diversion. *Because* is the worst reply. It doesn't soothe our soul, settle our mind, or direct our blame, but it may be all we get. When wracking our brains for perfect understanding, we may only get a headache. Sometimes I've finally filed unmet inquiries in "The things I don't need to know right now" drawer.

In Job's story, no one realized **there are simply dry, difficult seasons.** When God finally broke His silence, He never linked Job's suffering to punishment, nor offered satisfactory reasons. But His words and presence still deeply impacted Job. Imagine if every *why* was answered. Our finite minds couldn't grasp it all! Jesus wisely dispensed knowledge to His disciples in proper doses at proper times.

Ask *why* humbly, entrusting it to a very brilliant God.

Next, we'll observe the *where* and *how* about *why*.[14]

---

14 Dedication: Roy & Sally Ferguson. You consistently support people. Keep lighting fires!

Point: How can *why* be beneficial? detrimental?
What's your "go-to cause" for suffering?
Are there "simply dry seasons"?
Ponder some reasons for difficult seasons in the Bible. Job 1-2. Matthew 4:1. Proverbs 19:3. John 15:1-8. Romans 8:28. Hebrews 12:1-13.
What "whys" are asked in Psalm 43?
What's your biggest *why?* What's your assumed answer?
Prayer: Turn previous answers into prayer.
We ask *why* when things go wrong. Thank God for three things that *went right*. Why did *they* occur?
Practical: File an unanswered *why* in "The things I don't need to know right now" drawer.
Let go of blame.
Read John 9:1-7. What *why* was asked? What was their supposed reason? How did Jesus respond? Notice his quick transition from a theological or philosophical *why* to a practical perspective (verse 4).
Playlist: *No Matter What* by Kerri Roberts
Pocket:

4: The "Wait a While" Tree

Are you also going to leave (John 6:67)?

Rarely is the mind more susceptible than during seasons eliciting *why*. We can think superficially for decades, and in a moment of difficulty start contemplating the deep, mysterious workings behind the universe. *I'm being punished. It's my parents' fault. It's fate. Satan's messin' with me. All things work for good. Why* craves knowledge, but too often remains unsatisfied or confused. How should we respond when answers evade? What do we conclude?

The **Where** and **How** about **Why**

With the mind wide open, *why* **becomes a potential incubator of belief.** God and our enemy both teach in the classroom of suffering, so we must be alert to conclusions "discovered" there. Reflection and searching may positively yield understanding or change; however, convoluted ideas also lurk. One writer concluded, "Before I was afflicted I went astray, but now I keep Your word" (Psalm 119:67 NKJV); others conclude, "*Because* I was afflicted, I went astray; now I scrap Your word," Be slow to adopt new and improved belief systems in the dark, when the propensity to trade convictions for conclusions is high. Suffering doesn't automatically make a credible theologian or philosopher. Unanswered questions often breed doubt. *This God-thing doesn't work. Life is meaningless.* Unanswered questions also breed faith. *I don't know, God does. Life is hard, but we'll get through this.*

In confusing seasons, we incline to wander or quit. A bunch of Jesus' followers called it quits when they didn't understand what He was doing or saying. "At this point many of his disciples turned away and deserted him. Then Jesus turned to the Twelve and asked, 'Are you also going to leave?' Simon Peter replied, 'Lord, to whom would we go? You have the words that give eternal life'" (John 6:66-68). "At this point" attests to life's defining junctures, where we choose our next path. What is Jesus' answer regardless of the reason for the season?

Stay.

Sometimes all Jesus asks of us is to stay. "Remain in me, and I will remain in you" (John 15:4). He may not expect us to start, produce, or figure out anything right now, but merely stick around. Job demonstrates this amazingly, remaining with God even when he didn't feel His presence, experience His blessings, or understand His activity (or inactivity). When everything supposed God's unfaithfulness, Job kept trusting. What will be said at the end of your story? "Things got hard. He couldn't reconcile it with his faith. At this point he turned away." Or, "At this point he resolved to stay with God!" Determine your ending and hold firm.

The Bible occasionally enhances "remain" with a prefix, meaning *to remain under*. Often translated "endure," it encourages steadfastness under pressure. The book of Hebrews addressed Christians undergoing tremendous hardship. Their hope-filled eternal perspective had kept them going for a while, but they wore thin in the struggle and considered giving up. To them was written,

> *Let us hold tightly without wavering to the hope we affirm, for God can be trusted to keep his promise. Do not throw away this confident trust in the Lord. Remember the great reward it brings you! Patient endurance is what you need now, so that you will continue to do God's will. Then you will receive all that he has promised. We are not like those who turn away from God to their own destruction. We are the faithful ones, whose souls will be saved (Hebrews 10:23,35-36, 39).*

Hope is vital. It's often the first step in the process of restoration. It encourages us to continue when willpower vacillates or vacates. Paul the apostle prayed "that you will be strengthened with all his glorious power so you will have all the endurance and patience you need" (Colossians 1:11). We link God's mighty power to instantaneous healing and unexplainable miracles. And so it is. I've witnessed and experienced such. But notice the reasoning for *this* dynamic power— to help us endure long trials and difficult seasons with hope and even cheer. Staying requires the same power as the brilliant demonstrations of deliverance we seek. When winter passes, who knows what might spring up for those who remain?

Ask *why* wisely. It can lead to radical conclusions and destinations.

Why is the first question, not the *only* question. While I expected

Pastor Roy to confirm my assumptive *why*, he simply asked, "Does it matter?" I pursued the past to understand the present (mainly to blame myself), but his question indirectly scanned the future to gain wisdom for the present. Endless *whys* weld us to the past and gridlock us from the path forward. One guy supposedly uncovered the reason for his hardship: "My suffering was good for me, for it taught me to pay attention to Your decrees" (Psalm 119:71). It happened *because* he lived too carelessly.

Maybe.

Or maybe what he learned was *the result of his response* to suffering, a testament that God can manifest good in everything. When *why* meets silence, God is likely shifting our thinking toward the future. We may benefit from other questions. *How should I respond? How will God use this? How will I want this story to be told to my children and grandchildren?* Yancey adds:

> To backward-looking questions of cause, [the Bible] gives no definitive answer. But it does hold out hope for the future, that even suffering can be transformed or 'redeemed.' Sometimes, as with the man born blind, the work of God is manifest through a dramatic miracle. Sometimes it is not. But in every case, suffering offers an opportunity for us to display God's work.[15]

Ask *why*, but know there are other questions too.

Jesus urged His disciples to remain, promising reward will eventually follow. Those who stay with their Shepherd through desert places usually discover unknown streams rich in spiritual nutrition. **These treasures often become their greatest contribution to a needy world.**

Wag-n-bietje boom

A tree in southern Africa boasts pairs of thorns, some straight and some curved. Getting snagged detains passersby, as the thorns must be removed one by one. This characteristic earned it the nickname *wag-*

---

15 Yancey. (84-85)

n-bietje boom (vockh-abiki boo-em) in the Afrikaans language. The "wait a little while tree" beckons those who come near to linger longer.

The tree on which Jesus died pleads with those tempted to wander or quit: "Please stay longer."

Remain close to the tree with the crown of thorns.[16]

> **Point:** If w*hy* yields no answers, may God give "peace that passes understanding" (Philippians 4:6-7).
> Have you adopted new "beliefs?" Where did they originate? Where will they lead?
> **Ponder** how the past and future each help navigate the present.
> Count "remain" or "abide" in John 15.
> **Prayer:** My prayer after writing this chapter was for faith in Jesus to be preserved, restored, or discovered. Was that for *you*?
> "Lord, strengthen this reader with all Your glorious power so they'll have all the endurance and patience they need."
> **Practical:** Finish the sentence. *At this point I will*
> Consider at least one other question. *(How will I respond? What would faith say or do? When I tell my story, what do I want it to say? Will this make me bitter or better?)*
> **Playlist:** *I Still Believe* by Jeremy Camp
> **Pocket:**

---

16 Dedication: Tersia Downing. Thanks to you and your family for letting me stay a while in Africa!

5: The Story of the Captain
Written with Harmon Schmelzenbach III

> *As for me, God will redeem my life (Psalm 49:15).*

One night our church met Harmon Schmelzenbach, who was born into a legendary missionary family in Africa. Growing up on the front lines—watching firsthand the rhythms of God at work—struck a chord deep within him. His adult journey followed a traditional path toward ministry and missions. Within six years, he neared ordination.

That's when numerous unanswered questions hit. After much prayer, Harmon and his wife made the costly decision to walk away from his family's one-hundred-plus years of foreign missions involvement, as well as his own years of intensive personal preparation. Harmon commented, "What a waste! All those years. All that work! Everything I saw myself as...what a waste!"

They packed their essentials, sold their possessions, and bought one-way tickets to start a new chapter in the Caribbean. Harmon completed the United States Coast Guard's requirements for Merchant Marine Officer and launched a charter boat company. Eight years later, they made the agonizing decision to raise their growing family in New Mexico. Vast desert separated him from the nearest ocean. Harmon hung his hard-earned captain's license on the wall and thought, *So much effort, life, and energy for nothing. What a waste!*

The God who wastes nothing eventually called him and his family to a significant assignment in the South Pacific, where he drew extensively from his formative years in Africa. For example, campfires were the boardrooms where chiefs and tribes discussed important business, just like he experienced as a kid in Africa. The business knowledge acquired in the Caribbean became an inestimable asset. The "useless license" enabled Harmon to log over five hundred ocean voyages exceeding 36,000 nautical miles as a missionary captain into remote islands!

God's timing never seems to match ours, but unquestionably, God wastes nothing if we allow Him to redeem our messes, successes, and *every*thing that's happened to us, in the same way He redeemed our souls. God desires to use it all—*if we are willing.* I think of the stories Harmon shared that night, and how he enthusiastically bragged on the God who wastes nothing, who invites us into the story He's writing. I'm glad he didn't quit. God orchestrated all of life—Africa, the Caribbean, New Mexico, the South Pacific—perfectly.

I contacted Harmon years later, wondering where he was and what he was doing. He responded from the interior regions of Papua New Guinea. My heart soared! God called him to oversee his denomination's growing missionary operations across seven countries and four time zones. He was responsible for fifty missionaries, hundreds of churches, a hospital, clinics, institutions of higher education, and countless ministries. What if he quit in the season when everything looked like a waste?

You may think, "That's great, but my story isn't lined with exotic destinations and significant degrees." Don't get hung up on peripheral things. **God can take the elements of anybody's story and write a masterpiece, signed by His pen, bringing Him glory.** Harmon is the first to admit a high-profile leader in kingdom work is unusual. Often, when noting true "heroes of the faith," he speaks of unknown individuals in far-removed places, doing great things in partnership with the God whose love cannot be separated from His passion, power, and plan to redeem everything.[17]

Point: God can redeem *anything*.
Ponder: What segment of life seems wasted, from which nothing good could emerge?
Prayer: "Lord, I offer *this* for Your use."
Practical:
Playlist: *Road to Redemption* by River
Pocket:

---

17 Dedication: Captain Harmon Schmelzenbach III. I love your God-story!

6: (gasp!)

> *Bones... **covered** the valley floor (Ezekiel 37:2).*

"Let me see a giraffe today." Anticipating our safari in Botswana, Melissa asked the Creator one favor. And then this happened.

At 5 in the morning my car sputtered after sipping the last drop of fuel along a dark country road. I coasted to the side of the road, prepared myself for a three-mile hike, and opened the door. It happened.

Gold rays crested The Garden of the Gods national park in Colorado during an Easter sunrise service. It happened again.

The same occurred upon first glimpse of the Grand Canyon's depths, Victoria Fall's width, and beholding the height of New York's skyscrapers.

What happened?

Awe.

Something surprising invades the normal or exceeds expectations, leaving us in wonder.

Before reaching the safari, three giraffes crossed the road. Melissa's eyes widened with joy. But that was just the beginning. We nearly saw them around each bend! Total for the day: forty-two. Our guide said, "After dozens of tours, I've never seen so many giraffes!"[18]

After exiting my car, I looked up and gasped at the sheer number of stars adorning the black sky. I stood speechless.

The hues of an Easter sunrise revealed just how many gathered under the cover of darkness to worship the Risen Son.

Ezekiel likely gasped when beholding the inconceivable magnitude of bones strewn across the valley. Whatever happened affected massive quantities of people.

I reserved a gray Saturday morning to complete an application for a program I hoped would lead to a new, fulfilling season of life. Before diving in, I offered a compulsory prayer and read a list titled *Daily Reminders*. This was an ongoing attempt to renew my mind with certain truths. The fourth line read: *My worth and my identity are formed by Christ. To see how much I am worth, I only need to look to the*

---

18 If you're in need of seeing giraffes, have Melissa pray for you!

cross. I never made it to number five. Or the application.

It hit me—*multitudes* around the world feel worthless and broken *right now.* We're never the only one enduring a turbulent season. For the first time I ached for other modern-day dwellers in dry-bone valleys. I pleaded for God to work on their behalf, and humbly offered to partner with Him for their restoration. What followed was a furious three-hour tour through the Bible. An undeniable theme emerged—**hopeless-looking seasons are common; my situation was not some rare exception.**

Shocking numbers of people experience a level of brokenness assumed to be their demise. But maybe God-sized purposes exist for wasted seasons? Maybe Dead-Ends are God's Main Streets. The scribbled pages written that morning became the foundation for this book. I shared these findings with Captain Schmelzenbach, whose reply remains a personal treasure: "I'd encourage you that there are certainly untold masses of people who desperately need to hear what you are saying here."[19] Those two words etched my psyche—*untold masses.* Just like Ezekiel saw in the valley.

I reluctantly preached *"Simply Dry Seasons"* to 300 people. Assuming four or less would relate, I wanted something more conducive to a larger audience context. After repeated prayers for guidance met repeated silence, I figured God must be in this message. I spoke confidently and concluded the message by asking if anyone was in a dry season, knowing they would need the support of others. Nearly half the audience responded! I marvel at how many relate to dry bones. At any time, countless people are trudging some despairing wilderness.

The Restorer not only shared thoughts that Saturday morning. He let me lean against His passionate heart. Measly words could never convey how vibrantly it beats for those desperately needing restoration. "Jesus saw the huge crowd...He had compassion on them because they were like sheep without a shepherd. So He began teaching them many things" (Mark 6:34). **The heart of Jesus is huge for dry bones in desert places. I mean, HUGE.** Whenever I get bogged down in writing, I remember those sacred hours when I felt most vividly the Shepherd's heart pound for broken multitudes.

The number of people in the valley makes one gasp, yet *each one* is loved by the One whose heart beats big enough for all.[20]

---

19 This sentence was the primary motivation to write this book.
20 Dedication: Michele Tennesen and Kara Moore (*www.equippress.org*). This book wouldn't exist without you.

Point: Difficult seasons are normal. (I Peter 4:12) Do you feel like "the only one?"
Ponder: Jesus' heart beats vibrantly *for me*.
Prayer: For "the untold masses." (By name if possible.)
Practical: Tell someone you just prayed for them. What truth do you need daily? How will you remember it?
Playlist: *Love Song* or *Your Love Oh Lord* by Third Day
Pocket:

7: Desperados

> *They were **scattered…completely dried out** (Ezekiel 37:2).*

A dilapidated 60's-era car sank into the ground. Abused, then abandoned, it lay completely ruined beneath a bunch of pines. Parts were missing. Weather dismantled the interior. Everything was buckled, corroded, or broken. Labeling it irreparable would not be an exaggeration. It was too far gone, a pitiful pile of bones.

We just observed the surprising number of people in the valley, as well as The Restorer's gigantic heart for each one. The narrative now describes their condition. The portrayal as "bones" signifies extreme unraveling. A house may need minor attention like paint, moderate repair like a roof, or full restoration requiring a complete deconstruct. "Bones" describes the latter. It's life at the lowest, the bare minimum of existence. In a word—*decimated*.

> Some of you sit in a dark room amid piles of tissues—crippled by loss.
> Some struggle in a rehab facility or hospital. You've never felt lower.
> Some grieve the good 'ol days, or those meant to be.
> Some wouldn't mind if you didn't wake up tomorrow.
> Some feel permanently ripped apart.
> Some pace a jail cell, or feel walls suffocate you.
> Some are reading these words as a last resort.

One bitter soul lamented, "My heart is sick, withered like grass, and I have lost my appetite. Because of my groaning, I am reduced to skin and bones. I am…like a little owl in a far-off wilderness" (Psalm 102:4-6). *Withered. Reduced. Far-off.* **If you've lost everything, felt beyond repair, or hit bottom, you understand *bones*.** Bones were highly revered. Treating them with dignity and burying them properly honored the deceased. These bones, however, were *scattered like garbage* across the valley. Nothing good is said about scattered bones.[21] It disgraces the individual and desecrates the ground.

Sometimes leaders unearthed the buried bones of their enemies to

---

21 2 Kings 23:14. Psalm 53:5.

scatter them "like manure."²² It's the ultimate dishonor; insult to injury. God's people were thoroughly dismantled, then utterly disregarded. Too many, face-down in the dirt, hear: "You're a disgrace." Internal chatter screams *I'm dirty, toxic! I defile everything I touch!* David wrote, "I am poor and needy, and my heart is full of pain. I am fading like a shadow at dusk; I am brushed off like a locust. My knees are weak from fasting, and I am skin and bones. I am a joke to people everywhere; when they see me they shake their heads in scorn" (Psalm 109:24).

One more element describes their condition. They were not only broken apart and shamed, but completely dried out. This conveys pervasiveness of a condition or emotion, whether negative or positive. For example, *bad to the bone* or *fire in my bones*.²³ These were brittle bones, highlighting the prolonged duration of their impoverished state. They "died" so long ago it looked permanent. **Nobody trips on a skeleton and attempts CPR. It's *way beyond* too far gone.**

A certain Bible story always captivates me. During a lengthy national drought, Elijah finds a brookside retreat. Fresh water satisfies his thirst, and ravens claw-deliver his meals. But the drought refuses to relent, "After a while, the brook dried up" (1 Kings 17:7). Sparkling waters once cascading down rock faces now gather into miniature pools. Provisions require rations. We all experience the hardship of dried brooks. It's in the dejected demeanor of a man terminated from his job—the news echoes down the anxious hallways of his mind. Each replay dries his soul a little more. It's in the hollow eyes of a woman told she's no longer loved. It's carried on the slumped shoulders of a minister who, for whatever reason, is no longer "in the ministry." Souls resembling the radiant cottages of Thomas Kinkade's paintbrush now share the likeness of the Addams family mansion. Sources, seasons, ministries, dreams, fellowships—sometimes dry up.

Many recognize the proverb, "A merry heart does good, like medicine" (Proverbs 17:22 NKJV). It spotlights our need to be injected with joy. Cheer vaccinates against bitterness and other forms of spiritual heart disease. It's a great nugget, but only half the saying. "But a crushed spirit dries up the bones" (Proverbs 17:22 ESV). Many experience the crushing of spirit. A season of drought devastates us or those we love to the core, squeezing all marrow from the bones.

God wasn't surprised by the depleted brook, nor worried about

---

22 Jeremiah 8:2.
23 Job 4:14. Psalm 6:2; 35:10; 42:10. Proverbs 15:30 ESV.

Elijah's care. He had an unconventional plan—relocate him to another country to be helped by a widow. If God told me He commissioned someone to provide for me, I would anticipate a beautiful homestead and comfortable lifestyle, not a desperate woman scrounging one last meal. Nevertheless, that's who God chose to sustain His servant. In the end, they both experienced God's miracle of supply!

Backwarding

While preparing our childhood home to sell, my brother Greg and I coined the phrase, "When in doubt, chuck it out." Consequently, we infuriated everyone at least once…a week. Why? We trashed things they considered valuable. Sorry fam. Skilled restorers *first assess*, then carefully remove and retain valuables until the proper time of rebuilding. While some things need to be removed temporarily, the unhealthy needs to be removed for good! I heard a profound lesson taken from the recycling bin and the garbage can—sometimes we throw away what God intends to reuse![24] (And sometimes we keep what needs trashed.)

Why is demolition so fun, except when it's *our life* experiencing it? All that remained of the lives in the valley were *remains*. Being reduced is agonizing. It feels like we're being disassembled, even destroyed, and makes us wonder what we will have left when the dust settles. Anyone tackling projects knows things go backward before they get better. We shouldn't paint over rust or attach laminate to rotten wood. But sometimes we go back further than planned. *While we're painting, let's remove this wall, the old electric, and single-pane windows.* Next thing you know you're sitting around bare framing and general disarray, thinking, *that color wasn't too bad!*

Bones also carries a future significance. Because they outlast the body, they hint at eternity. One resource says Hebrew people regarded bones as symbolic of future resurrection. If true, it's fitting. **The "backwarding" of the old and broken makes way for the new and improved.** Dismantling something to its basic level precedes rebirth; it's starting over. God *loves* taking bare things and rebuilding them!

The bad news? It takes time. It's a difficult season, not just a bad day. There's little to look forward to.

The good news? It's a season, not forever. There's something to

---

24 Charlotte Gambill. K-Love Radio. *One Minute of Encouragement*.

look forward to—you just might not see it yet.

We may never plummet to these extremes, yet whatever downward or backward we experience, God can rebuild us. He knew what to do with a dry brook and empty cupboards. He knows what to do with modern-day dry bones and depleted lives. The "people of bones" were decimated, disgraced, and desperate. They suffered a long time, much like the car mentioned earlier. Little did that car know, someone hundreds of miles away was *looking for it*. Little did the bones know, Someone was looking for them.

For scattered bones to live again is hopeless. Or miraculous![25]

> **Point:** Have you experienced *decimated? disgraced? dried-up?*
> Even "small" losses can devastate. There's grace to grieve, hurt, and "not have it all together."
> **Ponder** gains from "backwarding." (Elijah gained a new friendship, testimony, and ministry.)
> Hopelessness often precedes miracles.
> Have you thrown something away that God wants to recycle?
> **Prayer:** "Lord, help!"
> **Practical:** Write a "psalm." In addition to the raw venting of feelings, include one truth and one element of gratitude or praise.
> **Playlist:** *Resurrection* by Nicol Sponberg
> *It is Well* hymn by Horatio Spafford
> **Pocket:**

---

25 Dedication: Edie Goon and Marie Hansen. Your hospitality and prayers have encouraged many.

8: Graveyard Walker

> *He led me **all around among the bones** (Ezekiel 37:2).*

Because I'm from western New York, I naturally envisioned the valley of dry bones with thick clouds and gloomy rain. Dense fog and plenty of human skeletons added a truly eerie atmosphere. Now I picture unrelenting rays from the noonday sun scorch beige sand. Arid draughts occasionally swirl like miniature tornadoes. Long, stern rock formations silently hem the valley from opposite sides. It's a forgotten place where nothing lives or wants to live. Not even a vulture circles overhead—it epitomizes gut-wrenching hopelessness and deep, deep sorrow.

The Lord didn't show this from a distance, nor briefly. He immersed Ezekiel in the experience, guiding him with precision, careful not to trample any sacred remains. A set of scattered bones rivets the Lord's focus, who pauses in holy silence. **It resembles the tenderness of a man at his best friend's grave.** They proceed to more bones. The Master, again moved, reverently kneels. He sees beyond the visible, knowing the bones are the fragmented remnants of what this life used to be. An atmosphere of loss prevails. They rise unhurried and locate another precious life.

They must have looked at every bone.

Eyes. Heart. Lips. Hands.

The Lord rises to behold the magnitude of this tragedy one last time. He's the embodiment of excessive compassion. There is no disservice of the Shepherd toward His sheep. He treasures them, feels for them, loves them. It mimics the way bystanders observed His uncontrollable weeping at the memorial of His buddy Lazarus:

> *When Jesus saw [Mary] weeping...he was deeply moved in his spirit and greatly troubled. And he said, "Where have you laid him?" They said to him, "Lord, come and see." Jesus wept. The people who were standing nearby said, "See how much He loved him!" Then Jesus, deeply*

> *moved again, came to the tomb. Jesus said, "Take away the stone" (Excerpts from John 11:33-39 ESV/NLT).*

His heart hurt. It was yanked out of position by severest love.
Have you ever noticed the little notation regarding the encounter Jesus had with the "rich young ruler?" Just before Jesus was turned down by this self-justified man, the story reads, "Looking at the man, Jesus felt genuine love for him" (Mark 10:21). Something profound rises to the surface in these accounts—hypervigilant attentiveness. Jesus intently, intentionally, sees. But there's more. The eyes of Jesus move the heart of Jesus, and when His heart is stirred, something will happen. Eventually His lips speak and hands move. Keen eyesight coupled with active love.

Hagar was a pregnant runaway. An angel finds her next to a spring and calls her name. He asks questions, gives instructions, and speaks kindly to her. So momentous is this to the single mom she renames the place. From then on, this desert oasis was called *The Well of the Living One who Sees me* (Genesis 16:14). She was overwhelmed with the fact that God saw *her*! God's Spirit still patrols wilderness regions for solitary, broken people. Maybe you'll rename a place because God unmistakably met you there!

A Shepherd's Task

When I think of God's works, some surface quickly—create, save, heal, comfort, guide. A less familiar, yet no less miraculous, ministry is restoration. When "Jesus noticed a man with a deformed hand, He said, 'Hold out your hand.' So the man held out his hand, and it was restored, just like the other one" (Matthew 12:13)! This hand once functioned efficiently. It could be relied on to perform a hundred tasks, but something happened—maybe disease, accident, or intentional harm. We don't know, but it dramatically affected his life. How do you do life with one hand, like zip your jeans or tie your shoes? Unfortunately, some have had to find such solutions, as did this man.

When some faulted Jesus for breaking God's law by restoring the hand on a sacred day, Jesus responded, "If you had a sheep that fell into a well on the Sabbath, wouldn't you work to pull it out? Of course you would. And how much more valuable is a person than a sheep" (Matthew 12:11-12)! He answers in the terminology of a shepherd whose sheep got stuck in a ditch. Maybe it wandered, got pushed, or noticed a shiny object. However it happened, the shepherd pulled it up and put it on its feet. What a picture of restoration!

Notice how David addresses God when praying for his nation's restoration: "Give ear, O Shepherd...Restore us, O God; cause Your face to shine, and we shall be saved" (Psalm 80:1, 3 NKJV)! Psalm 23 stands undoubtedly as the most eloquent tribute to God as a shepherd. David's heart is elevated in praise to his very-present God who provides, leads, cares, comforts, blesses, and encourages. Anyone who knows God the Shepherd can testify to these gracious workings. Yet another task of the shepherd is nestled in verse 3. With affectionate gratitude, the psalmist declares, "He restores my soul." David remembers when his soul wandered, withered in the wilderness, or shriveled in defeat. His body housed a dried soul, but the Shepherd sought him, pulled him up, and resuscitated him to life!

Phillip Keller offers first-hand knowledge about a shepherd's ever-watchful eye for sheep that get turned upside-down. "Sometimes it will bleat a little for help, but generally, it lies there lashing about in frightened frustration."[26] Time is limited as gases cut off blood supply and predators seek a free lunch. A cast-down state devastates that sheep, the shepherd, and the business. The loss of one is never just the loss of one. There's a ripple effect. Just one has a significant impact. Isn't that the opposite of the enemy's whispers to our downcast soul?

Nobody cares about you.
You don't matter.
You're a pathetic mess.
Nobody would miss you.
You'd do everyone a favor if you're gone.

Listen again to a shepherd's viewpoint: "Many people have the idea that when a child of God falls, frustrated and helpless in a spiritual dilemma, God becomes disgusted, fed up, and even furious with him. This simply is not so."[27] In stark contrast, cast sheep were a shepherd's *chief concern*. Perpetually searching for circling birds, repeatedly counting the flock, always ready to rescue—**good shepherds were ever mindful of sheep needing restoration.** Keller's explanation is worth retelling:

---

26 *A Shepherd Looks at Psalm 23.* Phillip Keller. Zondervan. 1996. (50)
27 Keller, 50.

> *Leaving everything else, I would immediately... count the flock to make sure every one was...on its feet. I would spend hours searching...I would see it at a distance, lying helpless. I would start to run...my very first impulse was to pick it up. Tenderly I would roll the sheep over. If she had been down for long, I would have to lift her onto her feet...I would hold her erect, rubbing her limbs to restore the circulation. When the sheep started to walk again, she often stumbled...All the time I...would talk...in language that combined tenderness and rebuke, compassion and correction. Little by little the sheep would regain its equilibrium. By and by it would...rejoin the others, set free from its fears and frustrations, given another chance to live.*[28]

When Jesus restores a cast down human, He's simply being a shepherd. His eyes still see. His heart still beats. His mouth still speaks. His hands still move.[29]

> **Point:** What about you or your situation do you think most grabs the Shepherd's heart?
> **Ponder** yourself as Ezekiel. The bones. The cast sheep. The Shepherd.
> **Prayer:** Pray like you KNOW God sees and hears you *right now*.
> Deeply contemplate Psalm 34:15 or Job 23:9-10.
> **Practical:** Where are *your* "God-places?" Name them. Go there literally or mentally.
> **Playlist:** *You Restore My Soul* by New Wine Worship
> **Pocket:**

---

28 Keller, 52-54.
29 Dedication: In memory of my first "shepherd," Pastor Fred Moore.

9: The Q&A

> *I will...transform the Valley of Trouble into **a gateway of hope** (Hosea 2:15).*

The Question

The Lord breaks the silence with a bizarre question, "Can these bones become living people again" (Ezekiel 37:2)? In other words, *can hopelessly broken people be restored?* How could Ezekiel say yes? Scattered skeletons becoming living, moving people with muscles, brains, and souls? That doesn't happen. Yet how do you tell God something is impossible? Some projects look hopeless, whether scattered bones, dilapidated structures, or long-forgotten vehicles rotting in the weeds. Wouldn't it be easier to buy a new one than salvage the old and damaged?

I walked with a handful of pastors through a massive, vacant building. Once a place employing hundreds, it sat cold and lifeless. A sad sight. A businessman with a love for God and big ol' buildings organized this tour. He envisioned a community center and wondered what we thought of the five-story structure. His broad smile never dimmed as he verbalized what could be. In a sense, he asked us Ezekiels: *Can this building live again?* Honestly, I didn't see it. I'm sure I nodded in agreement, but all I saw was a dead building requiring untold work and resources. I wanted a nap just thinking about it.

Again speaks of something that was, then wasn't, coming to life once more. A rebirth, if you will. When I was a kid, I considered a wrecked car final. Better write the eulogy. Now rusted shells with trees growing through the engine bay makes me think: *somebody could transform that.* We may assume the dry bones around us or in the mirror are permanently damaged goods. The desert has a way of reducing us. It's hard on the body, mind, and spirit. Things may appear hopeless. We may feel worthless, useless, fallen from grace. Meanwhile, The Restorer has a brimming smile and a vision. **No matter how low we feel or far we fall, several things can never be taken from us. They're built into us or bestowed on us by our Creator.**

- **Hope.** There's *always* an answer. We just don't always see it.
- **Worth.** If you can earn it or lose it, that's not what determines your true worth. Even cast sheep hold great value.

- **Purpose.** You're chock full of them. There are hurting people, broken people, and fallen people, but no such thing as purposeless people.
- **Grace.** It's unlimited goodness rooted in the heart of God—freely given to undeserving recipients!

Since 2005 that building has been a critical source of life to our community. When dedicated as The Gateway Center, our mayor commented, "In a sense, you could say this building has been redeemed. We need that to happen to more buildings around town." *Redeemed* also carries the theme of *Again*—something lost is found. True to its name, this building has served as a gateway for thousands to find hope, worth, purpose, and grace.

It's impossible to know the thousands of ministry and service hours accomplished throughout that building standing tall near the center of town. Meals served. Counsel, clothes, prayers, and furniture given. Unemployed have found work or developed marketable skills. Youth of all ages take to the indoor skate park. The half has not been told. This beacon of restoration is a living, breathing testament affirming, "Yes! Dry bones can live again!" What a contrast to that initial walk-through. I'm thankful for those who envisioned and labored for what could be, when all I saw was bird poop and lifeless rooms.

The Answer

I've always considered Ezekiel's response vague—an answer without answering. "Sovereign LORD, you alone know the answer to that" (Ezekiel 37:3). However, in one statement he avoids both hyped cliché and dishonoring unbelief. No flippancy; no faithlessness. **He simultaneously confirms the hopelessness of the situation while affirming God's wisdom and power.** *God, I don't see how it's possible, but You're far stronger and smarter than me.* Amid the dusty, empty ruins, I picture the Lord with a twinkling eye, infectious smile, and a vision for what can, and will, be.

Kintsugi

This Japanese tradition turns shattered pottery into surprisingly stunning art. Meaning "golden joinery," broken pieces are fastened with lacquer, then the fractures painted with powdered gold, silver, or platinum. There's no attempt to make the piece look perfect or hide the damage. The breaking and repair are viewed as significant components of the piece's story, even worthy of being accentuated and celebrated! Falling to the ground and shattering doesn't render it ugly and useless.

David Pike is a fanatic about every stage of this "art of repair." He can't get enough! Daily he extracts purpose from brokenness and transforms damage into beauty.[30] What he's been doing for years, God has been doing every day for thousands of years. He just can't get enough! He loves *every* stage of restoring broken things![31]

> **Point:** How would you have answered? (How do things "beyond repair" affect you?)
> God can transform troubles into gateways.
> **Ponder** which "thing you can never lose" is most important right now? Can you think of others?
> **Prayer:** *God, I don't see how it's possible, but You're far stronger and smarter than me.*
> **Practical:** Search "kintsugi" articles or images.
> **Playlist:** *God, Turn it Around* by Jon Reddick
> **Pocket:**

---

30 Christy Bartlett, "Flickwerk: The Aesthetics of Mended Japanese Ceramics." Kathryn Pombriant Manzella, "Beauty in the Art of Repair: Kintsugi by David Pike," 2014. *www.Traditionalkyoto.com*

31 Gary and Dawn Lynn, passionate investors in the lives of many. Thanks for "the greatest place to write!"

PART 2:
The Restorer *sprouts hope* in broken pieces who feel *unraveled*.

Dry bones, listen to the word of the LORD (Ezekiel 37:4)!

**The seeds of hope,
no matter how small,
can produce great things.**

**Hope is often the first stage of restoration.
Before God did anything for the dry bones,
He spoke words on which they could hope.**

**Elijah's story is a great example of how
The Restorer puts hopelessly unraveled pieces back together.**

10: There's Good News and Bad News
(Let's Start with the Bad)

> *"We have become **old, dry bones** – all hope is gone" (Ezekiel 37:11).*

God kept nudging Melissa toward Africa. Finally, like a sacred ultimatum, she said, "We have to do something about this." We contacted several connections and offered to serve. Our friend, Paul Mtambo, immediately invited us to his beloved nation of Zambia. Melissa, having a special affinity for African kiddos, looked forward to ministries involving children. I wasn't sure what my role would be, but a seedling desire to assist with WASH needs (water, sanitation, hygiene) sprouted in me. At Paul's direction, I took a course on teaching hygiene in developing countries.

The next summer we conducted a week of hygiene trainings for the Copperbelt region in the north. To come alongside these eager participants and extend practical, life-changing knowledge was highly rewarding, though I never imagined I'd be talking about poop in churches in Africa![32] Every night I fell into bed *joyfully exhausted*. Saturday was a travel day and Sunday I preached. By Sunday evening I was taxed. With wise sensitivity, Paul cleared our schedule for Monday. He acknowledged our service and knew we needed rest. That day in Zambia is one of the most poignant illustrations of the sheer gift God offers—a day every week to rest. I cherished it fully. Apparently, talking about poop makes you pooped.

Blindsided

As evidenced in this chapter's introductory quote, the dry bones considered their condition a dead-end. **Hopelessness is a dominant characteristic of the valley.** History has woven untold stories with the fabric of hopelessness—one of the most vivid is the narrative of Elijah (I Kings 19). It begins on the heels of extraordinary events. Boldly

---

32 My translator, Pastor Chileshe, called it "boom-boom!"

challenging his countrymen to stop vacillating between God and the god Baal, he orchestrates a showdown allowing the real deity to prove himself to the nation. Unlike Baal, who was vacationing or napping, God showed up. After heaven-sent fire ignited a sopping wet sacrifice, no one left the grandstands wondering who they should worship. What a spectacular victory for the kingdom of God!

Ironically, Baal's specialty was weather—storms, rain, thunder, lightning, earthquakes. These weapons in his arsenal supposedly impressed and blessed those who pleased him. As the nation reeled from a three-year drought, he ignored them. With a decisive death blow revealing the false god's impotence, it was time for God to manifest His gracious power. Following dismissal, Elijah ascended higher up the mountain and prayed hard for rain. God, who recently answered by fire, sent precious rain on a severely parched nation! Rising from victorious prayer, he ran down the mountain faster than the royal steeds.

Elijah was naturally exhausted. My schedule in the Copperbelt was child's play compared to the strain of his ministry on Mount Carmel. **Spiritual battles and spiritual service, even those with victorious outcomes, wax the people of God mentally, physically, emotionally, and spiritually.** Elijah was human, susceptible to the same weaknesses as us. He needed a good night's rejuvenation. Instead, he spiraled into a sleepless nightmare of the soul. Sometimes unexpected battles follow big wins, ambushing wary, weary fighters. Elijah was empty. He needed a day off, not a fight for survival.

How encouraging it would've been to open the mail and read someone's decision to come back to God. What a lift if someone stopped and shared what God did in their heart as they witnessed the fire fall. Instead, Elijah received a note from the government that produced a lump in his throat: "May the gods strike me and even kill me if by this time tomorrow I have not killed you" (1 Kings 19:2). Sincerely, *Jezebel.*

One blindsiding sentence devastated Elijah. It's the equivalent of going to bed after a perfect autumn day and waking up to crusty, blustery winter. This unexpected change of seasons meant life would never be the same. In response, the larger-than-life man of God flees in a frenzy of fear. **On one hand he feared death; on the other he feared living.** This is uncharacteristic of Elijah. He doesn't panic and run. He stands bold and tall. What's wrong with him? This seems unbelievable, even laughable—he just proved Baal false!

It's easy to offer critique or advice from a distance on how *others* should respond, isn't it?

He could've prayed and rebuked the fear.

Why didn't he just rip the note and have faith?
I thought he was better than this.

We have no idea. I envision myself responding with great faith, but I have no clue what it's like to be given twenty-four hours to live. The queen's death threat seized the control room of Elijah's mind. Any other day, it might not have hit so hard, but sometimes elements create a perfect storm. One dark note catapulted Elijah into a pit of hopelessness.[33]

> **Point:** Have you received bad news?
> **Ponder:** What news or change ushered your current season of life?
> Do I critique or advise others "from a distance?"
> **Prayer:** For new perspective or attitude. (Ephesians 4:23)
> **Practical:** Schedule a day (or hour) to rest, refocus, and replenish.
> What rejuvenates you?
> Devastating news makes life foggy. If that's your situation, let others help with perspective or decision-making.
> **Playlist:** *Scars* by TobyMac
> *Living Hope* by Phil Wickham
> **Pocket:**

---

33 Dedication: Paul Mtambo, my favorite Lion! Thanks to *www.lifewater.org* and *www.equipinternational.org* for tackling WASH needs in Jesus' name.

11: I Fly Solo

*He went on **alone** into the wilderness (1 Kings 19:4).*

Before relocating to Africa, we encountered countless challenges. With all those overcome, it seemed the struggles should be past, but some were just getting started. The first night was dark and intense. It lacked any romantic aura sometimes attached to international travel. The walls suffocated Melissa. She literally gasped for air. We had no friends nearby or any means of communication. The dream-come-true felt like a prison. We wanted to "go serve," not engage in serious battle. We prayed and quoted all the verses we could remember. It was the first of many long nights. Hope was slipping.

Without hope, we're susceptible to all manner of soul sickness—uncontrollable anxiety, numbing apathy, hollow depression, bitter anger, suicidal tendencies. Some assume God's children, at least the strong and mature, are automatically shielded from these, but the unfolding story of Elijah speaks otherwise. No one is granted immunity from such perils.

Too many military heroes return home to face unexpected struggles like depression and PTSD.[34] Spouses enduring the dark night of losing a child stumble into ugly divorce. Missionaries who sacrificed everything find themselves suffering at the hands of those they served, or served alongside. We presume sacrificial obedience guarantees immediate blessing, but too often it begets hardship and tests our faith and endurance. If a life-altering situation ever compelled you to think *I can't handle it; I'm not strong enough for this,* you understand Elijah's reaction. The man of God anticipated the mountaintop clash. He wasn't ready for the death threat. His story reveals three signals of waning hope.

I want to be alone

"Elijah went to Beersheba...and left his servant there. Then he went on alone into the wilderness" (1 Kings 19:3-4). This southernmost border

---

[34] Find help at *Operation Heal our Patriots. www.samaritanspurse.org*

town was still not far enough away. ³⁵ His sidekick during the "pray for rain" event was told to stay while he soldiered on solo. Alone is not inherently bad. Some battles we face alone, even when in the company of others. **Every believer is called to a personal relationship with God, and needs to know how to access the secret, solitary place with Him.** One person before God's throne can accomplish incredible things.

I need to acknowledge that on occasion God calls an individual to a season of extreme separation, often involving deep pain but fostering deep fellowship. God may reveal powerful secrets, but not let a word be uttered to anyone. Jesus, Paul, Jeremiah, and others throughout church history were temporarily set apart from crowds, noise, even socializing, to be strictly one-on-one with God. Think of it as *ordained isolation*. It's not always glamorous, nor to be entered into unless directed by God. Except for this rare exception, isolation can be dangerous, particularly when facing significant or prolonged battles. Be alert to the enemy's tactic of separation from the pack, physically or figuratively. **Even Jesus, during an agonizing night, asked friends to stay nearby and be available.**

Many, especially men, hide when they don't have a handle on life. *Better to be lonely than exposed as incompetent. I don't want to be seen like this or be a downer.* Not having answers makes us feel out of place, even at church. We sometimes don't know what's going on ourselves and can't explain it when people ask. We'd rather suffer alone. Was it wise for Elijah to leave his servant behind? Unless directed by God, I see valid rationale both ways. The point here is the danger of suffering in hopelessness and depression alone.

Depression is not a mark of shame, weakness, or spiritual immaturity. Countless good and godly people have descended its pit. Many find a way out by the ladder of hope. Charles Spurgeon, nicknamed "the prince of preachers," wrote,

> *I am the subject of depression so fearful that I hope none of you ever get to such extremes of wretchedness as I go to. But I always get back again by this—I know that I trust Christ. I have no reliance but in Him, and if He fails, I shall fail. But if He does not, I shall not. Because He lives, I shall live also, and I spring to my legs again*

---

35 Sounds like a town with a drinking problem, but there's no archaeological support.

> *and fight with my depressions of spirit and get the victory through it.*[36]

Point: Does it help knowing strong Christians struggle with depression?
Do you "just want to be alone"? Why?
Ponder: Unless a matter of obedience, should Elijah have gone alone? Why? Why not?
Would you rather feel safe but lonely or incompetent but around others?
Is there a place you can "be real" *and* feel safe?
Prayer: Psalm 91. Take comfort knowing you're never alone.
Practical: Do you naturally fight battles alone or with the help of others?
Develop your "weaker hand" by
—being alone with God (*just* your Bible, pen, paper) OR
—seek another's assistance.
Follow-up: How did it go?
Read "When a Preacher is Downcast" by Charles Spurgeon.
Playlist: *Just As I Am* by Travis Cottrell
Pocket:

---

36 "When a Preacher Is Downcast." Charles Spurgeon.
Dedication: Pat Fleming. Your heart and humor give hope to our military heroes.

12: Death Threat

I have had enough, LORD. ***Take my life*** *(I Kings 19:4).*

One sign of hopelessness is excessive isolation. The second is awfully malignant and must be dealt with *immediately*.

I want to die

Elijah "sat down under a solitary broom tree and prayed. 'I have had enough, LORD. Take my life, for I am no better than my ancestors who have already died'" (1 Kings 19:4-5). His prayer unveils the raw emotion of a man who loves God but feels deep despair. Many have prayed this same prayer. Some consider Elijah suicidal. Was his prayer a heartfelt desire, or spontaneous words puked out of intense angst? Whatever it was, his future looked grim, and he felt hopeless.

My conclusion—this isn't the prayer of someone planning to kill himself if God didn't oblige. It's possible to speak of death, even pray to die, without being suicidal. He asks God to take his life but appears to leave his life in God's hands. Paul, facing a life-or-death situation, said, "I trust that my life will bring honor to Christ, whether I live or die" (Philippians 1:20). If Elijah was suicidal, that doesn't make him bad or unusual, just human and overwhelmed. At any given time among any audience, it's likely at least one has dealt with suicidal notions in recent months. If that's you, you're not alone. Don't be ashamed to tell someone or ask for help.

Suicide is rampant. A growing chorus fantasizes it, even glorifies it. A sobering article references the Center for Disease Control's report of a consistent decline in the average life expectancy of Americans. "This time, neither war nor pestilence is behind the drop in life expectancy. The threats are not external, but internal."[37] In one year we lost 115,000 Americans to drug overdose and suicide. The article continues:

---

37 "The So-Called Deaths of Despair." John Stonestreet. *www.breakpoint.org.* Dec. 2018.

> *In the Christian view, despair is the opposite of hope. Thomas Aquinas wrote that despair "is due to a man's failure to hope that he will share in the goodness of God." For Aquinas, despair was more dangerous than unbelief or hatred of God because "by hope we are called back from evils and induced to strive for what is good, and if hope is lost, men fall headlong into vices, and are taken away from good works."[38]*

We desperately need hope. Without it, we naturally plunge into danger, including suicide. A friend, trying to detox from addictive painkillers, spoke of the incessant voices in his head urging him to end it. Insanely real, their suggestions rang crystal-clear:
When the road turns, go straight.
Take the whole bottle before going to bed.
Wouldn't you like to be free from all this?
Nobody will miss you.
Others hear voices of revenge and self-pity:
Don't you want to get even?
This will make them feel bad.

Let me speak compassionately, but firmly. **Suicidal thoughts are rooted in lies. They especially congregate where the past looks unforgiveable and the future unkind.** During the 2008 economic collapse, the news reported a man who shot his wife and children, then himself. He wasn't an angry madman; just lost his job, and with it, hope. He couldn't see how to provide for his family. I can't think of a single instance where suicide stemmed from truth. As we will discover, even Elijah's request to die stemmed from a false thread in his belief system. Suicide is the deeply unfortunate, final action of a valuable life convinced some lie was true. Please don't let your final deed be motivated by a lie. There *is* hope for you and your future; it's just not clear yet. My heart breaks for those so broken that death seems better, and for the untold needless pain carried day and night by the loved ones of those who ended their life.

---

38 Stonestreet.

There's More

At 3:00 in the morning, a lone man trudged the long city bridge toward his claustrophobic apartment. Hope for a fresh start dissolved when his family u-turned instead of coming to visit. That final nail of hopelessness pounded into the coffin his life built around him. To make it worse, *he* was the reason they left in the first place. Though turning to God thirteen years before, his destructive lifestyle proved too toxic an environment for others to breathe.

Halos from the streetlights glowed through the light fog. Without a single car or pedestrian, the aura was surreal—perfect for making a change. Onto the railing he climbed. Gazing into the dark currents below, he knew one more step would forever rid him and the world of his wretched life. *Well, this is it.*

A friendly tone from behind matter-of-factly said, "There's more." It was so calm it didn't even startle him. Those words piqued his addictive appetite. *Something I haven't experienced? Guaranteed to satisfy?* He faced the stranger with the wonderful secret, but no one was there! With two perfectly chosen words, God graciously spared him. He stepped from the ledge into his bonus stage of life. That was over thirty years ago.

His is not a magical "happily ever after" fairy tale; rather the testimony of a life put back together by the same God who restored Elijah. The process has been long and transformative, painful and joyful. Some relationships are mended, including his marriage; others remain severed. **He views every human interaction, flower enjoyed, lesson learned—*every* experience—as "the more."** A psychiatrist explained, with the "never-enoughness" of addictive behavior, those were *the only two words* that would've whet his appetite. What a testament to the masterful skill of God as an encouraging restorer!

If you wrestle with suicide, there's more, my friend. Don't forfeit future chapters because the current one feels hopeless. There's a way through this. You are not alone. Please reach out for help! After you've invited someone to come alongside you, may I humbly suggest offering your life to God and see what He can do with it? It may or may not be a dramatic turnaround, but I guarantee God has a plan, and a future He will unfold in its time. Someday you will look back and thank God you chose life.

God had more for this man, for Elijah, for the scattered bones. A lot more. He started putting their fractured lives together. When Ezekiel proclaimed God's hope in the valley, something powerful happened, "As I spoke, there was a rattling noise all across the valley. The bones of each body came together and attached themselves as complete skeletons" (Ezekiel 37:7).

Broken now doesn't mean broken forever.[39]

> **Point:** If you've been suicidal, reach out NOW! Not sure who to contact?
> **Focus on the Family:** Connect to caring counselors and find resources like their *Alive to Thrive* program.
> 1-800-A FAMILY (1-800-232-6459) Monday-Friday 8am-10pm EST
> help@focusonthefamily.com
> **Crisis Text Line:**
> Text: "connect" to 741741
> info@crisistextline.org
> **National Suicide Prevention Lifeline:**
> 1-800-273-TALK (8255) 24-hour availability
> TTY: 1-800-799-4TTY (4889)
> *www.suicidepreventionlifeline.org* with live chat network Monday-Friday 2pm-2am EST
> **Ponder:** Is your struggle external or internal? Though we can't control external pressures, we have some control over the internal. Does that change your attitude or perspective?
> **Prayer:** Lord, if this reader wants to give up and die, **please intervene!** Preserve their life and hold them close.
> **Practical:** Think of one reason to live. Who do you love most? Imagine how devastated you'd be if they ended their life. Choose life.
> If you don't want your life, offer it to God. Give Him a chance to do something with it!
> **Playlist:** *Rescue* by Lauren Daigle
> **Pocket:**

---

39 Dedication: Focus on the Family, for consistently valuing life. *www.focusonthefamily.org*

13: Five More Minutes

> *He lay down **again** (I Kings 19:6).*

Despair may lead to isolation or arouse a desire to die, but even if you can't identify with these, the next may resonate.

I want to sleep

> *As he was sleeping, an angel touched him and told him, "Get up and eat!" He looked around and there beside his head was some bread baked on hot coals and a jar of water! So he ate and drank and lay down again (1 Kings 19:5-6).*

Elijah is exhausted. The distance traveled by foot since the showdown is staggering, plus he's emotionally sapped. Sleep is vital and listed as a gift from God. Some need that more than anything, but there is a caution when it's *all* you want. If sleep stifles access to you, and doesn't replenish, but simply provides an escape from life's despair, it may be unhealthy.[40] There's also a time to awaken. To stir from slumber. To face it. To hear God's direction. To move. When inactive for too long, physical rest does not satisfy. True restfulness includes pause *from movement*. God made sure Elijah didn't get imbalanced in this regard. The angel advised practically, "Get up and eat!" Exercise and diet can go a long way toward combating depression.

Drawing again from Spurgeon's insights borne out of dark experiences:

> *A day's breathing of fresh air upon the hills or a few hours' ramble in the beech woods' umbrageous calm, would sweep the cobwebs out of the brain of scores of our toiling*

---

[40] Alcohol/addiction can produce the same tendencies.

> *ministers who are now but half alive. A mouthful of sea air, or a stiff walk in the wind's face, would not give grace to the soul, but it would yield oxygen to the body, which is next best.*[41]
>
> *The angel repeats, "'Get up and eat some more, or the journey ahead will be too much for you.' So he got up and ate and drank, and the food gave him enough strength to travel forty days and forty nights to Mount Sinai, the mountain of God" (1 Kings 19:7-8).*

These signals warn of hopelessness and depression. From my experience, apathy is another marker—we no longer care about anything. This is so difficult to overcome. It feels easier, even appropriate, to succumb. I remember once saying audibly, "I am depressed." The simple acknowledgment clarified the battle and redirected my remaining energies toward fighting my enemies instead of myself or others. Take inventory of these indicators and others like destructive behavior, poor eating habits, and mood swings.[42]

Point: Is sleep an escape?
Do you feel apathetic?
Ponder Psalm 40:1-3.
Prayer: Elijah walked 40 days to meet with God.
Exert some effort to do likewise.
Practical: Take a walk.
Do *one thing* to care for yourself. Adjust sleeping, eating, exercise, or downtime patterns.
Do *one thing* to care for another.
Playlist: You need something peppy! *Awake My Soul* by Hillsong (feat. Tasha Cobbs Leonard)
Pocket:

---

41 "When a Preacher Is Downcast." Charles Spurgeon.
42 Dedication: "Coach" Bill & Janet Carr. You've helped many ministers along their journey.

14: Everyone Needs a White Bench

> *I will open your graves...and cause you to rise again (Ezekiel 37:12).*

Melissa's family graciously invited us on their vacation. This critical getaway gave us a chance to breathe and thaw out from the north's unrelenting cold. I love the first morning of vacation. With the week still ahead, it feels so free. Grabbing my crutches and Bible, I headed to Kure Beach. The quaint community moved to the slow pulse of salt life. Some slipped into the corner diner for breakfast, while others were walking off breakfast. The pier was abuzz with fishermen seeking the big one. A swinging bench beckoned me to the warmth of the barely-risen sun. The tall reeds, soft tones of the sand, and rhythmic ocean waves provided a great setting to spend some desperately needed time with God.

Perhaps influenced by the nautical surroundings, I read about Peter's night-fishing saga. Within minutes *I* was hooked. A gripping discovery made it difficult to read through the warm tears. I thought I'd ruined everything and disqualified myself from serving God again. Not sure why; just assumed I blew it. Peter must've felt this way, but Jesus reached out to him and restored him!

Maybe He could restore me too?
Maybe my story isn't over.
Maybe He's been in this all along!
Hope cascaded like living water into my wilderness soul.
God can raise me to life!
He still has purposes for me!

I consider that morning on the swinging bench the beginning of my restoration, when a little *hope* tugged my line. **The seeds of hope, no matter how small, can produce great things. Hope is often the first stage of restoration. Before God did anything *for* the dry bones, He spoke words of hope *to* them.**

Superseding Whispers

Let's return to Elijah's story. An angel directed him to rise and eat in order to embark on a journey to the mountain of God. Though its exact location is uncertain, my best research suggests the trip from Beersheba required six miles of desert every day for forty days. The day-to-day lives of powerful men and women of God are not always glorious. But God was on the other side of this wilderness. Elijah headed to the same area where God encountered Moses centuries before. "There he came to a cave and spent the night" (1 Kings 19:9).

God broke the silence with a probing question: "What are you doing here, Elijah?" God often asks questions to those close to Him. It's a gesture promoting friendship. **The Almighty cared about the contents bottled up inside Elijah, so He offered a safe place for him to bare his soul, with no hint anything was off-limits.** Elijah immediately bit the bait. He had a lot pent up. "I have zealously served the LORD God Almighty. But the people of Israel have broken their covenant with you, torn down your altars, and killed every one of your prophets. I am the only one left, and now they are trying to kill me, too" (1 Kings 19:10).

The last statement reveals the fault line in his belief system. Beliefs have consequences and manifest in our prayers and conversations. Elijah believed he was the only committed believer left; hence, the last hope for the nation. Talk about a burden to shoulder! According to his thought pattern, if he dies, the kingdom of God collapses. He is the last voice pointing the nation to God, the final flickering flame, and he's about to be extinguished. Someone already told Elijah about one hundred godly prophets, yet Elijah still saw himself as the only one. He over-exaggerated his importance, unable to imagine God's work continuing without him. As my childhood pastor, the late Rev. Fred Moore, often said, "God is on the throne, and He ain't nervous!"

It's hard being God—if you're not God.
But if you are God, being God is a cinch.

God anticipated this meeting and patiently listened to the heartbreak of a tired, depressed minister. Many in Elijah's shoes have run to places and drowned their sorrows in worldly amusements or destructive behaviors. Meanwhile, God invites us to dump our stuff on the floor before His throne. Nothing is off-limits. After the prophet unearthed his soul, God told him, "'Go out and stand before me on the mountain.' And as Elijah stood there, the LORD passed by" (1 Kings 19:11). A terrifying display of God's power sent Elijah back into the cave's recesses, where **His fear of God rekindled.** It had been replaced by a fear of man (or woman, in this case).

God reminded him of His awareness and capability of handling everything. Something pivotal happened in the back of that cave. It's the greatest thing that can occur in the life of someone at wit's end. God whispered—gentle, powerful, peaceful, lifting. We don't know what He whispered. It remained secret, just between the two of them. There's nothing like timely words from God to spark new hope after the fog of despair has settled. God's clear word was what Elijah needed. It had the power to change his life, *if* he embraced it. I believe this *eventually* became his turning point. God repeats his question. The prophet repeats his response verbatim, which makes me wonder if he believed God's words the first time.

However long it took, by the time Elijah departed, God's words fortified him. The whisper of the Almighty superseded the thunderous threat of the queen. This new internal operating system replaced human voices. **Everything looked hopeless only because God hadn't spoken yet.** I'm glad the God of Elijah never scratches His head, wracks His brain, or paces nervously through the night trying to find a solution. What was such a big deal to the man was child's play to his God.

You'll never overhear God say:

Oops.

Uh oh, now what?

Angels, report to the conference room near the throne for an emergency meeting.

Hmmm.. Never thought of that.

I forgot.

Let me check with Oprah, Dr. Phil, and Wikipedia.

Amid a season of various pressures in college, these words anchored me: "Remember the word to your servant, upon which You have caused me to hope. This is my comfort in my affliction, for Your word has given me life" (Psalms 119:49 NKJV). When we descend to the lowest places where hope seems lost, even *there* God knows what to do. Even in the depths, "The eternal God is your refuge, and his everlasting arms are under you" (Deuteronomy 33:27).

New Tricks for an Old Dog

Without hesitation, desperation, or exasperation, God commissions Elijah to a brand-new assignment. In response, he seeks two young men to tell them God chose them to be kings. Amazing! God used this repurposed prophet to speak purpose into these guys. God was not only using him to confront kings, as in the past, but to call them! Next, he finds a young farmer named Elisha and takes him under his wing. This was new for Elijah. His ministry philosophy favored the lone-ranger approach. He gave his life to see national revival, but never saw it. Instead, God used the aging prophet to impart revival into one young man.

This morning I heard the dreadful news of a young minister who took his life. I met him at a picnic a few years ago—he was excited about new opportunities. But life went different than envisioned, and he ended it too soon. After the initial shock, I thought: *What would have happened if he endured this dark night and experienced God's mercies in the morning? What ministry would've been accomplished? How would God have redeemed his pain?* We'll never know. Hopelessness spoke last.

God can take our mess and make something beautiful, even as He used a broken veteran to mentor a man for the next generation. **Many have discovered fruitful new realms following long, barren nights.** A quick word to aging ministers—whether retired, forced out, or timed out due to personal limitations, the tendency is to feel dried up and useless. Don't underestimate the impact you can have, even if "just for one." Think of Moses nurturing Joshua or Barnabas encouraging Saul. Maybe God will use you to raise up someone whose life would never take flight without your imparting investment.

Jezebel's note, collapsing under a tree—these weren't Elijah's finale. Great contributions *followed* his pit of depression. Before descending the mountain, God told him something else: "I have reserved seven thousand, all whose knees have not bowed to Baal" (I Kings 19:18 NKJV)!

Elijah wasn't the only one. God's kingdom was still in good hands![43]

---

43 Dedication: Russ & Carrie Hamby. Can't thank you enough for that crucial getaway!

Point: Worn out from trying to "be God?" The world isn't on your shoulders.
Ponder what makes you feel hopeless. Where do you go when things feel hopeless?
What words frighten you? Could they be replaced with a healthy fear of God?
Prayer: Are you comfortable exposing your heart to God?
Practical: "Hope's List" (*Bonus Features*) proclaims God's greatness, which hopelessness skews. Read it standing to demonstrate trust amid struggle. (Ephesians 6:10-14)
God sometimes uses uncomfortable seasons to change our course. Record any recent stirrings toward a new focus, ministry, or career. Don't force it; just be alert.
Playlist: *Be Alright* by Evan Craft
There's Hope in Front of Me by Danny Gokey
Pocket:

15: I Have My Sources

> *I pray that God, the source of hope, will fill you completely with joy and peace because you trust in him (Romans 15:13).*

Where does hope originate? The verse above reveals the answer. When you pray, you're at the production plant where hope is manufactured and distributed! You may be in a crack house, jailhouse, schoolhouse, or God's house; at work, in the woods, or behind the wheel. Good news! You're in the presence of the inventor and bestower of hope. One ministry of the Spirit is to inject hope—overflowing, confident hope into God's people. He *wants* you to have hope.

The LORD instructed Ezekiel to speak a message to the dry bones. He could've done it Himself, but instead, He put life-giving words into a human mouth. God was restoring them *while* Ezekiel spoke! God does so much through words of truth! If you have been given a ministry involving speaking, seek His words, then speak confidently, knowing He works while you speak![44] Ezekiel told those old bones what God was going to do. This reveals something about hope. **It's rooted in the character, will, and ability of Almighty God.** Because God had a plan, there was hope.

Under New Management

I gave a tractor to a friend in exchange for some mechanical work. One sunny day he showed up, more a favor than anything. The old Cub didn't run, mice camped under the hood, the seat split, vines befriended it. Wasting no time, he unearthed it, inflated the tires, cleaned the seat, and removed the mouse nest.

"I can't believe those tires hold air. The metal is perfect. It's solid." Nothing negative came from his lips. We loaded the reclaimed jewel on his trailer. After thirty minutes with Ray, it stood taller. His enthusiasm raised as he spoke his vision. "I've got a battery and a seat. Amazing— the gas tank is completely free of debris. That slipping belt won't be hard to fix. We'll get it cleaned up and paint that yellow and that

---

44 Acts 10:44. 1 Peter 4:11.

white." It was contagious. I glimpsed what he saw. Every lap around the tractor brought more excitement and vision-induced words.

I was glad it went to him. I saw a broken, worthless, dirty old mess. I emphasized its flaws and pathetic condition. My only vision was to send it away. Then along comes a man with a tire inflator in his hand, who appreciated its qualities and verbalized its future. Broken things were handled with optimism, not critique. **Something powerful happened during that half-hour. It got a new owner!**

If the tractor remained in my possession, it rightfully had no hope. When it belonged to Ray, it rightly overflowed with hope! Why? Hope is rooted in the character, ability, and will of the owner. And just like God, who spoke to the old bones before restoring them, Ray first spoke. Those words, all kind, flowed from a keen vision powered by love and backed by skill. "You can see it done, can't you?" I asked. "Yes, I can!" he responded. He recently sent pics. It's beautiful and works perfect!

There's no such thing as a hopeless Christian. If you belong to God, you have grounds for hope, for He is the source of hope. Even when we don't understand, we can still have an expectation that God will be with us and work on our behalf. It doesn't imply our detailed plans will work the way we pray or envision. It doesn't always mean we know the outcome. We don't have to know how it will be answered in order to pray. Some prayers are *nevertheless prayers*. "Nevertheless we made our prayer to our God" (Nehemiah 4:9 NKJV). In other words, "I have no idea how this can be answered, but I'm trusting God." **Hope simply means there's always an answer. It expects God to be gracious.**

The dry bones represented people living against their will as strangers in a foreign country, who concluded there was no answer or remedy. "Our bones are dry, our hope is lost, and we ourselves are cut off" (Ezekiel 37:11)! God, eavesdropping on their conversations, adopted their analogy, then infused it with hope. "OK, if you're hopeless bones, I'm the One who will revive your bones and make you an army!" That's why God first instructed His servant to speak specific words of hope, comfort, and stability to them. Faith comes by hearing. His words sprouted hope, gave them something to believe in, gave them security amid insecure circumstances.

Their uncertain future was not dictated by what they saw or felt but by God's promised words. When they felt insecurity or despair, they could remember: *God said He will make us live again*. In His wisdom, it redirects our eyes from us or the situation to Him, His ability, and His words. They had hope because the Lord had a vision, which He revealed by His words, and eventually confirmed by His works. I lost hope most when I doubted God's character or words, but Peter's story sparked hope. God's stories are laden with situations of hopelessness. In fact, He majors in hopelessness.

Who Owns You?

Do you belong to God? If not, would you like to? You were created to know Him, to live in right relationship with Him. We've all gone our own way. Our sins distance us from the God we are meant to be close to. According to the Bible, there's a very uncomfortable truth—we either belong to God *or* the devil. There's no neutral ground. That's why one element of God's great salvation is described: "He has rescued us from the kingdom of darkness and transferred us into the kingdom of his dear Son, who purchased our freedom and forgave our sins" (Colossians 1:13-14). **He transfers us out of Satan's kingdom into Christ's kingdom!** What a glorious transaction. It's called redemption, meaning God paid an exorbitantly high price to forgive everything we've done wrong, and make us right with Him. Broken lives estranged from God find peace with Him!

> *You know that God paid a ransom to save you from [your] empty life. It was not paid with mere gold or silver, which lose their value. It was the precious blood of Christ, the sinless, spotless Lamb of God. God chose him as your ransom long before the world began, but now…he has been revealed for your sake. Through Christ you have come to trust in God. And you have placed your faith and hope in God because he raised Christ from the dead and gave him great glory. You were cleansed from your sins when you obeyed the truth…you have been born again (1 Peter 1:18-23).*

If there's a "tug" inside—a yearning, a pulling of your soul to these things—don't put it off. God's Holy Spirit is trying to reconcile you to God! This is what you were made for! God says, "Come now, let's settle this. Though your sins are like scarlet, I will make them as white as snow" (Isaiah 1:17). Our sins are highly offensive to God, but the blood Jesus shed when He horrifically died fully covers them. "Without the shedding of blood there is no forgiveness of sins" (Hebrews 9:22 ESV). Forget about being good enough or spiritual enough. Confess your sins to God, knowing Jesus saves sinners. "As many as received Him, to them He gave the right to become children of God, to those who believe in His name" (John 1:11-12 NKJV). When *you receive Christ* by faith to save you, *He receives you* as His own! You're completely forgiven and fully accepted by God!

It's settled.[45]

> **Point:** Hope is rooted in the character, will, and ability of the owner.
> God and hopelessness cannot coexist.
> **Ponder** God looking and speaking over your life as Ray did the tractor.
> Describe your situation. (Example: "I'm a trainwreck.") Write how God might infuse *your* description with hope. (Example: "I'm the God who puts trains back on track.")
> **Prayer:** Pray a "nevertheless" prayer.
> Which kingdom are you in? Would you like to transfer? Ask Jesus to save you! "He who calls on the name of the Lord will be saved" (Romans 10:13).
> **Practical:** Physically look up. You're in the presence of hope!
> **Playlist:** *Great is Thy Faithfulness* hymn by Thomas Chisholm or *Faithfulness* (Howland Mix)
> *Jesus Paid It All* by Kristian Stanfill
> **Pocket:**

---

[45] Dedication: Ray & Dar Lingenfelter. I learned a lot from you in 30 minutes around a tractor!

PART 3:
The Restorer *speaks* *greatness* over broken pieces who feel *unworthy*.

> *There was a rattling noise all across the valley. The bones came together and attached themselves as complete skeletons (Ezekiel 37:7).*

**The desert can decimate
our sense of value.
Countless voices suggest who you are.
God declares who you really are.**

Let Him have the final say.

**Moses' story is a great example of how
The Restorer puts unworthy pieces back together.**

16: Just Look at You!

*They were scattered everywhere **across the ground** (Ezekiel 37:2).*

My heart raced. Counseling myself to be brave, I nearly plunged, then chickened out. I'd served in pastoral ministry for a decade, been run over by a truck, rode a train for two days with people I just met to a place known for its hostility. But this? Nope. Couldn't muster enough courage to…

First, let me give some context. Nine months prior we moved to Uganda. Ninety days later we returned home due to an emergency. Life unexpectedly morphed into a very confusing, uncomfortable shape. January hit hard with my entrance into the forties. February left me limping with a broken ankle. March forced prolonged hibernation from Old Man Winter's bitterness. I watched Melissa work herself ragged performing a thousand tasks. I felt ashamed and worthless, knowing my injury dumped additional strain on her.

So what couldn't I do?

Look in the mirror.

Sounds ridiculous to some, hopefully to most. Yet, I'm guessing someone thought, *I'm not the only one?* Or maybe, *This guy is more messed up than me!* I was ashamed of what I had become, or *not* become. I didn't want to look at such worthless garbage. I've always gravitated to being hard on myself. **A slightly distorted self-perception can severely warp in low times.** I chose negative self-talk over God's unchanging truth and collapsed like the house built on sand. I blamed myself for everything. Life was hard and the future bleak because of me. *If only I was stronger, smarter.* In addition to the weight of the season's challenges, I lugged the unnecessary burden of worthlessness, making the wilderness far more difficult.

One night I couldn't sleep. I slipped out of bed, grabbed my crutches, crab-walked down the stairs, and laid on the couch. I started to weep, not because of the trials, but because of the way I treated myself. Something new washed over me—compassion. I had become a cruel, unpleasant tyrant, demanding standards no one could achieve. I didn't treat others this way yet felt justified in doing so to myself. In the wee hours of the night, I apologized to me! A little grace can work miracles, even the grace extended to the precious soul in the mirror.

After we muster the courage to look.

We noted the symbolism of bones. After reducing a person to their lowest, bones remain. They portray the core of you, thus, the part of the physical body most closely associated with the soul. They represent worth, but *scattered* bones are the ultimate disgracing of a life created in God's image. **If our value derives from possessions, positions, personality, popularity, productivity, or pedigree, we are building on very uneven ground.** Winds blow in different directions. Things can get stolen, but your worth can't. Jobs and associations, accolades and reputation, can come and go. They may describe, but they don't define.

The people shown to Ezekiel had nothing of external value. Nothing. Anyone walking that valley would have seen a sad scenario, but the Lord saw inestimable value. After God spoke hope-filled words to the bones, He started putting them back together. Normally, rattling means something is loose or falling apart, but in God's Restoration Shop it's the sound of rebuilding, much like those emanating from a furniture repair shop, construction site, or autobody garage. **If scattered bones signify degradation, The Restorer was undoing their disgrace by reattaching them.**

Walking with Moses

Moses has been a companion throughout my wilderness journey. His story has helped me tremendously. It's incredible that we can access biblical, historical, and contemporary people of faith. Whatever you face, you're not the first, and you're not alone. Find a man or woman in the sacred pages and let them mentor you. Find a missionary or pastor from the past or present and let them speak to you. During one season of depression, I consulted Pastor Charles Spurgeon. His insights gave hope. I was glad I could sit in his office through a simple internet search. **As we walked with Elijah, who encountered the God who restores hope, let us learn from Moses, who encountered the God who restores our fractured sense of worth.**

"A new king came to the throne of Egypt. This king exploited our people and oppressed them, forcing parents to abandon their newborn babies so they would die. At that time Moses was born—a beautiful child in God's eyes" (Acts 7:18-20). What a volatile time to be born! His people suffered as slaves for generations. As with all boys born during this time, he arrived with a federally mandated death sentence on his precious little head. His mom hid him until they could keep him secret no longer. Laying him in a waterproof basket at three months of age, she placed him in the Nile River, and ultimately in the hands of her God. Who found him and fell in love with him? The princess! Seeking someone to raise him until the proper age, she hired his mom.

Isn't that a story only God could write? These peasants, oppressed by the government, were on the royal payroll to take care of their own son! We don't know much about Moses as a boy. We do know, "Pharaoh's daughter adopted him and raised him as her own son, he was taught all the wisdom of the Egyptians" (Acts 7:21-22). These statements from childhood through young adult years are followed by a summary of his life as an adult. What had the promising star become?

Powerful. In speech and action.

The Bible doesn't expound, but I picture Moses in the debate hall silencing his rivals, none overcoming his intellect. I envision him on an ornate stage before the greats of the world who traveled significant distances to hear his oratory. Can you see him at the federal advisory table, or privately sharing counsel with Grandpa Pharaoh? Well-versed in numerous fields, he spoke authoritatively and skillfully. But Moses wasn't just brilliant, or one who could elicit a standing ovation. He acted powerfully. I see him developing business models, managing projects, inventing resources, and maximizing productivity. Moses was a superstar.

Hard to believe there could be a time *he* wouldn't want to look in the mirror.[46]

> **Point:** Does your worth derive from shifting things? (Possessions, positions, personality, popularity, productivity, pedigree.)
> **Ponder:** What does your mirror say?
> Does worthlessness keep you from attempting things or enjoying life?
> **Prayer:** Confess feelings of worthlessness.
> **Practical:** Look in a mirror and think nothing negative. Observe the image of God. Apologize if needed.
> **Playlist:** *I Could Sing of Your Love Forever* by Delirious
> **Pocket:**

---

46 Dedication: Dad. I'm honored to be your son. Thank you for always speaking worth over me.

17: The (Embellished) Autobiography of Moses

[While not equating this with the Bible, I've creatively pieced elements from the true story to emphasize an unfamiliar season of a familiar man. Let's listen to what the autobiography of Moses *could* sound like.]

I enjoyed the honors and attention. I worked hard to get them. While my future in Egypt couldn't get brighter, concern for my native people, the Hebrews, brewed inside. Eventually, I went to see them, but I gasped in horror at their cruel existence. How could my adopted family allow this, let alone order it? Guilt ensued as I witnessed their grueling tasks—making bricks, digging ditches, hauling burdens, building structures for Pharaoh's fame—without rest, pay, or mercy. The royal family and I lived proud, carefree lives at their expense.

My body lived in the palace with the world's elite, but my mind preferred my family in their oppressive, little abodes. I despised being introduced as the son of the princess, an accolade I formerly treasured. The massive bed where I fantasized of kingship now housed nightmares of my family being beaten. Their plight gnawed at me, and so did a divine assignment. I *knew* God positioned me to liberate them.

One day a commotion caught my attention. A foreman demanded silence, then lit into a Hebrew man. Terror seared the slave's face as he pleaded for mercy. Tears left trails down his dirty, sunken cheeks. Undeterred, the whip rose high. I recoiled as it fell with a hellish crack. The blow ripped bare shoulders and elicited a blood-curdling cry. Down came the whip again. *Crack*. He tried to take it, but it proved too much. *Crack*. The tyrant's muscular arm operated like a machine in perfect rhythm. Up, down, *crack*; up, down, *crack*. I wondered if this crumpled mess of blood and flesh would survive. The paralysis of my people stung my heart.

Except *I* wasn't paralyzed.

I was born for this. The courageous spirit of a hero quickened me as I approached the assaulter, who was no match for my surprise attack. I quickly buried that disgrace in the sand. The next morning destiny pulsed through my veins and a declaration of independence resounded in my spirit. *They'll know I've come to deliver them, and if they follow my lead, we can be free!* How indescribable to be chosen by the Almighty for such an historic task. Life was about to change!

I didn't expect *this* though. Instead of a ruthless tyrant, I witnessed Hebrews fighting. Knowing unity was imperative for our movement, I assumed the role of peacemaker and questioned the instigator. He pushed me aside, demanding to know who made me their boss! "Are you going to kill me as you killed the Egyptian yesterday" (Exodus 2:14)? His words made me flinch. In one moment, I fell from chosen general to guilty fugitive.

Can't you see God sent me to rescue you?

An unfamiliar emotion arrested me—fear. Egypt went on high alert as Pharaoh wanted me dead. How could I escape his trained search parties? Chariot wheels closed in as commanders urged their steeds to run like never before. The synchronized marching of soldiers coursed terror through my being. I could feel them breathing down my neck.

I ran as hard as I could, not knowing where to run. Chaos rattled my mind, compelling me across the desert floor. As dusk settled, my pace became a crawl. I collapsed in defeat. My body heaved uncontrollably against the surprisingly cool sand as the clamoring army circled. I waited for a punishing whip or the unsheathing of a sword. Would I hear the merciless barking of a commander I often dined with? Would my overtaxed heart explode first? My tongue stuck to the roof of my parched mouth; my clothing saturated in sweat. I awaited my imminent demise. It felt like eternity. Curiosity insisted I look at Egypt's new hero. I was shocked!

Nothing.

No vicious army or fearsome horses. No flashing swords or intimidating chariots. Straining, I raised on one elbow to look behind. Nothing. Silence you could feel swallowed the terror. I bellowed a long-pent-up sigh of relief and struggled to stand. Every direction displayed barren stillness. I staggered like a drunk man, my legs rebuking me. My weary hands raised in appreciation to the Almighty, who mercifully rescued me again from Pharaoh's wrath.

A raspy declaration of victory preceded my crumbling into the sand. The gnawing fear of death subsided, allowing my raging heartbeat to eventually regulate. I relished that celebration, but not long. New fears emerged. Waves of loneliness overtook me. Now a man without home or country, I scanned for signs of life or help, and prayed that my family wasn't paying for my foolishness.

Hot sun jolted my fitful sleep, forcing me into this new reality riddled with uncertainty. A 360-degree observation spoke one unified story—wasteland. Frenzied thoughts and emotions rushed in. Thankfulness ebbed with starvation. Regret mingled with frustration.

Maybe I shouldn't have killed that tyrant, but he deserved it. "I did this because You called me, God! I gave my royal position and good life *for this*? I should've left things alone. I need water, or I will have escaped Pharaoh only to die of thirst. What stinks? Oh, that's me. What I would give for a refreshing bath and great meal. Give? I have *nothing*!"

Eventually I reached Midian and, with great relief, found a well. They were distant relatives to us Hebrews. I hoped to find a place of refuge until I could develop a plan. A gracious community leader took me in, but I hated it here. It was too backward and bland compared to the modern marvels of Egypt. Their customs, food, and dwellings were so foreign. I didn't belong. Daily I worried about my people and struggled to reconcile my compelling sense of destiny with my current way of life.

In time I married and settled down, but it was challenging. When I became a dad, I named my first son *Gershom:* "stranger in a strange land." I provided for my little family, but not by teaching at a university or serving as a judge, though I was qualified to do these things and a hundred more. Talk about a humble road—the rising star, the chosen deliverer, has become a shepherd boy in Midian. Egyptians despise shepherds; now I am one.

I missed being a somebody.[47]

Point: Can you identify with *this* Moses?
Ponder: Obviously, creative license was implemented. What's Biblically accurate? inaccurate? (Exodus 1-4; Acts 7; Hebrews 11) How do you envision it?
Prayer: "Turn and answer me, Lord my God! Restore the sparkle to my eyes, or I will die" (Psalm 13:3).
Practical: Hate your job? Is it "below" you? Until another door opens, humbly work as if Jesus was your boss. *Everything* He did on earth was "below" Him. (Philippians 2:3-11)
Playlist: *Breathe* by Michael W. Smith
You are my Rock by Petra
Pocket:

---

47 Dedication: Annabel Bowerman. You were our solid rock in a foreign land!

18: Detour—Next 40 Years

> *Moses **settled** there (Exodus 2:21).*

Ever feel your soul shrivel at the close of another mediocre day? Or a detour disintegrate your "real purposes?" Maybe medical emergencies dictate your schedule, setbacks have blown you off course, or a regretted decision haunts you at night. Moses anticipated "the promised land." Instead, he got Midian. We may think he had it all together, grabbed life by the horns, never questioned God, never wrestled with regret or runaway emotions. We easily drain the humanity from men like him.

Was Moses in the pastureland having rockin' devotions with God, writing psalms, and enjoying this secluded phase of life? Perhaps. Was God "purging Egypt out of him?" Perhaps. The Bible remains quiet about this prolonged season, but I think it was brutal on his psyche. If Moses got close to God and clutched his dreams, why did he vehemently resist when God visited? Remember, Moses single-handedly attempted to liberate a multitude of slaves from a superpower! As he watched sheep, did he plead, "God, get me out of here! This isn't my calling. I'm wasting away!" This side-step continued month after month until a new calendar replaced the old. Another September, another April. Years accumulate. Gershom turns 35. Decades add up.

Forty...years.

Don't minimize that, especially when we get impatient at forty-second red lights. Maybe while the lonely wind howled across the plain, or the extinguished lamp bid farewell to another day, the last ounce of life vanished from his soul. It seems Moses finally accepted this lot in life. It wasn't what he expected, but that's how it went. It's a very sorrowful scenario.

Who did I think I was?
Did God forget me? I doubt He wants an old murderer.
I had so much to offer, so much I wanted to do.
I gave my best years for this stupid work.

Equipped for other things, he merely exists. It used to be you couldn't keep this good man down. Now you can't keep him awake. The wilderness has a way of stifling every dream and joy till its inhabitants are as empty as it is. **How many currently occupy a claustrophobic space that's stolen their sense of dignity and worth?**

Mental Midian

After pastoring I suffered a mental brand of Midian. Life's landscape was quite pleasant—we bought a charming little house, settled into Melissa's home church where my best friend serves on staff, and I enjoyed my behind-the-scenes work. Things were good, but I wasn't. Melissa asked why I didn't sing during worship. "I don't know. I just can't" (or wouldn't). I felt numb, unworthy, and lost; wanted to fulfill God's plan but wondered what it was or how my present situation could lead there. I figured God would someday visit me and restore my calling, but many mornings wrought dueling thoughts: *I hope this is the day. I hope this is not the day.* We can be satisfied with externals, while knowing a major internal component is missing or unresolved. The good news? **A map and census of Midian hangs prominently in God's office.** He always knows who's there.

God didn't forget Moses. Eventually the two encountered.

One day Moses led his flock far in the wilderness to Sinai, the mountain of God. Every life-altering event occurs *one day*. Sounds unusual, but intentional. What motivated him? Searching for God? Finding new pasture? Changing scenery? Whatever his reasons, nothing could have prepared the old shepherd for what was about to happen. I want to marinate a little in what this encounter meant for Moses, and what it can teach us who have detoured or dead-ended.

We Have Ignition

God arrested Moses' attention through a fiery bush. This arid climate should've consumed it in seconds, but this one kept burning. To a guy unaccustomed to excitement in his career, it must've been beautiful and mysterious. Inquisitive, he approaches, only to realize he's not alone! That spot became sacred territory as God called, "Moses! Moses!" Was this the first thing he heard from God in a while? How powerful and precious for the ears of this aging man to hear the Almighty utter *his* name! I envision Moses melting, not from the fire, but because the clear voice of God refreshes weary souls. Any distance or silence was swallowed in an instant. **God's methods of restoration are unique.** This wasn't some chance encounter or generic "Y'all come," but, "Moses, I'm looking for *you*." Mmmm, water to a parched soul.

Willie Downing served as our college pastor. I met him my freshman year and felt shocked whenever he sought me out. Everyone cherished his endearing presence because he exuded such a precious brand of love. It was impossible to be with him and feel devalued. He smiled like you were his favorite, and say, "Ahhh, you're special, the only one of your kind!" Such words never age. Willie routinely chose students to serve with him in South Africa. I watched jealously at others' invitations. Their stories and interactions were incredibly appealing. I never felt qualified, but secretly hoped for an invitation someday. It came my senior year. It was deeply moving.

Though not always dramatic, God plans these ultra-personal encounters with precision and sensitivity. As no one else experienced a flamin' bush, you will experience things crafted just for you. Beware of coveting the way God approaches others. You don't need some Jordan River episode or get a bush to ignite. Keep seeking God. He will meet *you*. It might occur in a mundane setting at an unexpected time, or in a special place where you intentionally approach Him. He simply promises, "Draw near to God, and He will draw near to you" (James 4:8 NKJV). Nowhere is off God's radar.

The wilderness is often where we question our worth. It's also where God proves He knows our name. That's the greatest testament to our value, to be able to say, "God knows and loves *me*."[48]

Point: Does *mediocre, insignificant, worthless,* or *unfulfilled* resonate?
Have you experienced "Midian?"
Ponder your *best one day* with God. (What if it's today?!)
Is God trying to get your attention? Are you trying to "manufacture" His?
Prayer: God, please say my name. Remind me You're with me.
Practical: Put some sand or salt in your hand and count each grain. Then read Psalm 139:17-18.
Playlist: *Faithful God* by I am They
When the Tears Fall by Newsboys
Pocket:

---

48 Dedication: In memory of Willie Downing, one of the best to ever walk this planet.

19: Who Am I? (And Other Gnawing Questions)

> *Who am I to appear before Pharaoh?*
> *Who am I to lead the people? (Exodus 3:11)*

After God called Moses and declared the place holy, He assured him He heard every cry, sigh, groan, and prayer of the people in bondage. They felt ignored and abandoned, yet their plight moved Him. From the bush, God prescribed an intervention. Then came the hitch—Moses would facilitate it. God ever seeks human partners to accomplish His purposes. Most who hear God's call consider themselves highly questionable or automatically disqualified. He doesn't offer an explanation. He just chooses who He chooses. Moses used to consider himself the right choice. Forty years earlier he would've run to Egypt. Now he's reluctant. His sense of worth must've drained into Midian's wasteland. *Who am I?* he questions.

I'm not enough.
You have the wrong person.
I can't do anything important.

When we question our ability to do God's will, He assures us of Himself and His ability, not ours.

Good Bones

A myriad of TV shows depicts the restoration of houses. We are introduced to a structure well past its prime because it's hardly entertaining to watch a furnace install or new paint in the bathroom. Viewers crave transformation, so hosts show a house as is, then unfold a vision of what can be. As the house is assessed, you often hear "...but it's got good bones." In other words, the structure is solid. Hideous wallpaper can be removed, the sagging roof shored up, the kitchen overhauled, the master bedroom expanded. All is possible, even makes sense, because it has *good bones*. At its core, it's unquestionably worth investing in! During the next hour, we witness a stunning metamorphosis.

Moses was "good bones" in God's sight, but not in his own. His first concern reveals a universal gnaw in the heart of mankind. *Who am*

I? What's my worth? During my dark night, I had to remind myself that Calvary, where Jesus gave His life for mine, forever determined my worth. **The cross is the grandest, loudest, most spectacular declaration of our worth!** Many voices, external and internal, announce your identity. The one you heed will dramatically affect the course of your life.

The first half of the book of Ephesians is an amazing proclamation of human worth, conferred on those belonging to God through Jesus Christ. It proves this is a major issue in our minds; it's also evidence **God wants us to think correctly—not just highly—about ourselves.** Paul nearly wears out a phrase describing our highest identity, superseding every other—*in Christ*. So much flows from that, literally, because what's in Him flows into us.

Other Gnawing Questions

Moses expresses another age-old concern. *They're gonna ask me stuff I don't know.*

Next, he addresses the "what ifs." *What if they question my calling, credentials, abilities, beliefs?* I don't have enough. The nation didn't exactly rally around him last time. What if he ruins everything again? God's assignments require more than we possess, yet He uses what we have. God asked, "What's in your hand?" He didn't ask what he *didn't* have. He could use whatever Moses possessed; in this case, a staff.[49] Oh the seemingly insignificant things God can use! A boy's lunch, words, seeds, ants, stones, dust, two coins, two wooden beams nailed together. **We have a little. God has a lot. God *loves* working with a little!**

The old man fails to deter the Divine, so he unveils his automatic disqualification. "Even…if I…wanted to…to…to do this, I can't. Because…I ca…I can't… speak goo…goo…uh speak well. Ph…Ph… Pharaoh won't li…uh listen to a stammering…fool." Moses thought he needed to speak well to obey God. Something affected his ability to speak. Maybe a stutter? Was this a handicap that developed over time, or a stronghold in his mind—a *believed* impairment? He told God he never spoke well, which wasn't true. He used to be powerful in speech. One category of surrender is relinquishing what we are *not* to God.

God answered every objection, so Moses unsheathes his greatest rebuttal, the clincher—*No. Find somebody else.* It wasn't motivated by

---

49 This ordinary piece of wood was later called "the staff of God!"

doubt or disqualification, but disobedience. God responds differently this time, not with assurance but anger.

Next thing we know, Moses is taking his first step toward God's call.[50]

> **Point:** What's your bigger struggle: doubt, disqualification, or disobedience?
> What makes you feel disqualified?
> **Ponder** the difference between thinking *highly* and *correctly* about self. How important is one's view of self?
> What's in your hand? "I have a little. God has a lot. He loves working with a little."
> **Prayer:** Surrender what you're *not* (what you *assume* you need to be).
> **Practical:** Read Ephesians 1-3, then answer "Who am I?"
> Repeated statements downplaying your value negatively affect demeanor, actions, and identity. Try repeating what God says about you. He's invested a lot in you. You're invaluable to Him. What voice declares your worth and identity? The one you heed will change your life.
> Can a step move you from feeling disqualified to empowered?
> **Playlist:** *Who Am I?* by Casting Crowns.
> **Pocket:**

---

50 Dedication: Brent Henderson, speaker, author of *Into the Wilds* and *The Roar Within*. Keep telling God's kids who they are! (*www.menministry.org*)

20: Back-Country Wisdom

> ***God called*** *to him from the midst of the bush (Exodus 3:4).*

Here are some gleanings from the burning bush that will hopefully encourage anyone, like Moses, who detoured into a wilderness. Read several times, note any that resonate, and use to springboard into prayer.

- Silent doesn't mean distant. I may not hear God, but He hears my cries, sighs, heartbeat, and mental chatter. He knows how to speak but sometimes remains silent. I must be careful about presumptions or false conclusions. By faith I know He's listening.
- God knows me *by name*.
- God has an assignment for me. Maybe I don't know it or believe it, but God never created anything devoid of purpose, and I'm no exception. Wastelands often precede promised lands (Psalm 66:12).
- When things look finished, God may be starting something new.
- God can breathe new life into an old one.
- God can meet me anywhere. There are no "insignificant" places. God is especially alert to those who feel broken beyond repair.
- God is undeterred by my self-inflicted disqualifications. Sometimes "disqualifications" are credentials.
- The truly great things about Moses were *ahead*. What if my best days, most fruitful years, and most exhilarating experiences are before, not behind?
- God isn't bound by time. Many are called late in life. Don't assume expiration dates.
- Take a step. Maybe nothing significant happens, but it could be a life-changing step. If I find myself on holy ground, I'll embrace it.
- Imagine if Moses went from the palace to delivering the nation! He had to first learn wilderness survival—its dangers, resources, climate—before leading the nation through it. Midian's wasteland was as essential to Moses' preparation as Egypt's classroom.
- Purpose doesn't imply ease. God's plans require faith, courage, and hard work.

When life is disorienting and purpose unclear, God often links us to others. The wilderness breeds isolation, so seeking key relationships is challenging. Moses likely *preferred* solo life now, but God connected him. Rarely does *just Jesus and me* work. Too much of my story reflects what I dub *preparation by separation*. Sounds super holy, but how many important partnerships have I forfeited over the decades? Yes, God sometimes isolates for a season, but the reality of *the body of Christ* is a clarion call to community. If we don't serve or use our gifts, others go without.

Roundabout

What if your future looks nothing like your past? These forty years hardly predicted Moses' following chapters. There are many phenomenal post-Midian experiences, but this lesser-known occasion yields insider secrets for wilderness travelers.

> *When Pharaoh finally let the people go, God did not lead them along the main road...even though that was the shortest route to the Promised Land. God said, "If the people are faced with a battle, they might change their minds and return to Egypt." So God led them in a roundabout way through the wilderness (Exodus 13:17-18).*

We get a rare glimpse into the thought process of God. He didn't choose typical navigational factors such as main roads, fastest routes, or most sensible. Don't some paths feel haphazard, as if He blindly shot a dart at a map and told us to start walking? In this case, God foresaw a battle scaring them back to Egypt's familiarity, so He guided them away from that possibility. We question the wisdom of the bumpy back road. *This cannot be of God!* What if God directed you into a bland wilderness to spare you from a battle that might defeat you, permanently detour you, or turn you from Him? The wilderness never feels best or fastest. It feels, well...roundabout. **There, our trust in God's wisdom is tested.**

With the Rocky Mountains as a breathtaking backdrop, I shared an engaging conversation with Paul (not the apostle), who spent years in an isolated, difficult season. God made him exit a smooth highway for a disorienting backroad requiring extreme dependence and painful waiting. He verbally sketched a God interested in the process, not just the final product or destination. The Shepherd wisely led him a roundabout way, and Paul willingly followed. God has since opened doors for powerful, fruitful ministry![51]

> **Point:** What lessons resonate? Why?
> **Ponder:** Read Exodus 3-4. See how God dismissed Moses' every argument. It's impossible to convince God that He chose the wrong person!
> Notice the difference in Moses from Exodus 3-4 and 14-15. What made the change?
> **Prayer:** Talk to God about a lesson.
> **Practical:** How can the backstory of God's wise leading be applied today?
> Who's the biggest encourager you know? Who's doing what you're called to do or would love to do? Is it time to connect?
> **Playlist:** *Higher Faith* by Rhonda Gunn
> **Pocket:**

---

51 Dedication: Paul Epperson, walker with God. Book this dynamic speaker at *ForgeForward.org*

21: The Story of G. Lee the First

*God bought you **with a high price** (I Corinthians 6:20).*

Just after my fourth birthday, life dramatically changed with the arrival of an orange 1969 Dodge Charger sporting *01* on the welded door. *The Dukes of Hazzard* gathered my family on Friday nights around the special treats of Pepsi and popcorn. My quality of life ratcheted up a bazillion notches. Some loved the human scenery, but I had eyes for *General Lee*. A few years later, a perfect replica slowly passed my school. My jaw relocated to my ankles.

I wasn't the only one. It's garnered a significant fanbase. One lifelong buff is Travis Bell, whose obsession towers most. He often visited the film's location, searching for anything to feed his fixation. He especially sought the original car that captured boys' hearts across America when it jumped Roscoe P. Coltrane's police cruiser. An undaunted hunt eventually led to the guys who painted, transported, and wrecked the numerous Chargers.

Soon he was en route down some North Carolina dirt road. The hills provided a retirement home for scores of cars. After securing "enough permission," he past the second Pinto and discovered a green Dodge. It lacked a door, but the engine and transmission were intact. Though sunk in the mud and consumed with pine needles, it was indeed a '69 Charger. Consulting the vehicle identification plate in the lower corner of the windshield revealed something extraordinary. An additional label read *Lee 1*.

He just located the original!

Travis eventually persuaded the owner to sell it for $400! After unearthing the car from its habitation since 1978, the legend was transported to Indy, put back together somewhat, and trailered to car shows. In time the novelty wore off and he sold it to a company who also eventually lost interest. A man from Florida bought it and hired Travis to oversee its restoration. The transformation was nothing short of spectacular. It became drivable, beautiful, and highly valuable, eventually selling at the acclaimed Barrett-Jackson auction in Arizona. Bids started at $50,000. Professional golfer Bubba Watson placed the winning bid at $110,000!

Think of its seasons of life: Brand new in a happy customer's driveway. Soaring high as a national celebrity. Irreparably broken and forgotten. Sought, purchased, and meticulously restored. Given new life by an owner willing to pay a high price for it. Like Travis, God relentlessly searches junkyard wastelands for a specific loved one. Undeterred by condition or circumstances, God rescues them from the mud and gives them a home. Dirt and brokenness are removed. Purpose and beauty recovered. Like Bubba, God considers those He loves so desirable He will pay a ridiculously exorbitant price to have as His own.

Countless lives can identify with General Lee's story:

- **The prisons of life.** Feels like nothing good will ever materialize.
- **The power of ownership.** The owner makes the difference, especially when it's Jesus!
- **The process of restoration.** This tale resembles the rise-and-fall-and-rise-again stories of many. What was dead can live again, often surpassing former greatness.
- **The price of love.** Crazy love does crazy things. Just look at Calvary.
- **The permanency of identity.** One thing about *Lee 1* never changed—its identity. No matter what, when, or where, it was branded forever as the original. Seasons are temporary; our value is not. We aren't defined by damage or cheapened by location. The Creator stamps our identity.[52]

---

52 Dedication: Scott Smith, best friend extraordinaire. This chapter reminds me of you for obvious reasons! Special thanks to Travis Bell. (www.celebritymachines.com)

22: Bible Study at the Devil's House

Listen to what they're saying: "There's nothing left of us." Tell them, "GOD, the Master says…" (Ezekiel 37:11-12 MSG)

I awoke early one Sunday to an angel hovering in my room! Needless to say, I didn't snooze my alarm. After waiting for a divine message, I mustered my courage to get ready for church. During worship, my spirit dialed in, expecting a revelation regarding the appearance, if it was one. I went straight home afterward and reverently descended the stairs. Hair rose on the back of my neck! It was waiting! I froze. Again, no heavenly instruction or sense of hallowed ground. I approached, trembling. As I opened a door, light from a window changed its shape. Yep, my great celestial visitation was a perfect combination of light and shadows!

Deserts are prone to mirages as conditions align to make things *look real*. Is the irresistible oasis or angelic visitation real, or only mind games? One of the devil's most powerful tactics is deception. He's a master illusionist and liar. He's the lurking lion ready to intimidate, the accusing prosecutor ready to condemn. His is the smooth tongue of a wolf-clothed sheep, the cunning voice of a slippery snake, the authoritative message of a handsome angel. His closet is full of disguises. Why? To deceive. He loves interpreting what we see and feel, ever eager to *shed light*.

Distortions often target God, faith, and life:
Nothing goes right.
Life is pointless.
If this is how God treats people, I want nothing to do with Him.
Why pray? It obviously doesn't work.
God hates me.
Sin is no big deal.
Jesus isn't the only way to be saved.
The Bible isn't as true as I thought.
I'm an atheist now.
I've committed the unpardonable sin.
Satan will gladly join your Bible study. Notice his strategies

during Jesus' temptation.[53] When Jesus quoted the Bible, he did too, but his manufactured misinterpretation promoted disobedience and violated God's character. He tried using the Word of God to trip the Son of God! He attempts to undermine the Bible's authority, but if he can't, he'll misuse it to deceive. I overheard a Christian classmate justify premarital sex to a friend. She didn't invoke a teen magazine, quote movies, or point to culture's acceptance. "Adam and Eve weren't married, so it must be all right," she said. She "used" the Bible to advise an unbeliever that sex outside marriage is OK, even though Genesis 2:25 calls Eve Adam's wife! The devil is a great distorter and a bold intruder. He will force entry, crawl through an opening, or jump a fence. Conversely, Jesus knocks on the front door, awaits our welcome, *then* enters.

Another target of deception is our perception of self. Ezekiel's audience saw old, dry bones in the mirror. Perhaps your mirror says:

I'm cursed, evil, bad.
I hate myself.
I'm a stupid piece of garbage.
I'll never amount to anything.
Why would anyone want to be around me?

The Devil on Mission

Our team spent several days in a remote, mountainous region of India. We performed mimes, handed out literature, and aired *The Jesus Film* on makeshift screens. It was exciting, but while there, a little thought seeded in my mind. *I'm not strong enough for this Christian thing.* It was extremely subtle, hardly detectable, and felt so natural I didn't think to tell anyone. Isn't that like the deceiving cockroaches of the enemy? They hate light. When exposed, they freak out and run to their precious darkness. The thought suggested action. *When I get home, I'm gonna quit.* I wasn't upset with God or cashing in the Bible. **The enemy tried to deceive me** *by attacking me.*

Thankfully, Mick, our leader, asked the team, "Is the enemy messing with anyone?" I didn't even consider it for me. Pride blinded me. Perhaps I thought it meant a flaw in my spirituality. We were about to close when it dawned on me: *Is that what I've been dealing with?* As I reluctantly voiced my recent thoughts, Mick erupted, "That's classic

---

53 Matthew 4:3-7

spiritual battle! The enemy is deceiving you! We need to pray right now!" The devil's plan was foiled, but he almost leveled me with one little distorted thought.

Satan's first two swings at Jesus included a subtle but direct mishandling of Jesus' identity. Notice it occurred in the wilderness—where maintaining our sense of God-given dignity is most difficult. He tries to redefine and warp the way we see ourselves too. If we can be deceived into leaving our faith during a mission trip, how much more are we susceptible in the wilderness? This doesn't make you unspiritual or weak. Don't let the enemy abuse you, sabotage your faith, or pressure you to keep quiet.

The desert breeds confusion and amnesia. Remember:
Who God is.
Who you are.
Whose you are.
What you have.
What Jesus has done for you.
Where you've been.
Where you're going.
How to laugh.
How to thank.
When you first believed.
Why God can be trusted.
Why you love Jesus.[54]

Some mirages warp our view of self; some warp our understanding of God, as we'll see next.

---

54 Dedication: Matt Fore, a hilarious illusionist who reveals truth. Author *The Truth Shall Make You Laugh*. Book your special event at *www.MattFore.com/Speaking*

Point: Is the enemy messing with you? Is your identity under fire?
Ponder your God-given *dignity*. (Psalm 139:14)
Prayer: Ask God to alert you to deception. Ask a friend to pray for you.
Practical: Reread the things to remember and think about one.
Playlist: *A Mighty Fortress is our God* hymn by Martin Luther
For a rockier sound try *Angel of Light* or *This Means War* by Petra
Pocket:

23: God Is Not Made in Our Image

*Then you will know that **I am the LORD** (Ezekiel 37:6).*

I enjoy the comedic wit of *Frank and Ernest* cartoons. Occasionally they broach matters of faith. One clip depicts a barrage of cussing arising from planet earth while God and angels sit on faraway clouds. An exasperated angel counsels God, "Give them another eclipse. The last one actually made them quiet for a few minutes!" God looks distant, annoyed, unsure, and unkempt. Always disgusted, He just wants us to shut up and behave. I'm sure the author isn't attempting a perfect theological rendition, but it gives opportunity to address distorted views about God. Having just discussed self-image, it's important to know that beliefs about God affect our beliefs about self. He's the starting point to accurately understand life and ourselves.

We need to let God speak for Himself! We naturally project our perceptions and feelings onto God.

God is mad at me. The church would collapse if I attended.
My dad ditched me. Why would God be different?
I feel insignificant—God agrees.
God let me down.

What the dry bones said was worlds apart from what God said. He's not the figment of our imagination nor created in our image. Circumstances don't define Him. He doesn't fluctuate with our fluctuating perspectives. He has chosen to reveal Himself primarily in the pages of the Bible and in the person of Jesus Christ.

When Moses neared the end of his life, he gathered the nation. Grabbing his journal, he tells the people their story. It's the story of God. Of challenges and miracles. Failures and forgiveness. Blessing and chastening. Good stories. Tear-jerkers. Funny tales. Some hard to swallow. But it's their story, and remembering is worthwhile as they prepare for the road ahead.

As the LORD our God commanded us, we left Mount Sinai and traveled through the great and terrifying

> *wilderness. I said to you, "You have now reached the hill country...the LORD our God is giving us. Look! He has placed the land in front of you. Go and occupy it as the LORD...promised you. Don't be afraid! Don't be discouraged!" I chose twelve scouts...and they reported, "The land the LORD our God has given us is indeed a good land." But you rebelled...and refused to go in. You complained in your tents and said...(excerpts from Deuteronomy 1:19-27).*

Pause a minute. What they said is too important to miss. They were miraculously liberated and overcame insurmountable odds. Just ahead lay the land God handpicked for them! Just one problem—the giants there made them feel tiny. The people started yacking.

> *"The LORD must hate us. That's why He has brought us here—to be slaughtered."*

Hate. Such a strong word. It was forbidden by my fourth-grade teacher. Imagine: God provided food, water, victory, and supplies. He chose, guided, taught, cared. He promised a fruitful land and His faithful presence. He worked powerfully on their behalf and patiently in their failings. Why?

Their conclusion: *He hates us, wants to feed us to these giants.*

Their minds painted a seriously skewed picture of the Divine. Their god was grotesque and sinister, untrustworthy and angry. He looked nothing like the God of compassion and mercy, slow to anger and filled with unfailing love and faithfulness. Challenges undermined the character of God in their eyes. **Their problem lied about God.** Moses corrected their misrepresentation:

> *The LORD your God, who goes before you, He will fight for you, according to all He did for you in Egypt before your eyes, and in the wilderness where you saw how the LORD your God carried you, as a man carries his son, in all the way that you went until you came to this place.*

> *Yet for all that, you did not believe the LORD your God, who went in the way before you to search out a place for you to pitch your tents, to show you the way you should go, in the fire by night and in the cloud by day (Deuteronomy 1:30-33 NKJV).*

What a tribute to the ever-faithful character of Almighty God. They concocted a god who fights against them. Moses described a God who fights for them. They forgot the things He did. Moses reminded them, employing a powerful image to recapture their lost understanding: **God carried you the whole time—as a strong father closely holds his son.**

God brought you here because He hates you?

He's been lugging you every step, and will continue, because He loves you!

We may caricature God as a Father who will give us up or, at best, hold us at arm's length, who says He doesn't have time for us, or nags because we never measure up. Yet, how does a father carry his infant son? Unless a diaper change is in order, *very close*. It portrays protection—eyes roaming for danger, arms embracing securely, lips whispering assurance. "It's OK. I'm here. Daddy won't let go." It depicts possession—"You're mine. I love you. I'm proud of you."

God doesn't hate you!

The Change

I was terrified of a teacher. He was nine feet tall and foreboding. Fears of his sternness were passed down by upperclassmen. Afraid of discipline, I over-exaggerated my laughter at his dry jokes. This went on for three weeks until something strange happened. I *liked* his class and appreciated his style. **The thing is—he didn't change. I did.** The assumptions I conjured, and those drawn by others, were highly distorted. The man who disquieted me became my favorite. Two years later I had the privilege of asking any teacher to introduce me for a special occasion. I chose him. I found him to be a great man and educator. The one I thought despised me stood tall on my behalf.

God gets bad press. Some is derived from our own conjectures, and a ton adopted from a million other voices. Satan and an ungodly culture will always sling mud at God's reputation and encourage us to join. If your view of God has become distorted, I pray you find Him refreshingly different. The real heavenly Father is One who will carry you and stand up for you. His joy is to raise you up, not beat you down. Has God "changed" in your eyes? Have you drawn conclusions that look nothing like His revelation? Chances are the master of disguise is nearby.

The older we get the fewer cheering voices we hear, leaving us bankrupted of affirmation. Your bank account may be full. The contents of your garage may be the envy of the cul-de-sac. Your church or business may be thriving. Many may admire your power or expertise. Yet deep down, you long for a friendly voice cheering your name and a strong hand patting your back. Jesus is a friend like that—maybe not the pseudo-Jesus you heard about or the one you dread from a distance. **He's more like the teacher I discovered than the one I imagined or heard about.** Many who dislike God actually dislike a tainted, warbled distortion of Him. Some discover a friend they can't imagine living without.

God brought us here because He hates us. Such was the conclusion of a nation content to keep their distance from Him. Moses introduced (or reintroduced) them to a God who holds them close, as a man carries his beloved son. If your view of God includes a flyswatter and deeply creviced brow, let Him reveal Himself to you. If we only know Him by hearsay, there's a good chance He's become a distorted caricature of the original. Study Jesus, "For in Christ lives all the fullness of God in a human body (Colossians 2:9)." He's the perfect portrait of God. One of your greatest purposes is knowing God as He is.

Those who know God best love Him most.[55]

---

[55] Dedication: Every teacher who goes the extra mile to lift a student.

Point: Did this challenge your view of God? How? Do you think God hates you? Why?
Ponder: God carries *me* like a son.
What are your "sources of revelation?" Do they make you think highly or lowly of God? Do they evoke praise, love, and trust, OR complaint, bitterness, and skepticism?
Prayer: Confess distorted views of God. Ask forgiveness.
Receive God's love. (Psalm 23:1; 99:8. John 3:17. Romans 5:8; 8:32.)
Practical: Search *Team Hoyt Ironman*.
Thanklessness breeds spiritual drift. Thank God! (Romans 1:21).
Playlist: *Such an Awesome God* by Maverick City
More Than You Think by Danny Gokey
Pocket:

24: My Dad, the Abolitionist

*You are no longer a slave but **God's own child** (Galatians 4:7).*

A dad's greatest joy is arriving home to the energetic pitter-patter of feet and an enthusiastic "Daddy!"[56] The day's junk vanishes in the exuberant love of a child. Remember the "prodigal son," who left Dad's estate with Dad's money to major in partying?[57] When funds and friends expired, he landed a job feeding swine. Desperate, he craved their food, but his arrangement didn't include a meal plan. He couldn't go lower. There among pigs, he came to his senses and thought of Dad.

The young man returned home with no cologne strong enough to mask his stinky body or life. He wasn't expecting home and a Dad though—that bridge burned long ago—he just needed an employer. He had no idea his Dad yearned for his return. Waiting. Praying. Watching. Every morning. Every evening. When the young man came into view, Dad bolted toward him. The regrets and shame of a rebellious life melted in an affirming embrace. *Maybe this is a good sign I can get a job.* **The heart of his father transcended having another worker on his farm. He wanted a son in his house.** To prove this, he gifted four things—a robe, a ring (equivalent to his signature), sandals, and a prime rib feast. These things belonged *only to sons*.

Independence Day!

> *God sent his Son…to buy freedom for us who were slaves to the law, so that he could adopt us as his very own children. And because we are his children, God has sent the Spirit of his Son into our hearts, prompting us to call out, "Abba, Father." Now you are no longer a slave but God's own child. And since you are his child, God has made you his heir (Galatians 4:5-7).*

---

56 Telling a "Dad-joke" is a close second.
57 Luke 15:11-32

God sent Jesus to set us free, not squeeze us into a fancier straight jacket. The father could've been a harsh boss, held the past over his son's head, watched him like a hawk, found pleasure in his errors. That's what slavery to religious laws looks like. Unbending, critical, condemning. It offers no help and is never satisfied. It cares not for friendship and leaves no room for grace. Christ frees us from the slavery of always trying to be good enough, living in the negative spiritually, and striving to stay above the waves of regret, failure, and shame. This religion-induced slavery says we will never measure up. The bar always exceeds the highest attainments.

It's precisely to this group of people Jesus says, "Come to Me, all you who labor and are heavy laden, and I will give you rest. Take my yoke upon you and learn from Me, for I am gentle and lowly in heart, and you will find rest for your souls. For my yoke is easy and my burden is light" (Matthew 11:28-30 NKJV). Jesus isn't talking about a good night's sleep or much-needed break after exhausting physical labor (although He knows we need that too). **He's offering rest for exhausted *souls* straining under heavy spiritual burdens. His solution: come to Me.** One hug by Jesus erases the long list of debts we owe. Hear His whisper—"All is forgiven, son. Leave that there, daughter." Let mercy wash over you.

The burdens of sin and shame have been carried by Christ to the cross and dealt with in full. If you've received Jesus as your Savior, your spiritual account is no longer negative! Jesus' perfect righteousness has been given to you. It's more than enough! Colossians 2:14 says, "having wiped out the handwriting of requirements that was against us, which was contrary to us. And He has taken it out of the way, having nailed it to the cross." It's the equivalent of mortgage burning. In those days, a paid bill was nailed above the debtor's front door, displayed for everyone to see that it was settled! **The record of our mountainous spiritual debt was nailed to the cross, which boldly proclaims: "Paid in full! This debt is finished!"** *Signed by Jesus in permanent red ink.*

Keith Green, 1970s musician, felt spiritually desperate. He wanted to be close to God but felt distant, like something sabotaged their relationship. Agony enveloped his soul. Songwriting stalemated. He went to his music room and slumped at the piano. A short time later, he emerged, bursting to share his new song:

"My son, My son, why are you striving?
You can't add one thing to what's been done for you.
I did it all while I was dying.

Rest in your faith, My peace will come to you."[58]

He aspired to write a love song to God; God wrote one for him instead!

No More Bill

One spring we visited the majestic Niagara Falls. I was pleasantly surprised there was no longer a toll to cross Grand Island. *That's great. New York is saving us money. I love New York!* A month later I got the bill for $2.00. I knew I was delusional. A few weeks later a bill arrived for $7.00. Really? A $5.00 late fee for a $2.00 charge? I thought it was stupid and put it on the pile.

A short time later a scary orange envelope arrived. With trembling hands, I tore it open. I owed $102.00! It became an urgent matter requiring immediate action. I prayed for divine favor and dialed the agency. Hope faded by Stephanie's short tone. I told my sad story, assuring I would resolve the issue. My goal was to get the fee reduced to $7.00. Instead, she offered an option that sounded too good to be true—convert to "E-Z Pass" and load the account with $25.00. That would *fully* remedy my balance *and* credit my account $25.00 toward future tolls. "Sure. I'd do that," I said coolly, then asked, "What about my bill? Anything else I need to do?"

Her reply was perfect, "Sir, there is no bill!"

I thanked her, hung up, raised my hands, and praised God!

"God sent him to buy freedom for us who were slaves…so that he could adopt us as his very own children" (Galatians 4:5). He delivered us from the bondage of a never-satisfied list of spiritual rules *so that* we could be adopted into His family. He's not content to have slaves in His field. He wants kids who sit at His table, enjoy His friendship, partner in His mission. He gives His name, privileges, promises, and care. He even lets us call Him "Abba"—like running up to God at the front door, shouting, "Daddy!" This was *never* uttered by servants. Only children used this term of endearment.

I met with a guy shortly after he got saved. Something was obviously wrong. After our discussion he asked, "So I don't have to keep beating myself up over the things I've done?"

"No. Jesus was beaten for all those things on your behalf. They're all taken care of!"

---

58 *When I Hear the Praises Start.* Keith & Melody Green. 1977.

Relief covered his face.

Every sin is wiped clean. If you inquire about your account, He'll say, "There is no bill!" It doesn't exist. There's no payment due! Abba loves you. Find joy in the incredible worth He places on you!

Live forgiven. Live free.[59]

> **Point:** Are you wandering? The Father is ready to welcome you home!
> Feeling spiritually bankrupt? Jesus gives rest for burdened souls.
> **Ponder:** God wants me as a son, not a slave. What difference does it make?
> **Prayer:** *"Abba..."*
> **Practical:** Are you beating yourself up for something Christ was punished for? Stop! If Christ forgave you, there's no bill! Demonstrate this definitively: walk across a stream to illustrate your sins washed away. Pound a nail (without hitting your thumb) and imagine the cross. Write your sin on a rock and throw in a lake. Look up and declare "I'm forgiven!"
> **Playlist:** *When I Hear the Praises Start* by Keith Green
> *Holy Water* by We the Kingdom
> **Pocket:**

---

59 Dedication: Dave & Tara Powers (*www.Mountaincitymusic.com*) and every songwriter or musician who strengthens our faith and love.

25: Hi, I'm Your Image Consultant

When you believed in Christ,
he identified you *as his own (Ephesians 1:13).*

A Veggie Tales animation introduces us to Khalil, a loveable little caterpillar. Well, that's only half true. He's half caterpillar and half worm. Apparently shy on affirmation, he bolsters himself with motivational tapes: "You are powerful and attractive. You do not run from your problems but confront them face to face. You are a skilled metal worker." He repeats in his classic accent, "I am a skilled metal worker. Aaaahh, I did not know that."[60]

If only it were that easy.

Just as God's "caricature" (not character) can be skewed, we can become a misshapen creature of our own making. These images are **voice-activated**—people's comments, internal ideas, comparisons, Satan's lies. Believing them fashions the way we see ourselves, which affects the way we live. Some voices inflict hefty blows like *stupid, ugly, defective, bad,* crippling their victims in Despair Alley. Other voices like *I am God, better than everyone,* proudly escort their victims to Pedestal Boulevard. Both pathways lead downward, short-circuiting well-being and kingdom usefulness.

The goal is not positive, but *accurate,* thinking. "Don't think you are better than you really are. Be honest in your evaluation of yourselves" (Romans 12:3). Another rendering reads, "The only accurate way to understand ourselves is by what God is and by what he does for us, not by what we are and what we do for him" (MSG). **How much strife is rooted in the quest for others, or ourselves, to think highly of us?** The only safe place for level-headed self-assessment comes from our Maker's voice, who wants us to think properly so we can live properly. *Accurate* or *inaccurate* is preferable to *positive* or *negative* because self-perception may be lofty, but false. Claiming to be an astronaut or NFL linebacker might make me feel good but wouldn't be true. Similarly, thinking I'm toxic trash would be wrong *and* make me feel horrible. We need level heads, not lifted high in exaltation or hung low in exasperation.

---

60 *Jonah: A VeggieTales Movie.* Big Idea Productions and F.H.E. Pictures. 2002.

Voices influence, but the room of self-imaging is accessible only to you—and those you permit access. One major source derives from what we think others think about us. How flimsy is that? Satan seeks to commandeer this control room to steal your identity and destroy you. How quickly we abdicate this place God entrusted to us! Jesus also seeks access to this sacred space, but His words lift. Seeing ourselves accurately—*chosen, believer, valuable, loved*—takes work. Hard work. Hence, tiring times make us especially vulnerable to the devil getting a foot in the door. **In the end, you alone sign off on the way you perceive yourself.** Don't let the devil or anyone else steal your identity. Let God declare it!

Seagulls and Sons

Craig's stepfather constantly belittled him. Bearing the nickname *Seagull* (for no positive reasons) affected him deeply, until something pivotal happened. He discovered his true identity after reading about the courage and godliness of his dad and grandfather—he hailed from much more honorable stock than seagulls! That awareness empowered him to reclaim his real family name. The transformation was remarkable.[61]

Maybe a name or comment pushes you down. It handicaps and confines. It's heavy and hurts. Your Abba has a different perspective; He speaks things so great they require faith.[62] Abraham, "the father of many nations" didn't have a kid yet. Peter "the solid rock" was still a small stone. Gideon "the mighty warrior" hid like a coward. "How can I rescue Israel? My clan is the weakest…I am the least" (Judges 6:15)! He could never fulfill his calling with this belief ruling his life. **God spoke identity over him before assigning his task to him.** Identity correlates with purpose. I love God's directive to Gideon the chicken, "Go with the strength you have…I am sending you" (Judges 6:14). *Don't worry about the strength you don't have.* Whatever strength he possessed, whether minuscule or mountainous, was sufficient. God planned to do the heavy lifting anyway.

The greatest credential is God's commission. It's not the only thing, but it's the highest authorization. By outward standards, Gideon ranked last. By God's standards, he ranked first for this task. He couldn't earn the title. It depended on faith, not emotion. Faith believes first;

---

61 *Wild at Heart*. John Eldridge. Thomas Nelson Publishers. 2001. (21)
62 Romans 4:17.

behavior eventually catches up. God's declaration changed Gideon, who subsequently acted as a warrior, not a wimp. Understanding his identity settled him so profoundly he named a place of worship *Jehovah Shalom—God is my wholeness and peace*. **The clumsy, constricting, condemning stronghold of his previous identity broke when he believed God's view of him.**

The Power of Identity

Like hope, worth is rooted in the will of the owner. Your value doesn't emerge from the perceptions of people or culture. Some may idolize while others condemn to hell. If you derive identity from something temporal, you'll fluctuate. It's not determined by ability or disability, accomplishment or failure. True worth is found in the unchanging truth God speaks over you.

Identity not only comforts but compels and challenges. That's why this is so crucial. If the enemy or the world can control this, they can stifle well-being, influence, and potential accomplishments for Christ. The gut reaction of Moses at the burning bush was *Who am I? I'm not enough. I don't know or have enough. I'm disqualified. Somebody else would do better.* Conversely, God saw him as chosen rescuer, author, leader.

We agonize over this heavy *Who am I?* question. It's the great unrest. The bloody civil war. It invokes intense searching and innumerable attempts to prove our worth to God, ourselves, our parents, and the world. We compensate, compete, and combat because of it. While the human psyche desperately seeks favorable answers, God's Spirit leads us to the wooden cross where Jesus proved—**you are loved and valuable!** An accurate view of self cannot be understood apart from our Creator and Savior.

The way you see yourself is surprisingly not for your glory or to make you feel better. **It's less about you than you think.** Accurate identity fosters the likeness of Christ. Paul knew he was a God-called preacher and leader. He rested *in* it, operated *from* it. But he also considered himself a servant, ready to obey his Superior. He stood confident before the most powerful, yet served the least desirable, because he knew who God said he was. We can feel ooey-gooey about being chosen, which is indeed phenomenal, but we are chosen—to be holy (Ephesians 1:4). *Oh, I don't care about holiness; I just wanna feel special.* Thinking we are chosen, special princesses can breed disobedient, self-absorbed brats. **A properly balanced identity quiets**

the soul, qualifies for action, and quickens godliness.

In the parable of the prodigal son, the father made sure everyone, especially his boy, knew he was his son, not an employee, slave, or loser. Imagine the son's liberation to hear those words spoken by the one who mattered most! Perhaps he heard people regurgitate his choices: *he's just a thief.* Maybe people at church treated him according to his sin: *how could he do that to his father?* Inner chatter may have caused insomnia: *you oughta be ashamed of yourself.* His dad's words superseded every voice: "You're my son. You're forgiven. I love you!"

Divine Photography

I strongly considered another subtitle for this book: "Where Broken Pieces *are* Masterpieces." It highlights the truth that even when we're broken and have nothing to offer, the Restorer still prizes us, still esteems us with dignity. We don't have to be one ounce better to become worthwhile! I chose the subtitle I did because it emphasizes the work of restoration and is easier to say.

Hear the valley reverberate with the sounds of broken lives being put together—sounds in the form of questions, cries, declarations, whispers, hammering nails into wood, ripping spiritual mortgages, and developing images. God is hard at work! If you bear a burdensome stigma, God wants to replace it! The labels attached to you through bitter words from broken people? Throw them in the garbage! God gave you a new name that needs to be discovered or recovered. You'll know you've grasped your identity when it settles you in peace and activates you in purpose.

A thunderstorm rocked a father's slumber. He was immediately concerned for his young daughter. Knowing she would be terrified, he hurried to her room, but she wasn't in bed! As lightning lit the darkness, he noticed her silhouette in a strange position near the window. "Hey Daddy!" She laughed, repositioned, and froze for a few seconds. "What are you doing?" he asked. With total peace she said, "I think God is taking my picture!"

Yes, child of God. He's taken your picture. He'd love to show you and tell you what He sees.[63]

---

63 Dedication: Rick Rohlin, who enthusiastically empowers people worldwide. Interested in sports and missions? *www.ISAsports.org*

Point: Do you gravitate toward "negative" or "positive" self-perception? "Accurate" or "inaccurate?" Who has access to your imaging room? You alone sign off on self-perception.
How much life do you spend hoping you or others think highly of you?
Ponder how identity comforts, compels, challenges. God-given identity requires faith.
If identity correlates to purpose, what might that mean for you?
Prayer: Read "The Father's Blessing" in *Bonus Features*. I hope it's a moving experience for you.
Practical: Have someone read "The Father's Blessing" over you.
Playlist: *Who You Say I Am* by Hillsong.
Pocket:

PART 4:
The Restorer *spends time* putting broken pieces together. His craftsmanship is *unparalleled and uncompromising.*

Sinews formed (Ezekiel 37:8 MSG).

Screws and nails are not exciting,
yet vital for strength and stability.

The Restorer doesn't do shoddy work.
Desiring to support you
and hold you together,
He links you to people and resources
at just the right time.

Be alert to the connections
He is fastening.
They are making you strong.

26: Shoddy Work Sucks

> *Sinews formed (Ezekiel 37:8 MSG)*

My youth pastor built a remote-controlled car when he was young. He meticulously followed directions and watched it take shape. Once finished, the final step instructed him to disassemble it and epoxy critical points. Considering it unnecessary, he installed the batteries and took it for a spin. Before long, a wheel fell off, then other parts. He learned connections are crucial but take a little extra time. It required stability to function properly.

While you hung around like a mooch in mom's womb, God knit you piece by piece, moment by moment, month after month. Spurgeon writes, "God made you. He fashioned your curious framework and put every bone into its place. He, as with needlework, embroidered each nerve, and vein, and sinew. He is your Maker. You are a mass of dust, and you would crumble back to dust at this moment if he withdrew his preserving power."[64] The marvel of the body is the exquisite result. We are complex, intricate creations, comprised of millions of parts that somehow intertwine. Each part is significant, perfectly fitted with all the others.

After God walked around the valley, He scrupulously collected every bone of each skeleton. Soon He would add muscles for activity and purpose. But first He sought careful fastening, so He grabbed the sinews, "a tough, flexible band of connective tissue that connects muscles to bone."[65] Its robust composition prevents unraveling or crumbling; its flexibility facilitates movement.

A restoration shop ensures every part is suitably connected. While tempted to throw on paint, crank the engine, and cruise by evening, the wise restorer works on the frame, electrical components, suspension, steering linkage, drivetrain, brakes, and a host of other non-glamorous elements. Why? Proper fastening is critical. Ever observed something that looks good, until closer inspection reveals it was thrown together as quick and cheap as possible? **God isn't throwing some low-grade, low-budget project together for the weekend.** He's building your life

---

64 *Questions Which Ought to be Asked.* Charles Spurgeon. 1880. *www.biblehub.com*
65 trc-leiden.nl, 2017.

to last for the long haul. No apologies. No regrets. You never hear "ehh, good enough" at God's Restoration Shop. Broken people need stability, and stability takes time. How often has a mechanic, therapist, doctor, or carpenter been asked:

How Long?

God is timeless. His energy limitless. His work effortless. His quality matchless. God can get stuff done quickly. Imagine His morning to-do list:
- Carve the Grand Canyon. Check.
- Set up Victoria Falls. Yep.
- Build Mt. Everest. Got it.
- Etch the Amazon's route. Done.
- Scatter untold islands. Complete.
He simply spoke these into existence![66]

- Finish everything needed for salvation. Check.
Done in six hours.

Some of His best work takes moments to accomplish, even though He might've spent thousands of years preparing for it. God also has a reputation for the slow build. Line upon line, little by little, like taking 1600 years to complete His manuscript! God's working in our lives often feels painfully slow. All saints question *How long?* sometime. Man's timeframe is "as soon as possible." **God's timetable is "at the right time."** God is not panicked, frenzied, hurried. The thorough craftsman may be criticized initially, but his work appreciated forever. Those who cut corners will be praised that it's done so quickly but cursed when the wheels fall off. When it comes to time, it's best to leave the details to Him. He restored Moses after 40 years, Elijah after 40 days, and Peter after a week or so. Each had to wait, but all encountered God *one day*. We trust a God who performs instantaneous miracles and takes His sweet 'ol time.

While building Rachel's playhouse, I noticed the middle sagged. Do I slap a support under it or dig a hole, pour cement, and ensure its stability? Knowing my tendency, I called myself in for questioning, "Keith, do you want it right, or have regrets?" Thankfully, I took the

---

66 Genesis 1. Hebrews 11:3.

extra time to make it solid. **When tempted to doubt God's character because of delay, He may simply be avoiding shortcuts.** God is unhurried when building something to withstand the test of time; yes, even to last for eternity.

Warning: Raw Content!

Paul prayed "that you will be strengthened with all his glorious power so you will have all the endurance and patience you need" (Colossians 1:11). Later he mentioned some who shelved Jesus, the solid cornerstone, for low-grade substitutes. He said they had "not held fast to the head from whom the whole body, supported and knit together through its ligaments and sinews, grows with a growth that is from God" (Colossians 2:19 NET). Abandoning their support system made them unstable and stymied their growth.

Job 10 records the unbridled anguish of a devastated man:
I'm disgusted with my life.
My soul is bitter.
My complaining is justified.
Why is God punishing me?
I feel rejected.
Why do others get ahead, especially those deserving punishment more than me?
My life used to be good when God cared about me.
God waited for me to mess up. He's mad.
I can't catch a break. God denies every joy.
Why do I have to live?
I want to be alone.
I want a moment of comfort sooo bad.
My future looks hopeless.

Amid all this he writes, "You clothed me with skin and flesh, and you knit my bones and sinews together. You gave me life and showed me your unfailing love. My life was preserved by your care" (Job 10:11-12). Later we hear his strained but determined muffle, "Though He *(heavy breath)*...slay me *(heavy breath)*...yet...will...I *(heavy breath)*...trust Him" (Job 13:15 NKJV emphasis mine).

That's tough sinew right there, folks.

Certain foods, vitamins, and supplements claim specific benefits. *Promotes joint health. Reduces inflammation. Assists memory.* I can never remember which one does that. God made us—so He knows how to maintain us. He seeks our well-being and stability. Consider these "sinews" promoting soundness:

- **Worship.** (2 Chronicles 16:9. Isaiah 30:15. Nehemiah 8:10.)
- **Timely Scripture.** (Psalm 119:105. Isaiah 40:8. John 6:63.)
- **Honest prayer.**
- **The Helper, God's Spirit.** (John 15:26. Romans 8:26.)
- **Helps**—books, resources, people. God gifted some to help others. (1 Corinthians 12:7, 28.)
- **God's love.** (Psalm 94:18. Ephesians 3:18.)
- **Faith.** (Psalm 91. Ephesians 6:16.)
- **History with God.** (Psalm 136. Revelation 12:11.)

Even one of these at the right time can stabilize you. It's not that we hold on to God so well, but that He holds us together so well.[67]

> **Point:** Aren't you glad God avoids shortcuts when it comes to *you*? Fastening takes time.
> **Ponder** I Samuel 30:1-6. David's predicament was severe. Amazingly, he encouraged himself. Sinew stabilized him. Have you ever needed to encourage yourself?
> **Prayer:** Sit silently for five minutes. *Appreciate* God. *Deeply* express your emotions.
> **Practical:** Practice one of the "sinews."
> **Playlist:** *I Will Rise Again* by Jason Gray
> **Pocket:**

---

[67] Dedication: Boyd Lawson & Bud Short. I've always admired your meticulous craftsmanship.

27: My, What Strong Sinews You Have!

*The whole body, **supported and knit together** through its ligaments and sinews, **grows** (Colossians 2:19 NET).*

Relax by the fire under a star-kissed sky as Jacob the patriarch tells his story:[68]

I ran away after swindling my brother. Oh, did he hate me! When God directed me to return home decades later, I asked Esau about getting together. He messaged back saying he'd come the next day, with 400 friends! Paralyzed with fear, I prayed harder than ever. It turned into an all-out wrestling match with a mysterious heavenly opponent.

We played for keeps.

I positioned my feet in the dirt. Next thing I knew I was on my back. Not to be outdone, I wrested my hands from his grip, knocked out his elbow, and cast him off. We regrouped under the moon's unpainted rays—dancing in circles, sizing the other, pining for weakness. The scrimmage continued for hours. Clawing, punching, blocking, spinning, kicking.

My bones ached, my clothing a mess of sweat and dirt. I had to win. Rousing my energy and will, I lunged with a loud whelp just before daybreak slipped through the trees. He read me like a book; with one swift movement he hammered my hip. I fell, stunned. He broke me. *(somberly)* Yes sir, broke me real good. He stood victorious, then turned to leave.

(The flame reveals a widening smile.)

I tripped him! Down he crashed. I couldn't wrestle, so I clung, as if letting go meant falling to my death. Ignoring his demand to let go, I tightened my grip, then made my own request. For too much of my life, gains came through grabbing and trickery—I didn't want to be that man anymore. I wanted God's blessing because He gave it to me.

God's messenger "wounded" Jacob by affecting the sinew in his hip, perhaps akin to a severely pulled muscle. An affront to his strength, this weakening blow suggested surrender. Strength is man's desire, but we are tempted to build our life with faulty boards if they look good or

---

68   Genesis 32.

save time. Jacob's deception made him strong, but manipulative. This strength was weakness in disguise. He could lie, trick, or cheat without batting an eye. Relationships were sacrificed to get ahead.[69] God targeted his defective props by asking his name, meaning *deceiver* or *heel-grabber*. Sometimes God turns unhealthy strength into weakness, to turn healthy weakness into honorable strength.

Jacob continues.

After he left, I slowly rose and brushed myself off. That's where this here limp began. Hurt like crazy, but it built my faith. I was depending on God's steady hand. The night before I was deceiver. By morning I was favored prince of God. I quit grabbing people's heels to get ahead. I learned to grab God instead. He awarded me a new identity and changed my name to *Israel*, saying I wrestled with God and prevailed!

Interestingly, when we fight God, and He wins because we surrender, He declares us the winner.

Wanna Sponsor Me?

Sinew figuratively refers to "that which supplies strength or power; knit together, or make strong with."[70] Think of multi-stranded rope for superior durability or rebar incorporated into cement. How appropriate that *Ezekiel* means "strengthened of God," for God strengthened him to make the dry bones strong. With the fallen in the valley, God meticulously sewed their sinews in place. Each critical component would eventually enable them to move, rise, and achieve. Because of the cords God ties together, we become stronger.

Ever asked sponsors to fund a trip or sport? Every donation, encouragement, and prayer is like sinew—strong connections, stabilizing links. They join you and your endeavor together, making it possible. Sinew is highly useful for thread, bowstring, string for instruments, cords. When life unravels, God precisely knits you back together. Nothing haphazard. Nothing wasted. **He intelligently and strategically fabricates you for the race He chose for you.** I've never seen monster trucks in NASCAR or Indy cars tackle off-road courses. You were built on purpose…for purpose. What's more, God is fitting you with others He's fitting together!

---

69 He hated his own medicine!
70 Websters Revised Unabridged. Noah Porter, editor. G. &C. Merriam. 1913.

Custom Fabrication

The previous chapter listed several types of sinews, available to all. These cohesive elements hold us together, keep us upright. However, the Master Craftsman forges *you* with custom parts! As none share your fingerprints, no one has your exact sinews. Consider Moses. Nobody would've hired "Midian Moses" for a significant job, but God was still connecting more sinews. Some of Moses' sinews included his name, upbringing, education, and employment. Family, siblings, in-laws. The development of patience, character, and humility. Egyptian life, wilderness life, and a bush experience. A calling, a regret, a staff. God was working all things together.

What about your sinews? Skills and resources. Family, friends, teachers. Body, mind, and faith. Experiences, education, and equipping. Weaknesses and strengths, plans and pains. What makes you angry, passionate, or fulfilled? God is writing history, working as locally as your heart and as globally as the ends of the earth. He's the director and plays the lead role but seeks supportive cast members. He assigns your role as He sees fit, then ties all the pieces of you together accordingly. You become connected…and interconnected.

It's Sinew Season

I hated my job. I felt out-of-place, worn down, forsaken. Every attempt to leave fell flat. I felt stuck, insignificant, uncomfortable. This season promised little value or hope. Looking back, I see God in the details. The effects of a stroke recently relocated my mom to a nursing facility, a move extremely hard on her. Our "unwanted places" were four miles apart, making daily lunch visits possible. God knew we would need each other's company. Additionally, a coworker developed my skills which led to another stream of income. This period of struggle, mediocrity, depression, and endurance primed me to seek my calling and become receptive to the message of this book. **God was setting things in place when I didn't think He was doing anything.**

- Sinew stabilizes. These connections are vital and personal, yet easily unrecognized.
- The assembling of sinews can seem mundane and time-consuming, even unnecessary. This is when we are most tempted to hurry God's work or quit.

- Sinew's toughness makes us strong; its flexibility makes movement, and thus achievement, possible.
Thank God for sinews!

The Prayer of an Unknown Soldier[71]

I asked God for strength that I might achieve.
I was made weak that I might learn humbly to obey.
I asked for health that I might do greater things.
I was given infirmity that I might do better things.
I asked for riches that I might be happy.
I was given poverty that I might be wise.
I asked for power that I might have the praise of men.
I was given weakness that I might feel the need of God.
I asked for all things that I might enjoy life.
I was given life that I might enjoy all things.
I got nothing that I asked for, but everything I hoped for.
Almost despite myself, my unspoken prayers were answered.
I am, among all men, most richly blessed.[72]

---

71 Also called *The Creed of the Disabled*. Author unconfirmed, though often attributed to Charles Nimitz.
72 Dedication: Don & Shirley Short, Craig & Kathy Short, Mark & Pam Eckendorf. This family knows how to sponsor others!

Point: Are you in a "sinew" season? God knows what He's doing.
Do you have weaknesses that are strengths in disguise? Strengths that make you weak?
Ponder Colossians 1:17. God presently holds you together physically and spiritually.
Jesus mentioned the heart, soul, mind, and strength. What's one way to promote emotional, spiritual, mental, or physical health?
Prayer: Are you wrestling God about something? He wants *you* to win!
Practical: Reread "Custom Fabrication" above. What "sponsors" belong to *your* story?
Search "Laminin Louie Giglio."
Devotional pick: *Streams in the Desert*, February 20.
Playlist: *Rattle* by Elevation
Pocket:

PART 5:
The Restorer *spurs* *purposes* in broken pieces who feel *unqualified*.

Muscles appeared (Ezekiel 37:8 NET).

There's no such thing as a
life without meaning.
You brim with divine purposes!
God has special assignments for you
and is passionate to reveal them.

The waste place is often
the unlikely ground where
God reveals your next big purpose.

Peter's story is a great example of how
The Restorer puts unqualified pieces back together.

28: El Diablo vs. Quickdraw Pete
The Throwdown

> *Satan demanded to have you,*
> *that he might **sift you** like wheat (Luke 22:31 ESV).*

Picture an old western TV show. There's a small town with a general store, saloon, sheriff's station, and post office. Horses are hitched to posts. Men stand on porches talking business. Women in long dresses and fancy hats cross the dusty street with their bagged goods. It's a scene of ordinary, peaceful life. But there's always a villain, sometimes a posse, whose arrival creates panic. The bad guy halts his mean, black stallion in the middle of the street, retrieves a firearm, and haphazardly fires into the air. The drama signals to the scattered townspeople he has unfinished business. The pianist abruptly concludes his happy pounding at the saloon. Across Main Street, the sheriff pulls back the curtain and grips his pistol.

"Where are they, Sheriff? I wanna teach 'em a thing or two. Where's Pete and Andy? I know you got Zeb's boys in there. And I'm looking for Bart and the coward tax man."

Sheriff had been meeting with his band of good guys. He'd be leaving for a position at federal headquarters and was putting them in charge. They respected the lawman and wanted to please him. They watched him live out his responsibilities with integrity, compassion, and courage, and would do anything for him, even taking a bullet. They pledged as much. Sheriff soberly calls his men in the back room. Their jabbering continues without hesitation. Light teasing becomes argumentative jockeying.

"Why should you get St. Louis? I've been here longer."

"That's not fair! I get it. You get Pierce's Creek."

"I'm not going there! That should go to someone like Phil!"

"What do you mean, 'someone like Phil?'"

"I don't care where I am if it's away from all of you!"

These were the men who'd oversee his district?

Well, shoot.

"Enough! I'll place you where I choose. Come see this." They shuffle obliviously to the stately man looking out the window. Holding a small stack of papers, he orders, "Jim, hand these out."

"What's this?" Pete demands before the page reaches his hand.

The page read:

> WANTED!
> Dead or Alive!
> Centered on the page was their picture.
> "I challenge you to a duel!"
> Signed in devilish cursive—*El Diablo*.

Sheriff gives them a minute to digest the throwdown. A shiver bolts like lightning down Thad's spine before Quickdraw Pete changes the tone. "Is this a joke? Bring it on, Diablo." A fiery smile consumes his face. "To make this fair I'll use my left hand."

"Why's that, Pete?" asked Tom.

"Cuz my right hand *(swiveling it back and forth)* even scares me! This thing is illegal in some regions!"

Pete kicks his head back and belts a hearty laugh. The spirit of confidence overtakes the group as they revel in the joke. Everyone soared on the wings of adrenaline...except Sheriff. He had been watching their opponent. Dirty. All business. Vicious as a pack of wolves.

Trying to tame the naïve jubilation, Sheriff looked each man in the eye. "Listen! This is big! You've heard of El Diablo, the meanest rabble-rouser in these parts. We've run into him before and he's nothing but trouble. He wants to destroy every town, family, and soul. He can't wait for me to leave because he thinks you're all child's play." *(Singling out Quickdraw Pete)* "El Diablo wants to annihilate you. He thinks if loyalty to me endangers you—jail, or death—you'd pretend you didn't know me. There's a big challenge coming. I'm praying earnestly for you."

"Sheriff! These boneheads will let you down, but I won't. Trust me!" His superior interrupts. "My prayer is when the enemy beats you...not once, but three times...and you're down in bitter defeat, you'll look me up, not avoid me. I'll dust you off and set you on your feet again. At that time, I'll call you to an important assignment. Following your failure, you'll become a force of strength for others."

Pay Attention!

The actual mid-eastern account occurred during the last supper, when Jesus eagerly shared His heart with His disciples. Just them. No distractions. Nobody demanding proof or begging for miracles. The atmosphere was rich with meaning and deep in fellowship. In this spiritually high context, Jesus shocks them with an announcement, "Simon, Simon! Satan has asked to sift each of you like wheat. But I have pleaded in prayer for you, Simon, that your faith should not fail. So when you have repented and turned to me again, strengthen your brothers" (Luke 22:31-32). Foreseeing the high-stakes test, Jesus repeats Simon's name to arrest his attention.

Satan didn't delegate this battle but saved it for himself. So he asked permission! I don't know if he asked God the Father, or Jesus the Son, but the chief opponent had to ask permission! This Greek word for *ask* is always used by an inferior to a superior. Its translation into English varies from polite request to explosive demand, as if calling someone to trial, but it's always a lower rank to a higher, such as a child to a parent or a human praying to God. [73] **Our mightiest adversary is still inferior to the Almighty.**

While Jesus specifically addressed Peter, Satan threatened them all. "To sift *you*" is plural. Reminiscent of Job chapters 1 and 2, the enemy's request to inflict severe trials is apparently granted. This seems harsh. Why didn't He say "No way?" Western culture doesn't find testing of this sort necessary, and it doesn't jive with any unspoken belief that God's great plan is my safety and happiness. But think of a world without testing. How do you know if products can withstand the pressures of use? It seems God allows testing to see what's in us (probably for us to see what's in us) and to make us stronger disciples as a result.

Destined for Trouble

Because some young believers were undergoing severe troubles, Paul sent Timothy to encourage them so they wouldn't be shaken apart. "You know that we are destined for such troubles. Even when we were with you, we warned you that troubles would soon come" (I Thessalonians 3:3-4). Apparently, Paul's new believer class had a lesson on the certainty of faith-shaking trials. *Destined* depicts commissioning. Perhaps you've witnessed a ceremony ordaining ministers, a commissioning of missionaries to distant lands, or soldiers ordered to a particular assignment. These are solemn occasions. The joy of past

---

73 A different word is used when Jesus prays to the Father—one pertaining to *equals*!

accomplishment tempers with the likelihood of future challenges.

Similarly, we have been *commissioned...*

...to undergo trials.

Rough times are in store for everybody, believers and unbelievers alike. After a house fire, people scour the devastation to see if anything survived. Does God allow fiery trials to burn junk away now so when we get to the fires of judgment, there will be things of value that please Him?

The enemy's purpose of sifting is to separate you from your faith, and ultimately turn you from Christ. He wants to beat the faith out of you and hopes nothing genuine emerges through the shaking; just a sham faith gone with the wind. Sifting reveals quantity without quality. How did Jesus pray for Peter? That his *faith* wouldn't fail, and that he'd return. Was Peter's faith shallow? Would he continue following Jesus?

If a difficulty is pulling you away from God, you're being sifted.[74]

Point: Are you being sifted? What's pulling you away?
Ponder why Jesus allowed Peter to be tested.
Prayer: "Lord, You've been faithful to me. Help me be faithful to You."
Practical: If you're being sifted, what will you do about it?
Playlist: *Somebody's Praying Me Through* by Allen Asbury. Even if no one on earth is praying for you, Jesus is!
Pocket:

---

74 Dedication: Solomon Mukonjo, whose faith has endured heavy sifting. It's an honor to know you.

29: El Diablo vs. Quickdraw Pete
The Showdown

> *I have pleaded in prayer **for you** (Luke 22:32).*

Jesus didn't cancel this showdown or fight it for Simon Peter. Instead, He prayed for him. In *The Chronicles of Narnia*, Peter rushes to rescue his sister, who climbed a tree to escape an angry wolf. Aslan, the good lion, stands nearby. When his army attempts to assist, Aslan strangely calls them off, "Back! Let the Prince win his spurs."[75] While Peter draws his sword against the mocking beast, yards away stands a force capable of instant victory. Yet they silently watch. Aslan is interested in more than ending this skirmish; he wants to develop a courageous warrior who can fight bigger battles. The opponents engage and quickly collapse to the ground. Concern turns to celebration as Peter rises victorious. Aslan proudly confers on him a new title of great dignity.

Sometimes the King's sons win; sometimes the foe prevails. Everyone has wins *and* losses, but Christ can use all of them. Doesn't it feel like we fight alone sometimes? *God, where are You?* We want Him to swoop in and save the day. Sometimes He does, and we praise Him for mighty interventions. Other times, however, He simply abides within. While Peter engaged in battle, Aslan was also engaged, undistracted, fully aware of His own in the struggle. Aslan and his armies were *near*, but *still*. Faith tells us God is close.

God, where are you?
Here. Inside you.
Greater is He that is in you.

Hugging God

One of the most powerful things I've ever witnessed occurred when Rachel was quite young. She was saying her good-nights. "Good night, Ben. Good night, Cal-Cal (our calico). Good night, Morden (Morgan, our golden retriever). Good night, Mommy. Good night,

---

75 *The Chronicles of Narnia: The Lion, The Witch, and the Wardrobe.* C.S. Lewis. Macmillan. 1950. (105)

Daddy." Without hesitation, she embraced *herself* with a mighty hug, kissed her heart, and confidently said, "Good night, God!" Then she walked like a boss to her bedroom as Melissa and I looked at each other with jaws dropped.

Silence doesn't imply divine distance or anger. Think about taking a test—the teacher is nearby, but silent. God does help and direct, and loves when we call, but sometimes chooses a more background approach. When this happens, He's likely providing an opportunity for our faith and fight to grow. Silence is sometimes the noblest gesture of attentiveness. Imagine watching the final play of a close game. Nobody switches to *Jeopardy* or asks a buddy about work. They're riveted. Maybe that's the picture you need if you're on the verge of giving up on God because it seems He's given up on you. **Tonight, when you go to bed, hug yourself, kiss your heart, and say *Good Night* to the One who chose to make you His dwelling!**

The Big Day

Quickdraw Pete eagerly waits for El Diablo to gallop into town. The showdown is his chance to shine for the Sheriff and impress his peers, but it seems his opponent might not show. However, a sinister plot unfolded against the Sheriff, who's now in an illegal trial.

The air was ripe with evil. Pete makes his way to the front porch of the hall where they're holding his boss. To his chagrin, a small crowd mills around. As he jockeys past bystanders to get a better look, a girl puts him in the spotlight. "I know him! He's with the Sheriff!" Normally he relished attention, but not tonight. "Mind your business, kid. You don't know what you're talking about."

Lowering his Stetson, he ventures down a dim side-street, seeking concealment. He hopes the Sheriff is OK and wants to be nearby if needed. Another girl recognizes him. "He's a deputy of that imposter sheriff!" Pete musters his best combative tone, "I don't even know who you're talking about!" He barely avoids the escalating situation. A deep exhale makes his breath visible in the cold night air.

Dropping his gaze even more, he can barely see five feet ahead as he nears the back door. *Can't these people go somewhere else?* Pete's hands are as cold as the faces of the crowd. He covertly makes his way to the yellow flames rising from a barrel. This proves costly. The fire's light allows several bystanders to notice him. Blood drains from his face and dread shocks his system as they boldly agree, "You're Quickdraw

Pete, the Sheriff's right-hand man!" Their circle tightens as a coalition of voices interrogate him. "They're trying the Sheriff now. He's not the saint he pretended to be. Doesn't look good. You're next."

They seize him. Another reaches for his hat. In these parts, you don't mess with a man's hat. His quick wit and flailing elbows stop them. "How can I be guilty? I don't even know this Sheriff. Dagnabbit! Get off me!" He wrestles himself from the mob, adjusts his hat, and storms off cursing. The door opens as a "juror" slips out for fresh air. Pete instinctively glances in. The smoky room was angry and chaotic, and there, in the center of those savage predators, stood the Sheriff. Clenched fists were inches from his face, the harassment relentless. A formidable attorney in a black suit slaps him hard across the cheek, jolting his head in Pete's direction. Their eyes lock before the door slams shut by a guard. "I said keep the stupid door shut!"

A rooster proudly announces the arrival of a new day.

He said this would happen. His mind flashed to the girl on the porch, the scuffle in the street, and the confrontation by the fire. He shut his eyes hard, hoping to wake up. The memory of the Sheriff's kind gaze broke him. *That look of abandonment!* He hastened through a deserted alley and out toward a patch of woods. Guilt barreled through his veins. Falling without regard for his body, he crumbled in a pile—a heaving mess of brokenness. There he wept.

Warmed by the Fire

I'm writing from a beautiful lodge in Pennsylvania. Thick hardwood trees abound. Nature's raw beauty somehow quickens and quiets me. It's January, and there's absolutely no movement. Though the trees are tall, they stand motionless. I anticipate wildlife rummaging for sustenance along the snow-crusted terrain, but there's no sign of anything, not even an antsy squirrel. A picnic table-turned-white and a firepit could share stories of bonfires and laughter, of friends gathered, and gooey s'mores enjoyed. But those are only memories. Today they sit cold and lifeless.

Though beautiful, it's also colorless. The ground is white, the trees dull brown, and the sky thick gray. Contrast that with the view inside, of beautiful log furniture and a massive stone fireplace where gentle flames provide warmth and life. Peter's inner life resembled the bleak outdoors. The adventures and dreams of the not-too-distant past turned cold and gray.

He needs someone to light a fire.[76]

> **Point:** Are you in a battle but God seems distant or silent? What if He doesn't miraculously swoop in, but wants you to fight without *feeling* His presence?
> **Ponder** Peter's denials and brokenness.
> Are you broken by failure?
> **Prayer:** Ask God to start a fire *for* or *in* you.
> **Practical:** By faith, give God a hug.
> **Playlist:** *Find My Peace* by Naomi Raine
> *Light the Fire Again* by Brian Doerksen
> **Pocket:**

---

[76] Dedication: Rachel McEntire. You're the only one of your kind! Always be a God-hugger!

30: Collecting Firewood

> *At dawn Jesus* was standing on the beach,
> but the disciples couldn't see who he was (John 21:4).

Peter, reeling from failure, leaves Jerusalem's noise and heads home to Galilee. He had been through a lot recently: the jubilant parade, the upper room, the denial trilogy, Jesus' crucifixion, the empty tomb. Maybe the tranquil sea air will help him detox. *Jesus said He'd meet us here, whatever that means.* Six disciples join him.[77] Peter crumbled as a stalwart follower of Jesus, but if there's one thing he knows, it's fishing!

This seems more than a weekend trip with his buddies. Was he returning to his old life, where things made sense? Three years prior, while Peter cleaned gear after a frustrating night at work, a nearby crowd listened to a preacher. *That's different. They don't talk to people like us.* As the growing audience nearly pressed the teacher into the lake, Jesus asks to preach from Peter's boat. So out they go. Just a few feet away from this fisherman sat a man whose words, demeanor, and presence bait him.

As the sermon concludes, Jesus tells Peter, "Go out where it is deeper, and let down your nets to catch some fish" (Luke 5:4). *I guarantee there's no fish anywhere.* Obediently, Peter unfolds the net and tosses it in. Within seconds, his boat nearly drowns! Amid a ton of squirming fish, in front of a jaw-dropped crowd, the rugged fisherman does something extraordinary—he bends a knee. By the time they reach shore, Peter decides to leave his business to be mentored by Jesus. He staked his life on it.

Yep, Jesus hooked a big one.

Peter heard His stories, watched Him heal broken people, rooted for Him when confronting the religious elite. He cherished the late-night discussions and mission trips. He felt so close to God around Jesus—so empowered, challenged, inspired. No one was like Him. Power, truth, and love all wrapped together. He knew Jesus was the Chosen One sent by God but couldn't understand why He took such interest in his ordinary life.

These memories were much better, however, than the recent irreparable mess he made. The man much at home in the limelight of

---

77 Where were the others? Are they breaking up the band?

Jesus' revolution returned to the rustic wood of a solitary fishing boat. *Not sure what those years were about. Maybe time to get back to normal.* Whatever his hopes were for fishing, they ebbed as fruitless hours wore on. Life is so upside-down he can't even do well what he does well.

Most likely he feels useless.

Meanwhile, Jesus is gathering firewood.

Some say it's darkest just before dawn. This is exactly when Jesus collected sticks and arranged them to receive the flame. Soon He'd invite seven weary men for rest, nourishment, and fellowship. **So many things the resurrected Lord could've been doing; here He is making breakfast!** What a demonstration of divine grace and down-to-earth servanthood!

I wonder Jesus' thoughts as He rose from the fire and looked toward His boys. I picture Him near the water's edge—infectious smile, arms loosely folded, eyes dancing. "Look at those knuckleheads! What a bunch! *(Feeling the scars in each wrist where nails bored holes)* But I love those guys! They're mine! I'd do anything for them. Die for them. Go to hell for them. Share heaven with them. They have no idea what I'm planning to do with them! *(Snickering innocently)* Seven men can't catch one fish!"

What a perfect setting to meet Peter. Jesus met him on this lake before and changed his life, calling him to more than he imagined (Luke 5:1-11). He would meet him here again. Peter's purposes, undimmed by denial, continued to radiate in God's heart, even though the disciple was completely oblivious to their unfolding. That's a trademark of "night life"—we don't see what God is doing at the time.

Job, a man who knew dark nights, captured it this way: "If I go to the east, he is not there; if I go to the west, I do not find Him. When He is at work in the north, I do not see Him; when He turns to the south, I catch no glimpse of Him. But He knows the way that I take; when He has tested me, I will come forth as gold" (Job 23:8-11 NIV). Job looked in every direction but couldn't catch the slightest sighting of God. **By faith, he *knew* God knew where he was. And he rested in that.**

Peter's night loomed long and dark. However, darkness was losing its grip as a glimmering hue peeked over the rural countryside. He would soon warm himself by orange coals and share breakfast with his best friend, who would light another fire—this one would melt the cold, barren regrets clinging to Peter's soul. But first, Jesus interrupts their dreadful night by asking if they caught anything. "No!" comes the strained confession.

At Dawn

Those two words move me. I realize they're to be interpreted literally; that is, these events happened early one morning. But they remind me of some figurative usages of darkness and light. "Weeping may endure for a night, but joy comes in the morning" (Psalm 30:5). "For God, who said, 'Let there be light in the darkness,' has made this light shine in our hearts" (2 Corinthians 4:6). Oh, when the night loosens, and new light emerges! *At dawn*. Glorious words of hope. What will your dawn bring? May the Light of the world shine on you! God does not waste the night; He works hard at night. **What He accomplishes in your night will be revealed in the morning. It will one day help others in the dark.**

A successful fishing expedition may have intoxicated ol' Pete and left him content with fishing for fish. Instead, he nets zero. We hate emptiness, but only empty things experience *The-God-Who-Fills*! You may be where you should be but coming up empty. You yearn for greener pastures and bluer skies. You plan to quit or move. The word for you is *endure* (Hebrews 10:36). You may be coming up empty because you're *not* where you're supposed to be, or pushing *your* agenda, not God's. The dead-end is His doing. The word for you is *surrender*. **If you're coming up empty, may God grant discernment to know if you should press on or move on. And peace to accept it.**

One Step

The voice from shore instructs them to throw their nets on the other side of the boat. It seems ridiculous, but they obey. The men spring to life as fish clamor their way into the nets! This jubilant commotion gives John a flashback. *I've seen this before. Oh yeah, Jesus in Pete's boat. Asked him to drop his net on the other side, though he hadn't caught anything all night. And there was this huge catch…(lightbulb)*

"It's Jesus!"

Peter's response is vital. He could ignore Jesus, sulk in shame, hide behind Nathanael, drown in guilt, row away. Instead, he plunges in and swims toward Jesus! How important is a step, especially the first step, in the right direction? It doesn't even have to be big. **The significance of a step isn't always determined by how grand it is.** Peter, though pathetic, did not become *a*pathetic. You might assume Jesus, obsessed with your failure, is moving away. Sometimes He stays on shore, throws a line, and waits for us to bite, but He's always seeking closeness. If you've gone the wrong way, turn around, take a step, and start over.

I love the story of Jonathan, son of King Saul. Saul and the army are parked under a tree while their enemy camps across a cliff-faced chasm. Neither army concedes or initiates. This stalemate continues until Jonathan has an *I gotta do something* moment. He pulls his friend aside, "Let's go across. Perhaps the LORD will help us, for nothing can hinder the LORD. He can win a battle whether He has many warriors or only a few" (I Samuel 14:6)!

He didn't know how it would play out. He just knew he had to take Step 1. Step 2: confirm whether Step 1 was of God or not. The enemy's response to their arrival would signal to Jonathan if they should advance or abort. I want all the steps before taking the first. To know I have what it takes, and the answer to every *what-if*. As a result, I've missed a lot. John Maxwell says, "It's on your journey that you make the greatest discoveries." There's liberty to explore a possibility. Jonathan testifies to the unlimited potential wrapped up in one step.[78]

> **Point:** God works nights on your behalf.
> Are attempts coming up empty? What if God is working another plan?
> **Ponder** Jesus looking your way. You may think He dislikes you. Truth be known, He might be making you breakfast!
> **Prayer:** "God, should I press on or move on?" It's not unspiritual to ask God to confirm the next step. (2 Corinthians 13:1)
> **Practical:** If possible, enter another room as if Jesus is there.
> Go fishing!
> Devotional: *Streams in the Desert*, March 14
> **Playlist:** *What a Friend We Have in Jesus* hymn by Joseph Scriven
> *What a Friend I've Found* by Delirious
> **Pocket:**

---

78 See what happens in 1 Samuel 14:1–23.
Dedication: Al Myers Sr, one of the best "fishermen" I know.

31: Breakfast on the Beach

*They found **breakfast waiting for them** (John 21:9).*

The trek through Amish country brought me to an informal Saturday evening gathering. They had no idea how the warm welcome blessed their guest speaker, who recently lifted his head from the dirty wilderness floor. It felt great to preach again after such a long hiatus. The next morning, we had another beautiful service. I freely shared my season of brokenness—loathing my existence, wanting to be done—when I spontaneously declared: "But I'm still standing!" They responded heartily and closed the service by asking God to restore me. More salve to my soul. Thank God the desert wasn't my grave. I lived to see more seasons.

After the first service, while walking alone, I blurted, "I can't believe I got to do that!" I just experienced what "fulfilled" feels like! Having compared myself to people who love what they do, the power of that statement touched my core. Envy is an aggressive cancer that clouds perspective. Before we know it, stage 4 "fulfillment envy" can infect our thought life with tension. When this occurs, the outlook is never good.

Upon reaching my forties, with the help of social media, I got updated on my peers. In a season where I felt like wasted potential, everyone seemed to be doing great. For the first time as an adult, I majored in comparisons with those having warm zip codes, new toys, large bank accounts, or "worthwhile" positions. You know, those brats deeply satisfied in life, who say, "I can't believe I get paid to do this!" To someone suffering from chronic "Sunday evening dread," it stung. I wanted that so bad but believed it was unattainable—for me. Brokenness wears down the soul's immune system. It makes us highly prone to envy, tells us everyone else has it made.

Listen to this honest account of a man succumbing to envy, "I almost lost my footing. My feet were slipping and I was almost gone. For I envied the proud when I saw them prosper despite their wickedness. They seem to live such painless lives; their bodies are so healthy and strong. They don't seem to have troubles like other people" (Psalm 73:2-5). Envy caused him to doubt his convictions, leaving him full of turmoil. "I realized my heart was bitter, and I was all torn up inside. I was so foolish and ignorant—I must have seemed like a senseless animal to You" (Psalm 73:21-22). Thankfully, he didn't remain in his mental languishing. "Then I went into Your sanctuary, God, and I finally understood." As he sought God in worship and prayer, new perspective emerged. The psalm ends differently. Fresh insight yielded peace and hope.

Don't interpret my story as the end of all sadness, doubt, or self-deprecating tendencies. I still dreaded my job, which I foolishly let define me. I had sloughs of depression. This wasn't a magical experience insulating me from future struggles; rather, a critical milestone of restored calling. When He saw my scattered bones, He didn't keep walking, but stopped and spoke purpose. Many wilderness seasons stem from unknown or unfulfilled purposes. **Purposelessness dries the bones.** When purpose is unclear, we flippantly chase "success" or apathetically accept mediocrity. Conversely, finding and fulfilling one's God-given callings often produces joy and contentment, and makes us less disposed to comparison.

Breakfast!

When Jesus' disciples reached shore, what did they talk about? Did they give bear hugs? Whatever happened, it's a scene of friendship and affirmation. Jesus invites them to a fire and breakfast. He enjoys their company at this private seaside retreat, and I'm sure they enjoyed His! Just the eight of them. He values quality time with His own! **Jesus is a master at embracing our humanity, especially when we hardly feel worth embracing.** Riddled with insecurities, awkwardness, and stuff, His warm welcome goes a long way to ease and nourish their souls.

After my college sophomore year, I spent the summer in Asia. God did some great things, but I struggled with sickness, severe homesickness, and questioning my purpose. I lost twenty-five pounds (when I didn't need to). Once home, I walked slowly through my backyard. Detoxing quietness and gentle warm sun replenished my body and soul. Knots of tension unraveled. I was home. I wonder if Peter experienced something similar while relaxing next to the coals. The presence of Jesus had been their home the last three years, and then He was taken away, catapulting them into untold levels of stress. Here on Galilee's quiet shore, they were home again.

After breakfast Jesus, ever the enthusiast of inquiry, initiates a heart-to-heart with Peter. As with Elijah, a probing question opens the conversation. He didn't ask if Peter learned his lesson or why he denied Him.

"Do you love Me?"

The question stung, but not to exasperate, condemn, or demean. We worry about all manner of stuff. Jesus sifts through it all. His question zeroed in on central things. About what's really going on inside. About motivation. About grace melting the heart's heavy baggage. "Peter, I'm not looking for superman. I'm looking for *you*. I'm not afraid of your flaws. I'm not hoping to be impressed.

I'm hoping to be *loved*."[79]

> **Point:** Have you experienced "I can't believe I got to do that!"
> Do you feel purposeless?
> **Ponder** what makes you envious. Do you wrestle with "fulfillment envy?"
> Ponder the chapter's last two sentences.
> **Prayer:** Lord, show me Your will. (Ephesians 2:10)
> **Practical:** Waiting periods can be times of preparation for fulfilling God's purposes in the next season (1 Timothy 1:18-19). Check out *www.myipsat.com* by Nexleader or *SHAPE assessment* by Rick Warren.
> **Playlist:** *Help Me Find It* by Sidewalk Prophets.
> **Pocket:**

---

[79] Dedication: Gowanda Free Methodist Church. Your willingness to welcome a broken preacher played a pivotal role in my restoration.

32: Good Morning, Mr. Failure!

> ***Cockadoodle-doooo!*** *(Matthew 26:74 paraphrased)*

Memories are powerful triggers, often woven into the fabric of everyday life. The smell of sanding wood makes me crave a bologna sandwich with Miracle Whip. Don't try to figure it out! Strange to you, it's reality to me. The energetic song "Sh' boom" transports me to the perfect date with my daughter Rachel in Warren, Pennsylvania. The words "blue heron" remind me of a funny conversation with a friend in eighth grade. The *Big Dipper* and *Southern Cross* dutifully testify of God's faithfulness.

Isn't it amazing how a song resurrects a strong emotion, or a taste activates a childhood event? I chose a few positive examples, but many "triggers" conjure painful emotions, crippling fears, and mocking hurts. Good days turn mentally ugly in a moment and leave us reeling and feeling out of control. I don't know if the power of those memories can be turned off. After all, how do I make a song or smell no longer remind me of that same old thing? I'm not a psychologist, but here's my two cents (which may be all it's worth): maybe we can't *control* triggers, but with a lot of work, can *re-route* them.

I've worked with guys who used the "f" word every time they exhaled. It made my mind heavy day after day. When I heard about a family trekking for a local ministry, I wanted to remember to pray for them. I chose that word as my reminder. It required plenty of mental workout reps, and didn't work every time, but it often guided me to a better destination. I couldn't change the external forces, but I could control where it took me. Instead of getting angry or sullen, I found a beneficial use of a negative stimulus.

Let's say the smell of cucumber reminds you of rejection. You religiously avoid them. Then a friend orders them with her salad at lunch. You bow your head to pray for the meal, burst into tears, and rush to the restroom. You regain composure and return to the table, assuring your friend it has nothing to do with her. She sighs in relief and offers to pay. You feel weird but vulnerably confess the power of cucumber's smell.

A month later your friend orders her salad with cucumbers again. The meal arrives and she remembers her crime. You brace yourself and tell her it's ok. This time doesn't require an escape or dampen the rest of the day, though it still has an edge to it. Your friend asks what changed. You tell her you consciously decided every time you smell cucumber to remember Ephesians 1:4, "Even before He made the world, God loved me and chose me in Christ." Sometimes it's harder than others, but the truth of being chosen is replacing the pain of rejection.

What do you think sent Peter jogging down memory lane? Let's review:

JESUS: All of you will desert Me.
PETER: I won't!
OTHER DISCIPLES: Ditto!
JESUS: Peter, before the rooster crows, you'll deny Me three times.
PETER: Even if I must die, I'll never deny you!
(Several hours later)
SERVANT GIRL: You were with Jesus.
PETER: I don't know what you're talking about.
SERVANT GIRL 2: This man was with Jesus.
PETER: I don't know the man.
BYSTANDER: Didn't I see you with Jesus?
PETER: A curse on me if I'm lying—I don't know the man!
ROOSTER: Cockadoodle-doooo
PETER'S MEMORY: *Before the rooster crows, you'll deny Me three times.*

(Bitter weeping)

Surely this etched his psyche. Certainly the crowing of any ol' rooster triggered failure. How could it not? The problem with roosters is they wake people up. How many times did Peter want to silence a rooster? (He was no stranger to swinging swords in the heat of the moment.) How often did he cover his ears to dull the sound of defeat? Imagine every time a rooster jolts your slumber, you relive regret, like an alarm saying, "You denied Jesus. You denied Jesus. You denied Jesus. Have a good day."

The memories must've ruined untold mornings—cowardice, naive affirmations of loyalty, the look on Jesus' face. He pulls the covers over his head. Whatever ran through Peter's mind and soul, Jesus sought to exchange it. **God isn't satisfied with your mental torment. He wants to replace it.** So much so, that when Peter heard a rooster crow, it could remind him of his Shepherd who made breakfast for him on a shore early one morning.

One of my earliest sermons was *Killing Roosters*. The next day someone sent a picture of a dead rooster on the side of the road. I didn't mean it literally! While it may be impossible to *kill* the roosters regurgitating those harsh memories, may God help us find a way to repurpose them as reminders of liberating truth and replenishing grace. When *cockadoodle-dooo* downloads failure and anxiety, God's Spirit says it's time to rise and shine.

A New Lane

Let's return to the breakfast story (excerpts from John 21:15-17):

"After breakfast Jesus asked Simon Peter, 'Do you love me more than these?'"

"Yes, Lord, you know I love you."

"Then feed my lambs."

"Jesus repeated the question: 'Simon, do you love me?'"

"Yes, Lord, you know I love you."

"Then take care of my sheep."

"A third time he asked, 'Simon, do you love me?'"

"Peter was hurt that Jesus asked the question a third time. 'Lord, you know everything. You know that I love you.'"

"Jesus said, 'Then feed my sheep.'"

Notice how restoration links with calling. As God restores our hope and worth, He also restores our purpose. Moses' restoration included an assignment of delivering a nation. Elijah was chosen to assist young leaders. Jesus *specifically called Peter* to lead an infant flock of disciples, but he is to fulfill this purpose motivated by love, not trying to repay failure's debt. Jesus reaffirms Peter—the man, the person, the friend. He reinstates Peter—the disciple, the leader, the worker. His story would've been radically different if Jesus hadn't met him for breakfast one morning.

Love Fuel

Many have emphasized the different Greek words for *love* in this conversation. Jesus asks Peter if he loves Him with *agape*, the highest dimensions of love, requiring self-sacrifice. Twice Peter responds with the lesser word *phileo*, still rich with meaning, but based on affinity or affection toward someone. It could sound like: "I don't know if I'd die for you, but I care about you." The third time Jesus adopts Peter's word. "Do you even care about me?" Peter responds, "Lord, you know all things. You know I care."

Three times Peter confessed he didn't know Jesus. Three times he confesses his love. This raw exchange is deeply humbling. No platitudes or pretenses. Notice Jesus didn't berate his word choice, shoot a disappointing look, or enlist guilt. Instead, He met him at the point of his love. Jesus earlier predicted Peter's denials. He predicts his future again—Peter would glorify God with his life...and death.

Three characteristics about the greatest of loves:

Agape **is more about the one loving than the one being loved.** The lover's entire being is consumed with love for another, independent of the performance or loveliness of the loved. It doesn't rely on externals, but springs within the one who loves. *Phileo* may secretly ask, "What's in it for me?" This mindset strangely escalated in the disciples the closer Jesus neared death. *Agape* seeks another's well-being at one's own expense. *Agape is the love God has for us.*

Agape is more about decision than affection. *Phileo* feeds on emotion and admiration. "I love you *because* you're hot or kind or supportive. You have qualities that *make you loveable*. I love you *because* of who you are, and it's cool we like the same things." We translate love as liking someone. What about choosing to obey Jesus regardless of what He does for us or asks us to do for Him? *Phileo* is fairly natural. *Agape* is supernatural.

Agape **is constant.** It's not shiftless, doesn't quiver with changing feelings. An advertisement highlights exact toys with different batteries. All start great, but the inferior brands eventually die. One keeps going. *Agape* continues after lesser loves burn out. This matters because ministry, relationships, and life require steadfast love. Face it, isn't this everyone's desire? *Agape* is the craving of mankind. Just like their Creator.

Oswald Chambers wrote, "It never cost a disciple anything to follow Jesus; to talk about cost when you are in love with anyone is an insult. Love for the Lord is not an ethereal, intellectual, dreamlike thing; it is the intensest, most vital, most passionate love of which the human heart is capable."[80]

Impress or Impart?

Sometimes brokenness exposes why we do what we do. The greatest, most effective motive is *agape* love for Christ. Peter wasn't

---

80 *My Utmost for His Highest.* Oswald Chambers. Dodd, Mead, & Co. 1935.

there yet, but Jesus wasn't done either. What motivated Peter thus far? I would sum it up in one word: *pride*. He had to be first. Certainly he participated in the arguments about who was best. Fame. Power. Control. These fruits stem from the root of pride. **Love for applause compelled him to impress others; following his restoration, love for Christ compelled him to impact others.** Jesus was transforming his internal operating system, installing a new "love mindset." Stripping his selfish ambition, He clothed him with an interest in the faith of others.

Peter would've been a brash, graceless minister if not for his brokenness and restoration. Jesus moved him from exhibition to exhortation, from strutting to strengthening. He learned to come alongside others for *their* benefit. When he met the disabled beggar (Acts 3), old Simon would've tried to heal him for Simon's sake. Peter healed him for Christ's glory and the man's well-being. I've preached for praise, and I've also preached to build up. God, in His grace, uses us even with skewed motives, but they will limit our capacity to serve. As with Peter, He meets us at the point of our love.

And graciously compels us to greater.[81]

> **Point:** God loves you based on His heart, not your performance.
> What roosters crow in your ear? God isn't pleased with your mental torment.
> **Ponder** your motives.
> What if Jesus asked, "Do you *agape* me?"
> **Prayer:** Tell God you love Him or sing a love song to Him. See *Playlist*.
> **Practical:** Try rerouting a trigger. Where does it lead? Where do you want it to go?
> **Playlist:** *Arms of Love* by Vineyard
> *I Love You Lord* hymn by Laurie Adams-Klein
> *Here I Am to Worship (instrumental)* by Lincoln Brewster
> **Pocket:**

---

[81] Dedication: Eddie Kizito ("Pastor Smile"). Your *agape* shows, my brother!

33: Jesus' Death Wish

> *Jesus took hold of me* (Philippians 3:12 NIV).

The pomp and circumstance of a commencement ceremony creates a serious atmosphere. It can make you feel big *and* small. One aspect of mine stands out—our class banner that hung directly in front of me. In the middle was a cross. Though a symbol seen a thousand times, this one captured me. I considered Jesus' bloodied arms and the intense expression on His face, but what seized me is what I *heard*.

Aaaaaaaahhhhhhhhhhhhhhhhhhhhhhhhhhhhhhhh!

The Savior's passionate war cry rattled my entire being.

"Jesus, again crying out loudly, breathed his last" (Matthew 27:50 MSG). Why this loud cry? Why was He giving everything? What was He thinking about? Me. He was accomplishing my salvation. **With the last breath of His life, He eagerly took hold of mine.** When I gave my worst, Jesus gave His best. "God demonstrates His own love toward us, in that while we were still sinners, Christ died for us (Romans 5:8 NKJV)." The Message says, "God put his love on the line for us by offering his Son in sacrificial death while we were of no use whatever to him."

Hear the zeal in His parched voice? If you doubt your value, let His fervent cry reverberate into your soul. Taking hold of *your life* didn't come easy. His pursuit of you cost Him His life. It reminds me of a missionary's emphatic determination, "I will bring the gospel to this land...*or die trying*!" Paul writes:

> *Not that I have already obtained all this, or have already arrived at my goal, but I press on to take hold of that for which* **Christ Jesus took hold of me.** *Brothers and sisters, I do not consider myself yet to have taken hold of it.* (Philippians 3:12-13 NIV emphasis mine).

Repetitive words and phrases in the Bible reveal major points. Sometimes they're obscured in modern translations, while obvious in the original languages. The context highlights a few "big ideas" like *already/not yet* and *press on/strain.* The key one, triple-stacked, is *take hold.*[82] I'm guessing vocabulary lessons rarely escalate your pulse, but this one might. To "take hold" means (drum roll please) *to eagerly seize or apprehend.* (I see that blank stare and raised eyebrow.) This isn't fetching socks or getting $1.37 in change. No! There's fervency in it! It's holding something long-awaited for the first time, like a newborn son or daughter! Speaking of daughters, I watched Rachel research, save, and wait for a new phone. Finally, after trading a cache of funds, *she eagerly grabbed the object of her pursuit.*

That's "taking hold."

Jesus did the same thing when reaching with every muscle to take *you* as His own!

Still Holding

Maybe you trusted Jesus years ago. He forgave you, received you. Everything was new! Maybe years passed, and after failing some tests and regretting some decisions, you doubt God loves you anymore. Maybe grace expired, or you used it up? **Good news—God's love continues for the saved who struggle and fall short.** It hasn't lapsed one millisecond or diminished one millimeter. Listen to this:

"Much more then, having now been justified by His blood, we shall be saved from wrath through Him. For if when we were enemies we were reconciled to God through the death of His Son, much more, having been reconciled, we shall be saved by His life" (Romans 5:9-10 NKJV). Notice the twin usage of "much more." If He demonstrated superior love when sin made me His enemy, will He do less now that I'm His child? Absolutely not! It costs God a lot to love me, both past and present, but it's as potent *now* as ever! **The best part—His love doesn't *depend on me.***

What does a shepherd experience after finding a lost sheep? Joy! Here's this dirty, wandering animal, *eagerly* sought by a man with gentle hands and beaming smile. Don't know how much sheep think, but this one may ponder, *I don't deserve to be loved like this!* Right on, lil sheep, neither do we. "Taking hold" means someone considers something so valuable he will pursue it at great cost—until clutching it with both hands. This brings such joy He doesn't plan on ever letting go!

Two hands stretched across an unsympathetic beam on a hill

---

82 The root is additionally found in the word *obtained.*

outside Jerusalem. What were they straining to reach?
You.[83]

> **Point:** Christ died to eagerly *take hold* of you.
> **Ponder:** Is it easier to believe God loved you as a sinner than it does as a saved person needing grace?
> **Prayer:** Are you convinced God loves you right now? Ask Him to show you.
> **Practical:** Gaze on a cross. Listen.
> Choose a "sign of love" between you and God. Every "sighting" will remind of God's special love *for you*.
> **Playlist:** *So Great* by Compassionart
> **Pocket:**

---

83 Dedication: Philemon Setyabule. Jesus eagerly took hold of you! As I write this, you're getting married!

34: Grab *That*

> *I press on to take hold of **that** (Philippians 3:12 NIV).*

Twice I've had to use crutches—after dislocating an ankle playing basketball at age thirty and after breaking the other ankle playing volleyball at forty. I'm contemplating songwriting or art when I turn fifty. During those armpit-chafing weeks I discovered additional purposes for crutches. Flip the light switch from the comfort of your chair. Challenge your kids to basketball. A raised crutch deflects any offensive attempt. Wide puddle? Swoop across like Tarzan. Add his cry for effect. Accessorize with cupholders and a rearview mirror. I won't share further examples in case I write *101 Uses for Crutches* someday, but I will say, grabbing my crutches often meant *extending my reach*.

In the last chapter we spoke of Jesus taking hold of us. But there's more! **He grasped us so we could grasp some things on God's heart.** Put simply, it's taking hold of something so that something can take hold of *that*.

Huh?

Here's some examples:

A hard-working student eagerly receives a degree that will help him change the world.

Police rally every resource to stop a dangerous suspect. Sweat. Focus. Adrenaline. Sirens. Everyone gives all. The culmination occurs when they seize the lawbreaker. What's reported? "They *apprehended* their suspect." This guarantees a safer neighborhood.

An athlete surges at the perfect time. His open hand greedily extends back toward an approaching teammate. The baton isn't the end goal. Gold is. But grabbing the baton is necessary to grasping gold.

A quick-witted teacher reaches toward a hopeless teenager on a ledge. After intense conversation, the teen slowly accepts the open hand. Grabbing that hand becomes the first step to holding everything else for the rest of her life—keys, a degree, a husband, a baby, a grandchild's artwork.

Commencement Revisited

During commencement, I heard Jesus' cry for my reconciliation. **But He died for something else—my ministry.** For the first time I realized how passionate Jesus is about my purposes. He died to make them possible. Christ not only thought of *you* as He reached toward you, but of *that* which He wants you to accomplish. What all is wrapped up in such a little word? *That.*

A faithful saint named Gail Olofson confided in me, "I'm not a preacher, but if I had the chance, my title would be 'That.'" Wish I could've heard that sermon. I've considered preaching it on his behalf but never felt qualified. I never heard his sermon, but I watched his life and heard him pray. He had a soft heart, habitually asking God to rid anything in it not pleasing to Him. It broke at the news of divorce or backsliding. He and his wife Betty beamed about missions and gave generously to it. He quickly offered a smile, encouragement, and prayer. He often affirmed, "God is the great heavenly orchestrator." This made him confident in prayer. These were some of *That* which Jesus made possible for Gail to grab.

Our lives are not meaningless piles of mess! They overflow with purpose and significance, which our Creator infused into us, and our Savior made possible. Purposes don't always come easy. God wants us to eagerly pursue them. I believe *that* comprises two main categories: God's work in us (character—who we are) and God's work through us (ministry—what we do). He's passionate about both. **The zeal which Christ pursued *us* is how we are to pursue *that*.** "It is God who works in you to will and to do according to His good pleasure" (Philippians 2:13 NKJV). Both elements in one statement—God developing you, then leading you "to do" ministry.[84] Another way of saying this, "Jesus fervently looked for me. When He found me, He held me tight. He's got some things for me to grab too. I want 'em all!"

You're Part of My **That**

I kissed Melissa and Rachel goodbye as they headed into the frosty cold to visit family. The temperatures wouldn't top zero all weekend. Perfect for hibernating. As I closed the door, I verbalized my longing, "Lord, I'm shut in with You." I needed to hear God. My only plan

---

84 Any God-honoring action, not excluded to pastors or missionaries.

was to seek God's purposes for my life. Internal restlessness signaled God had intentions I was not fulfilling. *I'm not getting younger. I need to figure this out.* Time to face the tension head-on. I didn't have a clear plan, wasn't sure how to begin, so I simply told God my concerns about my unfulfilled purposes.

His kind Spirit assured me the Father has purposes for my life *and wants to reveal them.* "We are God's masterpiece. He has created us anew in Christ Jesus, so we can do the good things He planned for us long ago" (Ephesians 2:10). We act like this is something to coax out of God, hoping He will spill the beans in a moment of weakness if we pray just right or long enough. **He likes when we ask; He wants to show you His plan for you!**

A manual from a seminar I attended twenty years earlier popped into my mind. Not knowing if it was heaven's nudge, I prayed, "If this is You, help me find it." I had moved four times since then. Searching felt like a potential waste of time. Five minutes later I held it in my hands. *Hmmm. This is more than coincidence!* I read, "Your destiny is the sovereign purpose(s) for which you have been created that when fulfilled brings God the greatest glory, brings you the greatest joy, and most significantly advances the Kingdom."[85] The concept of a destiny marker intrigued me, defined as an "event, experience, or circumstance that reminds us God has a sovereign purpose for our life."[86]

I pondered some of mine:
- Special heritage
- Parental oath/contract
- Prophecy
- Preservation of life (three checkmarks)
- Divine contact

An undeniable theme surfaced, nothing short of a revelation. These seven witnesses testified of a call to preach. I can't explain the importance of seeing these specifics about *my life*. It was there, tucked in the pages of my story but buried beneath life's rubble. Sometimes we need to remove ourselves from life's frenzied pace long enough to pray, hear, think, dig. Schedules and demands tell us to keep running. *There's no time for time-outs. Maybe next season when things slow down.*[87]

Look ahead to the next three months. Designate a weekend for

---

[85] *Charting the Course.* Steve Moore. 1989.
[86] Moore.
[87] Spoiler alert! It won't slow down. You must be intentional.

mandatory shut-down or earmark several shorter periods. This is an invitation. (First, I used "challenge," but Your Creator *invites* you to seek your purposes!) This brings Him so much joy He promises to reward those who do! **You don't have time to *not* do this!** I'm not implying a formula guaranteeing some great breakthrough. I've had retreats leave me confused and dry; I didn't "get" anything. Such times are frustrating, but we can't let this stop or discourage us. There's no such thing as wasted time spent with God. **In fact, time with God *is* one of our biggest purposes.** This time-out brought amazing clarity. My life changed because I could confidently step in alignment with God's blueprint. Peter needed to know Jesus still had purposes for him. We do too.

Closer Than They Appear

We often mistakenly confine *purpose* to the magnificent and the future—the lifelong career, the big assignment. Purpose isn't singular; there are numerous objectives to heed. Many are deemed so insignificant or simple we don't recognize them. For example, giving thanks is a God-ordained task we can do today. Encouraging someone, mundane service, loving your spouse, time with your kids, prayer, choosing right, paying bills—belong to our purposes. Some aren't about doing, but being. Seek your calling, ask God to reveal your special assignments, but understand many purposes aren't a distant mystery to be discovered. **They're right in front of us, to be exercised.**

My professor, Gary Cote, answered the door. A friendly salesman asked him to write his goals inside a circle, confident the goods he sold would help him achieve them. The teacher guaranteed, "If your product helps me reach my goal, I'll buy it." The salesman's eyes gleamed, again asking his goal. Cool and collected, he wrote one word: *Jesus.* "I want to be more like Jesus." The dumbfounded salesman left without a sale. **Purpose isn't always an assignment, but a person.** Whether known or liked, one of God's major goals is fashioning us into the likeness of Jesus.[88]

---

88 Dedication: Steve Moore. God used you tremendously to clarify my calling! Founder of NexLeader. Author of *The Dream Cycle* and *The Top 10 Leadership Conversations in the Bible.*

Point: Do you feel the gnawing of unknown or unfulfilled purposes?
Do you know what God wants you to accomplish? Does it stir? settle?
Ponder Jesus' passion for *your purposes*.
God wants you to resemble Christ. (Romans 8:29)
Prayer: "I cry out to God Most High, to God who will fulfill His purpose for me" (Psalm 57:2).
God *wants* to reveal His divine intentions. Ask confidently. (Psalm 105:3. Lamentations 3:25. Jeremiah 33:3. Matthew 6:8. Hebrews 11:6.)
Practical: Schedule a purpose retreat.
What purpose can you accomplish *today*?
Playlist: *Take My Life* hymn by Frances Havergal
Pocket:

35: Defying Gravity

> *I still have **a long way to go** (Philippians 3:13 ERV).*

We rode bikes everywhere. School. Church. Down to Wendy's to redeem our Frosty coupons. My best friend Scott lived three miles away, but the route was laden with hills. Going down you could reach thirty-five mph without effort. Going up involved sweat, pain, thirst, and sometimes anger. Paul could've coasted to heaven and still received gold medals. Instead, he rode uphill because he wanted *all that*. His lifestyle stance involved straining, focusing, expending, extending. "I press toward the goal for the prize of the upward call of God in Christ Jesus" (Philippians 3:14 NJKV). After relishing that Jesus eagerly took hold of him, Paul humbly admits he hadn't yet grasped everything Christ earmarked for him.

Rearview Mirror

As Paul presses on, he notices an obstacle to overcome it if he would reach his goals. It's true of us as well. Think of a leading racecar driver with a few laps to go. His laser-like focus and skillful driving situate him at the top. But something changes, though not with his car, crew, or capability. He's been focused out the windshield; now he's mesmerized by the mirror. What's behind steals his concentration. Some is good—maneuvering the wreck on lap fifty-two, winning California, landing his biggest endorsement—all great accomplishments. But they've become distractions. Even enemies.

His crew chief notices and urges concentration. The reset helps, until something catches his eye. The emblem on the car behind him is getting bigger. Jitters shoot through him like nitrous oxide. *Can I hold on?* breeds doubt and surfaces past mistakes. *If I didn't get that pit road penalty I wouldn't be in this predicament. Why didn't we change two tires instead of four?* His mind races to last season when he lost five positions in the final two laps. He shakes his head in disgust. *It took months to recover.*

The car behind him advanced three car-lengths as the white flag signals the final lap. *Come on, focus ahead!* His pep talk garners a clean turn 1. Slight ground is lost around turn 2, but not bad. And like a chronic habit, the mirror usurps what's ahead, causing him to ride too high around sweeping turn 3. *Where is he?* His driver's side window reveals a bumper. The lower line advances his competitor through turn 4, aligning their noses down the straightaway.

The crowd on the right stands to their feet. The fender to his left holds steady. All he can do is pedal to the metal and go straight. His senses hyper-ignite as the checkered flag falls. The roar of the audience rises above the engine's lowering RPMs. He checks the towering digital leaderboard, awaiting official results. After an eternity, the lumens at the top spot form a number.

It takes a second to process. "That's *me!*"

Time to celebrate! He salvaged the win but learned something about chronically looking backward.

Held Back

Have you watched a dominant team switch from pursuing points to watching a clock? Reckless abandon morphs into tentative safety. **Fear of messing up ironically becomes the greatest liability to messing up.** These tales from the sports world illustrate how hard it is to win while looking backward. Distractions in the mirror include things we label bad…and good. In fact, Paul highlights the latter. Past *achievements* can hinder forward progress. "Good enough" has waylaid untold future greatness. Past *failures* have impeded multitudes of future victories. To those straining uphill, and those afraid to begin the climb, the past can weigh down like gravity. Paul recognized the barrier called "the past" and intentionally worked to overcome it.

My pastor had a sign hang in his office: "The past ended a second ago." Reflection and remembrance offer wisdom and experience, like the markers God wrote into my story, **but when the past impedes forward movement, it's dangerous.**

So how did Paul deal with his past?

Before we find out, let's discover some interesting things about his past! That's next.[89]

---

89 Dedication: Duane and Becki James. God had more for you to see through your windshield! Becki is a talented writer and speaker. (*www.beckijames.com*)

Point: How can "rearview mirrors" be a tool? a detriment?
Ponder your current strategy for the game of life: clock-watching? Satisfied with past achievements? Hindered by mistakes?
Prayer: Talk to God about your past.
Practical: List some of your "good things" and "bad things." Beside each, note how it *could* help or hinder.
Playlist: *I Will Fear No More* by The Afters
Pocket:

36: Bad Credit? No Problem!

> *Whatever former things were gains to me [as I thought then], these things [once regarded as advancements in merit] I have come to **consider as loss** [absolutely worthless] for the **sake of Christ** [and the purpose which He has given my life] (Philippians 3:7 AMP).*

From all valued standards in his day, Paul had everything going for him. His religious, educational, and moral resumé shone impeccably. He had lineage, heritage, privilege, and prestige. His portfolio boasted achievements and affiliations. If anyone impressed God and men, it was him. Some people are cream of the crop in one or two realms. Paul was top dog in everything. And proud of it. He was not only good enough—but best.

God doesn't view things as people do. Like Paul, we may assume our objective is to impress God with credentials. How absurd! Frail creatures wanting to be worshiped by their Creator! **God isn't looking to be wowed, but worshiped.** We need a major turnaround in our thinking. A *repentance* if you will. That's what happened to Paul. As always, it came with great tension. He employs accounting terminology to illustrate the credits he inherited or earned.[90] (I've added modern equivalents.)

- Circumcised the eighth day (huge credit with God, as some view baptism or confirmation)
- Stock of Israel (the nation God "likes best")
- Tribe of Benjamin (good family and reputation)
- A Hebrew of the Hebrews (high-ranking)
- A Pharisee, the most powerful religious leaders of the day (Globally regarded as a top spiritual leader)
- Unrivaled zeal for God
- Flawless morals

They total an impressive bottom line. He was the perfect man in the eyes of men. Perhaps in his own. Notice the cataclysmic shift in Paul's thinking:

---

90 Philippians 3:4-6

> *But what things were gain to me, these I have counted loss for Christ. Yet indeed I also count all things loss for the excellence of the knowledge of Christ Jesus my Lord, for whom I have suffered the loss of all things, and count them as rubbish, that I may gain Christ and be found in Him, not having my own righteousness, which is from the law, but that which is through faith in Christ, the righteousness which comes from God and is by faith (Philippians 3:7-9 NKJV).*

Paul realized his accolades *prohibited* him from receiving God's righteousness! He reassessed his portfolio, his prized masterful work, and shredded it, threw the contents in a trash bag, and pitched it in the dump! How hard and humbling this must have been for big man Paul. Seems radical, but he didn't need his spiritual resumé anymore. This took faith, but Paul recalculated his balance sheet. Like an accountant finding clerical errors, he transferred his credits (gains) to debits (losses). He exchanged it all for one big credit—knowing Jesus!

Jesus and Jesus alone made him right with God! Paul employs the accounting metaphor elsewhere to describe the phenomenal transaction of the ransomed soul: "Abraham believed God, and God counted him as righteous because of his faith. When people work, their wages are not a gift, but something they have earned. But people are counted as righteous, not because of their work, but because of their faith in God who forgives sinners" (Romans 4:3-5). This is included under the section about purpose because one of God's purposes for you is to meet Jesus and be reconciled to God!

Honest Appraisal

Ever seen shows where people bring items to a professional appraiser? They want to know how much an antique or possession is worth. The appraiser examines the item and often shares facts about its time-place in history. They listen attentively to his number. It isn't factored by how much he likes the owner or some subjective sentimental value, but its actual valuation. Sometimes they walk away dejected, realizing their treasure isn't worth a dime. That was the revelation Paul received about his self-righteousness. And because it previously kept him from turning to Jesus, he labeled it garbage.

Things changed for Paul. Once a member of the spiritual elite, he became a member of Christ! He transferred his confidence of salvation from *himself* to the perfect blood Jesus shed on his behalf. No wonder his previous glowing achievements seemed like thrown-away leftovers in comparison! That way is superficial and uncertain. God's way is divine and unchanging, like an anchor for the soul! **If I point to things related to *me* as the basis for good standing with God, I've missed God's message.**

A friend mentioned his relative. "He's a good guy. In fact, he's *too* good. His goodness is keeping him from Jesus." It wasn't the obvious sinners who dismissed Jesus, but the moral and religious. We don't need spiritual accolades to impress God. Salvation is offered freely to all, regardless of background and experience. It's not guaranteed to someone because they're wealthy, nice, reputable, or a church member. This gives great hope for those with a grim spiritual balance sheet because God's way isn't about earning credits in the first place!

The cross of Christ alone can save. Now that's something to brag about!

Persuasion

Paul's past almost blinded him permanently. Then he met Jesus. No longer striving to earn salvation, he gladly served the One who saved him. He became a great preacher of a great salvation, extended to all kinds of people of all nations. He worked hard and accomplished a lot for God's kingdom. Concerning future goals and further gains, Paul resisted the lure of clinging to past achievements. If he rested in knowing God used him to write *Galatians* or start the church in Philippi, subsequent ministry may have never materialized. As he didn't let past accolades keep him from choosing Christ, he wouldn't let past gains impede future progress.

Paul's past wasn't all wonderful, however. He broke into Christians' homes and ripped parents from their screaming children. He condemned innocent people to prison and even death. Later he realized with horror that he was persecuting Jesus Himself. Even as a minister, he had such a sharp disagreement with a godly coworker they parted ways. These certainly kept him awake at night, even after meeting Jesus.

An unparalleled debater and skilled intellectual, it was near impossible to persuade Paul, yet he recalls such a scenario, "I am persuaded that neither death nor life, nor angels nor principalities nor powers, nor things present nor things to come, nor height nor depth, nor any other created thing, shall be able to separate us from the love of God which is in Christ Jesus our Lord" (Romans 8:38-39 NKJV). We don't have to be persuaded of things we believe. You don't have to persuade me that New York winters are too long. No need to stiff-arm a staunch Republican or Democrat to vote the party line. In other words, Paul didn't believe this naturally.

God had to *persuade* him of an undying love that covers the past. [91]

> **Point:** "People are counted as righteous...because of their faith in God who forgives sinners" (Romans 4:3-5). Would you rather present *your* righteousness, or that of *Jesus*, to God?
> **Ponder:** Does a former "spiritual valuable" seem like garbage now?
> **Prayer:** Confession means "saying the same thing." Do you need to agree with God about your sins, and that Jesus is the only way to be saved?
> **Practical:** Is something "good" or "bad" keeping you from Jesus?
> **Playlist:** *Thank You for Saving Me* or *I Found Jesus!* by Delirious
> *Free* by Steven Curtis Chapman
> **Pocket:**

---

[91] Dedication: To anyone who hasn't yet received Christ. He's your good credit with God! Find out more at <u>www.keithmc.org</u>

37: What Was This Chapter About? I Forgot

> *I focus on this one thing: **forgetting the past** and **looking forward** to what lies ahead (Philippians 3:13).*

A funeral reunited me with a man I hadn't seen in ages. I wondered how he was doing, as immense pain devastated him fifteen years before. Within a minute, he voiced the hurt. It didn't resurface; it never left. I tread humbly and delicately, for I've never walked that road, and am not offering a "get over it" tone of condescension. I was saddened by the tremendous weight carried so long, and for things never grasped, because of the past's tight grip. Life for him stopped in the '90s. Some pains, I suppose, are so deep they last a lifetime. What does "forgetting" look like in this scenario? Is it possible for a day when past things loosen enough to allow the captive to walk, even stumble or crawl, into things ahead? As a friend enduring an ongoing unimaginable circumstance says, "You may not be able to handle it today, but you might tomorrow."

Back to our question. How did Paul ensure his past didn't interfere with things ahead? I can't remember. Oh yeah, he forgot about them. *Forget* can also mean "to neglect" or "be ignorant of." "Forgetting did not mean obliterating the memory of the past, but a conscious refusal to let them absorb his attention and impede his progress. He didn't want his great heritage, nor his previous Christian attainments, to obstruct his running of the race. No present attainment could lull him into thinking he already possessed all Christ desired for him."[92] Sounds idealistic or overly simplistic, but this requires discipline and determination. "I focus on this one thing: Forgetting the past" (Philippians 3:13).

Life is filled with cuts, scrapes, bruises, and scars. While whitewater rafting as a teenager, I noticed the trees were keeping up with us. Yep, we were stuck between two rocks. The only way to dislodge was reverse, but the current rendered it impossible, so the guide instructed

---

92 *The Expositor's Bible Commentary, Vol 11*. Homer A. Kent, Jr. Regency. 1978. (142-143)

us to evacuate. I was the first onto the rock. While repositioning to make room for others, I slipped down the rock face, etching an eight-inch scar into my leg. It remained more years than I believed possible. (I just looked to verify, and it is gone.)

I'm glad I don't carry every physical scrape and bump. Neither do I have to carry every emotional scar, anxious weight, or spiritual failure. What a tremendous gift from our Creator! I wonder how many miniature or miraculous acts of healing the average human experiences in a lifetime. We would be a walking knot of mess otherwise. Some things fall like water off a duck's back while others require time, surgical procedures like confession and forgiveness, or assistance from a pastor or counselor. *Remembering* something doesn't mean it determines the future.

God always has something to say about domineering pasts. The powerful work of the cross and the ministry of the Spirit make it not only possible, but likely, to overcome. History highlights countless testimonies of those who left the old behind, allowing them to press ahead. The Restorer can take our scars and redeem them for notable purposes. Some of the greatest ministers, athletes, scientists, and leaders belong to this group. Author Joni Erickson Tada hasn't let the wheelchair from an accident dictate her life. David Ring, sought-after speaker, says, "I have multiple sclerosis, but multiple sclerosis doesn't have me." Michael Jordan overcame rejection. John Newton traded the chains of his vile lifestyle for a pen, with which he wrote "Amazing Grace."

Paul learned the secret that the past doesn't have to control the future. My best attempt at translating his phrase is: "I myself am presently forgetting the past in order to eagerly grasp the future." He had to overcome heart-searing regrets by relying on the love of Christ, from which he could never be separated. "The steps of a good man are ordered by the LORD, and He delights in his way. Though he fall, he shall not be utterly cast down; for the LORD upholds him with His hand" (Psalm 37:23-24 NKJV).

Does failure define you? Shame bind? Do big accomplishments chain you? What about rejection or praise? We can't let the past rob the present. **With all the things we need to tend, nurture, and pursue, God gives us permission, even blessing, to let our past go.** We can quit watering, worrying, and keeping those toxic gardens alive. Let it overgrow with "shoots of grace." God allows you to neglect, even act ignorant of, the things in your past that restrict you from moving ahead. We can stay in the past or go with Jesus but can't walk closely with both.

New Year feels like a reset, a fresh page. It holds new potential, perspective, and optimism. That, to some extent, resembles the spirit in which the apostle lived. When I read about mercies baked fresh every morning, God obviously wants us experiencing a new start regularly, not just yearly. John Wesley, eighteenth-century preacher, coined the phrase "the radical optimism of grace." It's the confident hope that God's graces can accomplish great things in us.

Don't forget to forget. There's amazing grace for your past. Just ask John Newton.[93]

Forget About Me

You will never get over me, or ever outlast me;
you can stay close beside me, but don't get past me.
You usually carry me wherever you go;
you wish I wasn't so cumbersome though.
I am there when you wake, and every time you fall,
and will gladly remind you of them all.
I'm your lifelong companion, at least I want to be.
You maybe not so much, but can you imagine life without me?
The thought sounds great, too good to be true,
but I'm just behind to make sure I'm remembered by you.
I'm full of pain, heartache, regret, and shame.
I come across as passive, but I'm far from tame.
I'm not all bad, or negativity;
I also house the successes that tie you to me.
These great things are what you're most proud of,
and sometimes you believe these make you enough.
Don't press on, or proceed with determination;
Please! think of me as your final destination.
Don't look ahead, keep looking back,
I promise to keep you on track.
There's one place that threatens to unchain you from me,
where Christ dealt with me…at Calvary.
Now I no longer have hold on your life,
forgiveness and grace put an end to my strife.
Leave me now, move to what's ahead;
Don't look back, consider me dead.

---

93 Dedication: James and Phoebe Ochan. You allowed a good God, not a horrific past, to write your future.

Though I've tried to control you and weaken your pace,
your future is brighter if you put me in place.
If my glories make you lazy, if my follies push down,
it's time to get over me so that you won't drown.
Either one can keep you from moving toward Jesus,
so whether we hurt you or sparkle, feel free to leave us.
Enough of me now, move onward at last!
Rise to new heights and forget me
    - your past.[94]

Point: God permits and blesses you to "neglect" your past (elements holding you back).
Ponder how to "ignore" your past. What obstacles or blessings might surface?
Prayer: Unforgiveness is perhaps the biggest chain to the past. Ask God to free you from it. (Ephesians 4:32)
Practical: Do you need to let something go? Write it down, then destroy the page. If necessary, tell someone.
Playlist: *My Chains are Gone* by Chris Tomlin
Pocket:

---

94 Keith McEntire

38: Fruitless in a Fruitful Land

> *Let us...**spur one another** on toward love and good works (Hebrews 10:24 NIV).*

This chapter arose out of nowhere, which sometimes means "inspired by God's Spirit," so I trust the directing of the true Author, who alone qualifies me to write it. I hope it doesn't come across as unseasoned words from someone who thinks he has it all together. It will be challenging, even a rebuke, for some, but I hope God uses these words to spur someone to good works, thus changing a life, and potentially the world.

The burden God shared with me about restoring invaluable people has always sparked images of lifeless ones face down in the wilderness. Of desperation, depression, and hopelessness. Of dried-out bones and broken spirits. However, God expanded the scope to include those not in a dry, difficult desert. In fact, they may be in a season where all is well.

Maybe too well.

Life is great, struggles minimum. It's a land of plenty. Like David said, "The lines have fallen to me in pleasant places; yes, I have a good inheritance" (Psalm 16:6 NKJV). They may even acknowledge God as their source of blessings. Plenty is not wrong or cause for guilt but can result in becoming unfruitful in God's kingdom. Many have retired from their career, to which I say "Congratulations!" Hard work has paid off and it's time to rest from those labors and enjoy the reward. But some have assumed such includes retirement from God's service. **Heaven's hotline doesn't have a retirement department.** We may quit working for bosses or companies but are never given permission to indefinitely quit serving God.

Can you really hear God say, "Now that you have resources, health, time, wisdom, and skill, just sit around and take it easy. Your remaining time is yours to use however you want. You don't have to serve or show up. Relax. Watch TV. Camp. Fish. Eat. Collect." It sounds ridiculous to put it in such earthly words. Please don't hear me say these things are inherently wrong, and everyone should sell their TVs, campers, fishing poles, and classic cars. If you have them, enjoy them! But if they consume, blessings can distract from the things of Christ and render us unfruitful. How is it some who live each week with six Saturdays are too busy to give *any* time for eternal things? God blesses for our enjoyment, but also to position for impact!

I formerly assumed every parable was only about salvation, including the story of the four soils.[95] I interpreted it to mean 25% will be saved, as represented by the good soil. Some see it that way, but may I offer another perspective? Jesus' explanation doesn't refer to the good soil as saved, but *fruitful*. God's desire isn't just for us to receive His message, but to receive it *and* bear fruit.

Sadly, scores of God's people have a track record with Him but have become like the soil among thorns. "The message is crowded out by the worries of this life and the lure of wealth, so no fruit is produced" (Matthew 13:22). The cares of the world, or we could say, *the things the world cares about*, have stunted what God planted. Observation says soils can change. Rocky ground can become cultivated and fertile. Moisture and tilling make hard ground soft and receptive. On the other hand, good soil can become barren and unproductive.

Claiming Mountains

Caleb was about forty when he exited Egypt with Moses. Nothing negative is said about him, and he remained wholehearted for God every phase of his life. Few share that testimony. When the nation neared the Promised Land, Caleb served as his tribe's delegate to assess it. He encouraged the nation to go in, but the people refused, and God reprimanded them with decades in a desert.

Their rebellion forced Caleb into a protracted time-out, but the wilderness wasn't powerful enough to quench his spirit or strength. Forty years later he awoke, smiled in the mirror, and said *adiós* to the desert of discipline. Deep in his gizzard, he wanted to do something for God. The undying tune in his spirit rang, "Give me that mountain!" A few years later, he and some tribal leaders approached Joshua. What was so important for this elderly man to take the precious time of the nation's leader?

A promise God gave him.

Forty-five years earlier.

"The land...on which you were just walking will be your grant of land and that of your descendants forever, because you wholeheartedly followed the LORD" (Joshua 14:9). Caleb clung to that promise with

---

95 Matthew 13:3-23

clenched fists all those years, but now he wanted it. This was the same territory others were afraid to possess Giants lived there, but Caleb asked permission to fight for the land. He begged for battle.

His family could've said, "Pops, you're getting older; take it easy. Once we get some land, you can build a little house and settle down." I can see Caleb dropping to the ground, rattling off some push-ups, then jumping to his feet. "Settle down? I'm fired up! Yes I'm older, but I'm not done. There are things I've had my eye on that I haven't attained yet. I've got some battles to win with God's help! I'm going for it!"

The desert didn't erase God's promise from Caleb's memory.[96] He could've become ornery, resentful, and weak. Many would have. Many have. After all, he didn't deserve to be there. But he didn't let a bad deal give him permission to make excuses. I think he was preparing in the desert—in the gym, getting stronger; in the tabernacle, getting stronger, and in his home, strengthening his family. Knowing God would one day dismiss them, he'd be ready.

Is there an unfulfilled promise God made you?

Did He speak something years ago that's been forgotten?

Two quick observations from Caleb's latter years.

He was willing to fight. Remember, these things happened in his eighties! He saw the promise of God fulfilled *during his retirement years* but wasn't just waiting for God to do it. Caleb fought for it. Some things aren't given like gifts on Christmas morning but labored for like gold medals on the Olympic stage. The battles won toward the end of your life may be the best and may influence your family for generations. That brings the second point.

His willingness to fight left a lasting benefit for his children and grandchildren. They reaped what he sowed. This may sound compelling, but you question your resources or abilities now. Caleb didn't fight solo. He fought with his tribe. Your tribe may be your relatives, Sunday School class, or breakfast buddies. Pray for some willing tribesmen who can fight alongside you for what God placed in you.

A Gift for Solomon

You may have a desire or burden *you're not meant to accomplish*. What starts in you might transfer to another and become their crowning achievement. King David lived in a beautiful palace, but the

---

96 Read about Caleb in Numbers 13–14 and Joshua 14:6-15.

Ark of God resided in a tent. This was unacceptable, so he determined to build a temple for God, who appreciated the gesture but informed the king he wouldn't build it. David spent his elderly years planning for the Temple. His labors were invaluable to Solomon, who witnessed his father's dream become reality. It became one of his noblest tasks (2 Samuel 7). Maybe your passion will become your son's ministry. Maybe what you most want to do will become the calling for your daughter.

Many of God's people, rich in wisdom and experience, resources and time, need to conquer mountains, but have settled in the plateau of thorns. Years of preaching, praying, teaching, leading, witnessing, and serving have become years of little to no benefit for the kingdom. This is not a rebuke for enjoying life or wealth, but a challenge to examine whether you've become unfruitful. Some of God's servants have forgotten to serve. Some chosen instruments are out of tune. Some clarion voices have laryngitis. Some warriors have traded weapons for remotes. Some who walked with God the longest have placed a sign on their door: "Out of Service." Not because they're broken. Rather, they're saying, "Send someone else."

Don't forget "that!"

We can be so satisfied with the earthly and temporal we have no desire left for the heavenly and eternal. **If you're alive and born again, you have a *current* call and assignment.** Whatever fruit your life has produced, perhaps this season of plenty will yield the most. You may need to revisit a dream that once stirred your soul. It may need rescued from life's junk drawer. Maybe the timing wasn't right, or the necessary ingredients never transpired, so you abandoned it. Take another look. Maybe now is the time. Maybe God brought all the components to you, but you haven't discerned it. Take that mission trip. Start that ministry. Pray into that dream. Don't have a dream? Support one who does. Mentor that young person. Raise that voice. Write that song. Create that video or artwork. Fix that car for the single mom. Buy someone coffee and lend both ears for an hour. Give that wisdom. Lead that group. Disciple that new believer. Reach that nation. Invest those finances. Fan into flame the gift God gave you. Possess that mountain.

Kingdom Veterans

The kingdom needs children, youth, and adults. It also needs seasoned veterans. I'd like to honor several whom I've been privileged to call teachers, examples, and friends.

- Steven Schank earned his doctorate in his 70s. Why? Decades ago, God whispered to him while driving truck that he would.
- Roy & Valerie Miller have a tireless passion to see God work everywhere around the world.
- Al Myers loves fishing but became addicted to fishing for men. He's personally distributed tens of thousands of tracts.
- George and Marie Hanson bore good fruit even in old age and never forgot how to serve. They witnessed to neighbors in word and deed, started ministries late in life, and battled in prayer.
- Don and Shirley Short are marked by love for God and selfless sacrifice for others. Sometimes when I ask for Don (in his nineties), Shirley tells me he's mentoring a new believer.
- Edie Goon, while in her seventies, reluctantly started a Sunday school class for adults. Her obedient, heartfelt labors became an incomparable lifeline to "her kids."
- An older South African pastor brimmed with gusto: "I want to collapse across the finish line—sweaty and exhausted!"[97]

> **Point:** Did this spur you or rekindle a shelved passion? Describe it.
> **Ponder** Matthew 13. What best describes the *current* state of your soil? What do you want it to be?
> Who is your tribe?
> If your burden or dream isn't for you to accomplish, who should inherit it?
> **Prayer:** For unfulfilled promises or dreams.
> **Practical:** How can you use a hobby for eternal purposes?
> What "spiritual veterans" do you know? Find a way to honor them.
> **Playlist:** From the album *Fly in Your Presence*, songs 3-5, by Kent Henry.
> **Pocket:**

---

[97] Dedication: Dr. Steven Schank, friend and teacher. Your spirit resembles Caleb!

39: The Story of J. Mark, Author

> *Bring Mark…he is useful (2 Timothy 4:11).*

The narrative of the early church in the book of Acts includes, but never spotlights, John Mark. His name pops up randomly, always relegating him to the shadows. **But background people are never deemed unimportant in God's kingdom.** We first meet Mark attending a prayer meeting at his mom's house, likely a normal gathering place for the church.98 This urgent meeting was to pray for Peter, who had been imprisoned. Unless God intervenes, he's a dead man. Their plea rose to heaven's throne late into the night, until interrupted by a knock. Any anxiety this caused was consumed in wonder as Peter walked in! Mark witnessed it. This event became part of his spiritual story. Mark heard the apostles teach in his living room! He conversed with Peter and the brothers of Jesus. His was a unique heritage for sure.

The Jerusalem headquarters selected his cousin Barnabas to oversee an exciting movement in Antioch, third-largest city in the Roman Empire. As the revolution spread, Barnabas needed help. He sought Paul (at this time still named Saul). Imagine these two on your church staff! For the next year they led the exploding group of Christians. After hearing of famine, these believers sent Barnabas and Paul three hundred miles to the church in Jerusalem to deliver a gift of money.

Unfit Missionary Trekker

They arrived as two but left as three. Mark was chosen to accompany them to Antioch. During a leadership prayer meeting, God commissioned Paul and Barnabas as the first overseas missionaries. Soon they boarded a ship with Mark as their assistant. God used them mightily on their first stop, Cyprus. They ministered in every town on the island, and even preached to the governor. Miracles, salvations—it was a productive trip for the gospel. Despite all this, before reaching their second destination, Mark "deserted them…and had not continued with them in the work" (Acts 15:38).

---

98 Acts 12:1-17

He quit.

But oh the stories Paul and Barnabas shared when they finally returned! After some time, their hearts stirred. "Let us go back and visit the brothers in all the towns where we preached the word of the Lord and see how they are doing" (Acts 15:36). While prepping for their second excursion, a major decision arose. Barnabas wanted to take Mark, but Paul questioned his competence. Their differing perspectives escalated into a sharp rift. The two greatest Christians in Mark's life split because of him. Paul grabbed Silas and went his way. Barnabas took Mark and returned to Cyprus, but nothing is written about it. In fact, the biblical record of Mark goes silent for a long time. Imagine the restless nights and heavy shame. *He* was the reason Paul and Barnabas no longer served God together. He blew the once-in-a-lifetime opportunity to assist these two greats. He let them down. Let the Church down. Let God down.

He was a hindrance.

A detriment.

An embarrassment.

Called to the Office

We could be hard on Mark, as Paul appears to have been. Was Paul right in a way? Maybe Mark *wasn't called* to this missionary work, tackling the incessant rigors of life on the road and at sea. He wasn't Bear Grylls. He was more like Lee Strobel—right at home in an office, who could interview key personalities, and craft words accurately and persuasively.

God had a unique use for Mark

How many "Marks" occupy the planet right now? They consider themselves disqualified, or others count them unqualified, because they didn't excel in a pursuit. Learning what you are *not* to do helps discern what you *are* designed to do. Maybe you wish you could trek like Paul, taking the gospel to places it's never been. And if you can't, you question if there's *any* place for you. How many believe they are un-useful because they can't preach like Graham, write like Lucado, defend the faith like McDowell, pray like the saint in their prayer group, or give gobs of money like so-and-so?

Perhaps God hasn't called you to preach, but to pray for your pastor. Perhaps you haven't been called overseas as a missionary, but you love visiting shut-ins. One caution—take preaching for instance.

Something as powerful and important as preaching doesn't necessarily come naturally or happen overnight. Just because it's hard, or the first time resembles a train wreck, doesn't imply you should dismiss it. It may not go well at the beginning, but skills, experience, and wisdom can develop, leading eventually to positive outcomes. Look at a light bulb and think of the hundreds of failures it took before becoming a glowing success. If you know God's calling, pursue it without doubt or reservation. If you called yourself to something, be willing to surrender it. Not sure? Question, explore, experiment.

Mark is a good example here. He quit the first time, but when given another invitation, tried again, though nothing suggests anything significant came of it. Perhaps he found his niche after that. I love the important task God assigned him—to pen the Gospel of Mark! We don't know what all Mark did, where he lived, if he continued missionary work, or if he settled down in one place. One thing we know: God's Spirit inspired him to write the earliest account of Jesus' life! *That's* how Mark best honored God and made his mark for the kingdom.

Paul later mentions Mark three times. He's not the same person who quit years earlier. Paul calls him a great coworker and comforter, and repeatedly instructed the church to *welcome* him (Colossians 4:10-11)! As Paul neared completion of his life, a bunch of names surface—some positively, some by way of update, and some for negative reasons. One is mentioned as a former companion who deserted Paul "because he loves the things of this life." Is it Mark? Nope. But in the next verse Paul mentions him, "Bring Mark with you when you come, for he is useful to me for ministry" (2 Timothy 4:11). That's an exclamation point statement! Paul, who refused Mark, endorsed him in the end as a godly man of extreme benefit!

Paul reserves "useful" for just three occasions. This word doesn't drip off his tongue. It's an exclusive word, hard-earned, like the professor who refuses to give an "A." It carries the force of being "*highly* useful, *very* profitable." One occurrence is for Mark! Of all the people Paul met over the decades, when it came time to etch his final thoughts on paper, he honored Mark's contribution to the kingdom, and to him personally.

Mark the deserter became Mark the faithful. He who crumbled when things got hard became a tireless worker. **Next time you read *Mark*, reflect on the man God used to author the book. Truly, God can make broken things useful!**

I Hated It!

My friend relocated overseas following college. Moved by the plight of the disabled, he sensed God calling him to do something. He took the assignment seriously, though not always certain how to accomplish such a tremendous task. He pursued an occupational therapy degree, knowing he could help many with that knowledge. Before enrolling, he was required to intern fifteen hours.

Experimenting with therapy saved him a ton of time, money, and frustration. It was torturous! He wasn't called to therapy, but to pioneer an organization (which has grown significantly and become *very useful*.) The other side of the story tells a tale only the heavenly orchestrator could accomplish. While he scrapped this degree, many miles away a young woman pursued it. God linked her to the ministry, and she has joyfully served many with the skills she developed.

If a role in ministry is perpetually boring, frustrating, and ill-fitting, I would urge you to reflection and trusted counsel. **Generally speaking, don't assume this chapter into your circumstance and immediately make a major decision like resigning.** I stepped down from the pastorate after seven months of deliberate thought and prayer, conversations with Melissa, multiple confirmations (2 Corinthians. 13:1), and wise guidance (Proverbs 15:22; 24:6). One nugget of helpful advice was to "take periodic soundings of the Spirit," to test the stirring every week or two. Does it intensify or mellow? Does it only surface after a bad Sunday or board meeting? Many well-meaning believers make extremely crucial decisions based on one impression. If unsure, don't force or rush. God confirms His leading.

If you question your current post in ministry, probe. Maybe the position is right, but methods need tweaked, a skill needs honed, or further education or a mentor is key. Maybe a sabbatical is in order. Perhaps you're pursuing what "makes sense," but hate it because you were designed for something else. Maybe you've quit, or feel like quitting, because you try to keep up with Paul on life-defying trips when you should be writing. Or to be fair, maybe you're bored out of your mind and ready to quit because God is calling you to the dangerous parts of the world.[99]

One helpful piece of advice from my friend Gary Lynn: calling

---

99 If *dangerous adventure for God* resonates, search *www.unusualsoldiers.com* and see what happens.

often flows from your greatest pain. No matter what you've been designed to accomplish, chances are some church, organization, or group would love to talk or work with you. Consult your spouse, books, friends, pastors, the internet. God can change your heart or your role; He can open doors or close them.

If you're not sure about this, forget what I say.
Grab your Bible and read *Mark*.[100]

> **Point:** Does Mark's story clarify anything regarding your calling?
> **Ponder:** Have you found your niche?
> Read *Mark*.
> **Prayer:** Lord, show me what I need to see.
> **Practical:** Search a ministry/activity of interest.
> **Playlist:** *Use Me* by Ron Kenoly
> **Pocket:**

---

[100] Dedication: Tim Swauger. How I appreciate you! Thanks for your friendship and support, and forwarding "17 Reasons Pastors Should Write a Book" to me!

PART 6:
The Restorer *spreads grace* over broken pieces who feel *unclean* or *unacceptable*.

Skin formed to cover their bodies (Ezekiel 37:8).

We wrestle with guilt,
regret, and shame.
They remind us we fell down
and got dirty.

God anticipated our failings
and provides a powerful remedy
to overcome them.

Rest under the covering of grace—
for the first time or once again.
Only through the graces of God
can those who fell
help others up.

Adam and Eve's story is a great example of how
The Restorer puts unclean and unacceptable pieces back together.

40: One Great Big Dysfunctional Family

You will remember your past sins ***and despise yourselves*** *(Ezekiel 36:31).*

I had great toys as a kid—matchbox cars, remote controls, an Atari 2600, the dirt pile. Wow, did I love that pile in the side yard under the pines. Tunnels and roadways were built with the excavating abilities of bare hands. My plaid pants often bore brown stains in the knees, symbols of joyous play on that sacred soil. I'm guessing Mom viewed them differently.

Not far away, a pothole grew in our driveway that jarred the wood-grain station wagon every time we arrived home. Donning my thinking cap, I resolved to rid this nuisance. My John Deere backhoe and a high-mileage dump truck were commissioned to the dirt pile, center of operations. After the tractor loosened the dirt and scooped it into the truck, I drove seven miles (Tonka scale) and dumped it in the unloved chasm. After many loads the hole disappeared. It felt great knowing my labors meant no more kidney-busting for the family. Blacktop with a dirt patch never looked so good.

Reality hit, however, during inspection. The supervisor appreciated my work but revealed a major mathematical flaw. I used H+D=S: "Hole plus Dirt equals Solution." The advanced formula was D+R=MM. "Dirt plus Rain equals Mud Mess." My one-man crew was hired to return the terra firma. If I'm not mistaken, the company parked the truck and invested in a wheelbarrow. The business closed but the dirt pile continued to provide hours of personal enjoyment. As a result, my hands were always dirty. Though constantly told to wash them, they just couldn't stay clean. Dirt flocked to my hands like animals to Noah's ark.

Wash Up!

Life requires constant cleaning—things get dirty, we get dirty. For kids, dirty hands and faces are normal. As adults we experience dirty minds, hearts, souls, and consciences. It's impossible to remain unblemished with gravity pulling us into the dirt and covering us in guilt. **What chance do we have in our sin-saturated world if Adam and Eve fell in their perfect paradise?** Here's what happened:

> *She took some of the fruit and ate it. Then she gave some to her husband, who was with her, and he ate it, too. At that moment their eyes were opened, and they suddenly felt shame at their nakedness. So they sewed fig leaves together to cover themselves. When the cool evening breezes were blowing, the man and his wife heard the LORD God walking about in the garden. So they hid from the LORD. God asked, "Have you eaten from the tree whose fruit I commanded you not to eat?" The man replied, "It was the woman you gave me who gave me the fruit, and I ate it." Then the LORD God asked the woman, "What have you done?" "The serpent deceived me," she replied. "That's why I ate it" (Genesis 3:6-8, 11-13).*

Their sin violated God and caused havoc on their own souls, each other, and all of creation, including you and me. Like parents ordering children to wash their hands before dinner, God seeks our attention when we err. Far from a "guilt trip" conning us into unwelcome chores, guilt's godly purpose awakens us to wrongs so things can be made right, to reveal what's broken so it can be fixed. **If we *are* guilty, we should *feel* guilt.** God uses several alarms to get our attention.

Conscience. God built this "right and wrong" buzzer inside us. Nobody told Adam and Eve they sinned; they instinctively knew.

Conviction. God's Spirit nudges using the Bible and other "voices." "All Scripture is inspired by God and is useful to teach us what is true and to make us realize what is wrong in our lives. It corrects us when we are wrong and teaches us to do what is right" (2 Timothy 3:16). The "sound of God" walking through the garden quickened Adam and Eve. (Peter heard it through a crowing rooster.[101])

Confrontation. This is bold, in-your-face, "you're under arrest" territory from God Himself, as in His questioning of Adam and Eve. It may also come via human voice, such as Nathan's "you're the man" bombshell on David (2 Samuel 12:1-12) and Paul's severe leveling of some church folk (2 Corinthians 7:8).

Confinement. When warnings go unheeded, sometimes we're sent to a figurative (or literal) jail or desert.

---

101 2 Kings 22:11-20 gives another historical example.

Desert Heat

***Sometimes* sinning leads to deserts.** When disciplinary in nature, a desert becomes the waiting room in the clinic where God seeks to administer treatment. Such was the case with the scattered bones in the valley. Listen to God's blunt charges: "When the people…were living in their own land, they defiled it by the evil way they lived. To me their conduct was as unclean as a woman's menstrual cloth. They polluted the land with murder and the worship of idols, so I poured out my fury on them. I scattered them to many lands to punish them for the evil way they had lived. O my people…you should be utterly ashamed of all you have done" (Ezekiel 36:17-19, 32)!

God pointed out their habitual sinful choices, but their stubborn refusal to listen eventually led to detention. They ignored every call, so God turned up the desert heat to arrest them. He knew things considered "not too bad" were or could become matters of life and death. Deserts can make us more attentive to what God has been trying to say.

Taste it Again

Two weeks before returning to Bible college for my senior year, I had a home-alone weekend. My holy ambition craved God. Friday evening was young, so I clicked on the TV. As channels flipped, I realized my quest was no longer holy. Though conscience and conviction rang warning sirens, I continued like I was powerless—until eventually hitting the power button. *How do I pray now?* Though I never "saw anything," the Spirit revealed sin in my heart. I felt so guilty. I *was* guilty. **How do we approach God with an unclean conscience? Dirty things don't draw near; they repel.** Shame enveloped me. I felt torn, wanting to hide, wanting to be close. I hoped to experience God, maybe even pray for nations to know God's salvation. *I was the one in need of saving tonight.*

I played a song in the darkening living room.[102] God met me powerfully through it four years earlier in this exact spot. I felt unworthy to have that holy song reach my dirty ears. "As I come into Your presence, past the gates of praise, into Your sanctuary, till we're standing face to face." I lowered my head in disgrace before a perfectly clean God, my dirty lips not daring to utter worship. I longed to be clean, longed for fellowship with my Savior. I had a strong feeling He wanted nothing to do with me.

---

102 *Awesome in This Place.* Kent Henry. Hosanna! Music. 1993.

It hardly seemed the time for religious platitudes or vain promises. I was like a cornered criminal, caught red-handed by the Spirit of God. The song continued, "I look upon Your countenance. I see the fullness of Your grace. I can only bow down and say…" I crumbled. Tears soon dampened the carpet. "You are awesome in this place, mighty God. You are awesome in this place, Abba Father. You are worthy of all praise. To You my life I raise. You are awesome in this place, mighty God." My heart broke, knowing I broke God's heart, and I lamented, "You knew I'd hurt You, even after You saved me. Jesus, You suffered for me on the cross. Now I'm hurting You again. Why didn't you just let me drown in my sin? Why not let me fall to the bottom where I couldn't hurt You again?"

The picture of falling to the floor of a dark sea of sin and guilt overwhelmed me. **The thought of drowning without hope of rescue revealed how utterly dependent I was on a merciful God.** As the song repeated, pure, powerful, lifting grace heard me, embraced me, and chaperoned me to God. I didn't deserve it. I remembered I never did. An old Corn Flakes commercial beckons cereal eaters to rediscover its simple goodness: "Taste 'em again for the first time." *You've forgotten how great they are.* That's what happened that August night. I tasted the purest grace of Almighty God again, and remembered it was grace alone that saved me. **When I finally rose, I knew God washed me, forgave me, restored me.**

I tasted His goodness for the first time—again.[103]

> **Point:** God restored the dry bones, who were confined to the desert because of sin. Does that give hope?
> **Ponder:** Is God seeking your attention? Have you been trying to ease or silence it? Could it have greater consequences than initially presumed?
> **Prayer:** God, don't let me hurt You.
> **Practical:** Try something you enjoyed as a kid!
> **Playlist:** *Awesome in this Place* by Kent Henry
> *Immeasurably More* by Rend Collective
> **Pocket:**

---

[103] Dedication: Kent Henry. You know the way to God's throne. Thanks for leading me there many times.

41: A Big Fat "F"

> *Remember how the LORD your God led you through the wilderness... **humbling you and testing you to prove your character**, and to find out whether or not you would obey his commands. As a parent disciplines a child... God disciplines you for your own good" (Deuteronomy 8:2, 5).*

Wilderness seasons make us wonder why God is doing this to us. If it's meant to be disciplinary, though, the reason is usually obvious, and warnings were likely ignored. Most incarcerated arsonists or grand larcenists aren't scratching their heads wondering what they did. However, a wilderness can be a natural phase of life or a perfect venue for testing. Sometimes we pass; ***sometimes* deserts lead to sin.** Desert winds howl untold stories of those who failed there. Consequently, many feel captive to guilt, regret, and shame. Some die naked and afraid while others discover a gift that clothes and cleans. **Getting dirty surprises us, not God.**

The Test of Failing a Test

The unseemly motivation for God's discipline or testing is to produce good. Satan's goal is to separate us from our faith, to pound any love for Jesus out of us. When Jesus warned Peter of Satan's test, He didn't pray for Peter to pass. **Instead, He prayed Peter's *faith* would survive failure.** In one breath Jesus prophesied Peter's fall; in another He encouraged Peter to get up. What's more, He forecasted restoration, stronger faith in the aftermath of failure, and greater purpose. God, with gracious forethought, has an answer for those who fail tests. **Only in the amazing grace of Jesus can those who falter in sin become a means of strength to others.**

Peter bombed the test of loyalty to Christ. This "F" led to a secondary test of how he would deal with the "F." Failing a test is always followed by the critical test of failure—when we face guilt and its posse. The bad news? The faith of many dies here. The good news? The faith of many thrives here. Failure doesn't have to be the end. We aren't helpless victims at the mercy of guilt. Good *can* emerge. It's possible to lose a spiritual battle, yet not lose faith. In fact, it can be where we turn around and find a better way. First, we must tackle this thing called guilt.

Friend or Foe?

Guilt is a power tool. It's helpful but dangerous and must be handled wisely. In careless or ill-intentioned hands, it causes untold devastation. In skilled, benevolent hands, it yields untold benefits. One way or the other, it's a game-changer.

Guilt is a one-liner, a messenger with one message: "You're guilty." When legitimate because of sin or error, it speaks what we need to hear, so the goal is not to oust it as quick as possible or ignore it until it dissipates. Though a factual statement, it unleashes strong emotions. That one line is easily misunderstood and misinterpreted, and when guilt tries to say more, it trespasses its authority. Guilt isn't the problem, nor inherently bad. It can be the warning that saves lives. Guilt is the bitter pill washed down with the sweet taste of grace.[104] Anyone unable to feel guilt after sinning lives on hard soil.

Guilt is popular, attracts a plethora of emotions and feelings interested in its fresh prey. One counselor wrote, "Guilt is at the basis of much human suffering. Perhaps no other topic so consistently pervades all of the problem areas [of counseling]."[105]

Guilt is a temporary custodian, designed by God to chaperone us for perhaps a long mile, but not two. It's not intended to be a lifelong acquaintance, nor equipped to take us home. Satan tries to hijack guilt so it leads us down unhealthy roads and traps us in bondage. God employs guilt to chain us until transferring us to Christ, who holds the key that unlocks us from guilt.

Guilt is like the airplane transporting us to Guilt City, where we transfer to another vehicle that takes us to our destination. Travelers know transfers can be overwhelming. Exiting the airport often lands us center stage before a sea of people and taxis vying for our business. Signs and voices clamor for our attention. This is critical. The wrong vehicle or individual can take you far from where you hoped to go. The right one gets you safely to your destination.

Let's meet some folks awaiting your arrival:

---

[104] Romans 3:19.
[105] *Christian Counseling.* Gary R. Collins. Word Publishing, 1998. (135)

Miss Shame bombards you immediately and won't leave you alone. "Look at you! You're filthy. Don't you know better? You oughta be ashamed of yourself!" She's embarrassing, but you know you deserve her. As she heralds every flaw, you drop your gaze, unable to look anyone in the eye. When you think it couldn't get worse, she gives a spit bath.

A billboard announces **"Guilt City Accommodations!** Stay! Work! Live!" You wonder if you might be here awhile.

Trio Tours. *The Original*, they boast. A respectable-looking woman named "Cover-Up" shows off their fig-based apparel, supposedly able to conceal dirt. Her brother "Hide" chimes, "No one will find you at my getaway, but if anything happens our brother 'Blame' will sue somebody and get you off the hook." Adam and Eve were their first clients.

Hoppin' music draws your attention to **Earplug Excursions**. A friendly crew puts you at ease, eagerly showcasing their goods guaranteed to help you move on quickly. "Everything is fine. Getting dirty is no big deal." Funny comedians, full-service bar, places to go, things to do—they thought of everything to deny, ignore, or downplay guilt.

The Sorrows Singers. Their music breaks your heart. These gals look alike but differ greatly in demeanor and outlook. They never work together.

"W," or "Dubs," hangs with hardcore bullies like Despair, Addiction, and Suicide.

"G" prefers the Dynamic Duo, "Repent" and "Believe." **Repent** is muscular, intimidating, comes off like a bulldozer, even an enemy. He's not afraid to get in your face and call you out. Before long, you'll be on your knees begging for mercy, confessing wrongs, making things right. He knows this is critical to restoration. His many five-star reviews share two themes: nobody likes him; nobody regrets his influence. Repent coaches you to think and live differently, while his gentler, extremely skillful brother **Believe** refocuses your eyes from failure to a Savior. He shares the hope that Jesus removes dirt, lifts up, makes new! In one ear, Repent declares your need; in the other Believe reveals the remedy.

Once guilt's message has been received, its mission is accomplished. The question becomes *Where do we go from here?* **Thankfully, God prepared an "A" (answer) long before we got an "F."** Guilt has the potential of leading to death's door or God's door. Personal responsibility or a harder heart. Repentance or denial. Stronger, or shipwrecked, faith. Unexpected ministry or destructive addiction.

The choice is literally ours.[106]

> **Point:** God anticipated failure and has a remedy for it. What tests have you encountered recently? Any victories? failures?
> **Ponder** your usual companion(s) on "guilt trips"? Would others be better? Is failure a test?
> **Prayer:** Clean me, O God. Remove my guilt.
> **Practical:** Watch a video about product testing.
> **Playlist:** *I Need You* by Donnie McClurkin
> **Pocket:**

---

106 Dedication: Chris Miller. Thanks for lunch at Ashville General! You encouraged me greatly when I felt like an "F."

42: Where are You Going on Your Guilt Trip?

> *I was **so swamped by guilt** I couldn't see my way clear.
> More guilt in my heart than hair on my head,
> **so heavy the guilt** that my heart gave out. (Psalm 40:12 MSG)*

A favorite childhood playground sat one minute down our busy country road. Clyde, for some reason, let us roam his farm. The outdoors provided sights to see and fields to peruse. The long driveway proved a biker's dream. Treasures awaited in the barn if we could get past "the guard." One brother distracted him until the others made it inside. He then had to muster his courage and wit to face the violent rooster alone. Eventually a lane allowed him to run to the barn's half door and hurdle it, barely escaping the clutches of the cranky bird.

After breathing a collective sigh of relief, we paid homage to the towering pair of Clydesdales and spied on the cows under the floorboards. Then it was full-on masculine play like hide and seek and jumping from the second floor into the massive pile of sawdust below. Our favorite, though, was tumbling down the haymow, which had no adverse side effects, until bath time when the hay-induced scratches screamed.

One day we beat each other with the large straw Legos. It was the most fun ever had at Clyde's barn! It was also the last time we played there. Caught up in our revelry, we were blinded to the bails that lay disheveled in a heap below. Seeing our error and fearing eviction, we feverishly lugged the bails to their rightful places. Though exhausted we continued, until our worst fear transpired. The hired hand caught us! We were red-faced from guilt and the humid summer heat. Our pledge to repair the damage fell on deaf ears.

Clyde never wanted us back. We silently rode home, overcome with the dread of punishment and the reality of banishment. As time went on, we adopted first-class retaliation. He made us pay. We'd make him pay. We used to wave and smile when he drove by; now we ignored him or glared. Our relationship severed. Find out the rest of the story in the next chapter.

Wronging Wrongs

Adam and Eve's disobedience ushered guilt's dreadful invasion, and with it, ferocious torrents of shame, regret, and fear. These are so intertwined sometimes it's difficult distinguishing them. Generally, guilt means *I've done wrong*; shame is *who I am for doing wrong*. **Guilt says, "I failed, missed the mark." Shame says, "I'm a failure, will never measure up,"** One counselor illustrates guilt as water overflowing the riverbanks and shame as the resulting "fetid swamp once it settles into the valley. So guilt becomes a stagnant shame after it has flowed from one thing we did over all…we are."[107]

Here are my simplistic definitions:
Guilt—I fell down and got dirty. I did wrong.
Shame—I *am* dirty. I *am* wrong.
Regret—I wish I didn't get dirty and hurt myself and others.
Fear—What if people or God find out?

This was pioneer territory for Adam and Eve. How should they respond? While wanting to make things right they chose inferior methods and materials. We haven't fallen far from the tree. It's like they sat us down and said, "Mommy and Daddy have something to tell you. When you fall, get dirty, and feel guilty and ashamed, cover it up, hide from God, and if necessary, blame others." We listened, but their attempts to right wrongs were wrong.

Let's revisit their story, appropriately dubbed "the Fall" (Genesis 3:6-13): "She took some of the fruit and ate it. Then she gave some to her husband, who was with her, and he ate it, too. At that moment, their eyes were opened, and they suddenly felt shame at their nakedness."

Notice their three-pronged approach to failure:
1. "They sewed fig leaves together to cover themselves." They instinctively sought covering, but assumed they had to make the clothing. "Those fig leaves represent man's earliest attempt to cover up his sin, to provide himself with a covering to cloak his guilt and shame. They represent every effort made by man to do something to make himself fit for the presence of God."[108] Their first concern? *Appear* **respectable, acceptable.**

They hid their bad things behind good things. Everything God

---
107 *Shame and Grace*. Lewis B. Smedes. HarperCollins. 1993. (17)
108 *Exploring Genesis*. John Phillips. Loizeaux Brothers. 1992. (59)

made was deemed good, including the fig leaves for their new guilt-and-shame-hiding wardrobes. We don't use fig leaves but still try to pay guilt's debt in the currencies of morality, charity, or religion. When I offend Melissa, I often tackle dishes, laundry, the vacuum. Why? I'm trying to appease my wrongs without approaching her to make it right, hoping good works prove sufficient. But it makes things worse. She wants to talk, wants to hear me own it.

We can be the same way after offending God, hoping chores satisfy Him. Get religious. More religious. Super religious. Ridiculously religious. Suffer the uncomfortable chafing of self-inflicted penalties. Win God with penance. Promise church. Volunteer. Give a Hamilton, maybe a Jackson. Give up sweets. Pray before meals. Read the Bible, or more of it. If you read three chapters, do ten. Whatever you're doing—is not enough.

It never is.

Good things, if used to right wrongs, make for a long, exhausting road with guilt. This is futile, frustrating, and fear-driven. Good deeds can't remove one dot of dirt. God calls these charades "dead works." From His perspective this equates to appeasing an offended person with a dead animal. Ironically, good deeds don't promote reconciliation. As we'll see, they allow safe distance *from the offended*.

2. "They hid from the LORD God among the trees." Their uniforms suddenly looked lame at the prospect of standing before God. **Their next reaction to guilt was to stay away from God and anything to do with Him.** Christians know they can't hide forever. Even when all seems well on the outside, those experiencing this unresolved tension rank among the planet's most miserable creatures. Eventually we need to show up, but it's uncomfortable.

The story of Peter approaching Jesus on Galilee's shore includes a fun fact—they caught exactly 153 fish. Why is that recorded? I have a theory. Peter craved fellowship with Jesus but, feeling guilty and awkward, found a distraction. *There He is. Should I say "Greetings, Rabbi" or give a hug? No, that's dumb. What were those lines I rehearsed?* (Clears his throat and walks toward Jesus, then notices the fish.) *Wow, that's a lot of fish! Maybe a record. Wonder how many are there? (Turns aside) 1, 2, 3...87, 88, 89...151, 152, 153.* Whether the reason or not, we're all familiar with diversions when we should be dealing with spiritual things. It's easy to assume guilt means "God hates me; there's no remedy." This causes many to never approach God again. **If only they knew—incredibly, surprisingly, God craves fellowship with those hounded by guilt, and holds the power to free them from it.**

3. GOD: "Have you eaten from the tree whose fruit I commanded you not to eat?"

Adam: "It was the woman you gave me who gave me the fruit, and I ate it."

GOD (to Eve): "What have you done?"

Eve: "The serpent deceived me. That's why I ate it."

They spontaneously learned the art of blame. Adam pointed fingers at Eve, with a subtle accusation against God, who gave her to him. He would rather condemn his wife than lose face. Then Eve invented a classic—*the devil made me do it!* Confession excusing self or indicting others is not much confession at all. It's like saying, "I did it, but it's *their* fault." Failure is inevitable, so is guilt; and guilt is powerful, so our handling of it is critical.[109]

> **Point:** Are you trying to remove guilt by morality, charity, or religion?
> **Ponder:** Have you verbally or secretly blamed others for your sufferings?
> **Prayer:** Are distractions keeping you from settling something with God?
> **Practical:**
> **Playlist:** *Glorious Day* by Passion
> *Our God is an Awesome God* by Rich Mullins
> **Pocket:**

---

109 Dedication: In memory of Granddad and Grandma, who covered us in prayer.

43: I Hear Footsteps Approaching

Where are you? (Genesis 3:9)

I thought of Clyde and the wrong we did. I wanted to make things right, offer an apology. Christmas break from college afforded the opportunity. His farm was a relic. His wife gone. He lived a solitary life in his old farmhouse. After much prayer for favor and courage, I drove my Buick up the not-so-long driveway and grabbed my offering on the passenger seat. I hoped to win him over with ice cream! My trembling hand knocked on the door. No answer. A little louder, then louder still, to the point the beating sounded angry. That did the trick. The weathered farmer cracked the door, wondering who I was and what I wanted.

I identified myself and offered my penance of sweet cream. His response shocked me. "Where have you been? Why didn't you boys come back? Did I do something wrong?" Expecting a spew of hatred, my relief spiraled visibly into the bitter air. During that reunion, my emotions flared gladness and sadness. Rekindled friendship felt great, but sorrow from the cumulative losses incurred for more than a decade tasted bitter. Our conversation that cold December night revealed the ugly fly in the ointment, the single perpetrator of division. The hired hand lied. He never liked us (what's not to love about three boys in your workspace?) and used the occasion to rid us once and for all. Clyde never told him to evict us. He never even knew about our mishap.

Guilt is a strong message, but too often is misperceived as the hired hand kicking us out of the owner's place. **If we assume guilt means God no longer wants us around, days, decades, or an eternity of fellowship can be lost.** Some retaliate with resentment or a cold shoulder. As the farmhand attached lies and assumptions to guilt, so does Satan. Bold lies: "You're too dirty! A shameful piece of crap!" Subtle suggestions: *You think God wants to be around you?* Or, *Quit worrying. Turn up the volume till it leaves.*

Guilt is often misquoted, radically misinterpreted, easily misrepresented, and dangerously misapplied. While I refer to guilt resulting from one's own sin, the Lord ministers to all our varied struggles with guilt. Have you noticed how unwarranted guilty feelings feel the same as legitimate guilt from violating God's commands? Many carry tons of guilt for every imperfection, or from others' sins.

We need to hear what God says about it, not the voices claiming to speak for Him. The difference is as vast as Clyde and the hired hand.

Of Debt and Distance

Debt breeds distance. Chances are you've seen relationships soured by it. Watch someone who hasn't paid a friend back and you'll witness avoidance until its unavoidable. Then awkwardness. That's how it feels with God after we sin. *How do guilty souls approach God in worship?* Are we banned? Will the church building collapse? Will a livid Coach Jesus demand endless suicides to atone for our bonehead mistakes? Do we pretend nothing happened? When I feel guilty, I get hesitant around God. I fear judgment, knowing I deserve it. Corporate worship feels hypocritical. Spiritual exercises don't shed the pounds of guilt and shame. The conscience keeps nagging. **An elephant in the prayer closet makes it hard to pray.**

Adam and Eve knew God as creator, good, bountiful, friendly. His presence brought light, joy, peace, and deep love. His assignments gave purpose and precipitated togetherness. Using His own image as the template, He crowned them with extravagant honor and significance. Though master, He bestowed unlimited freedom minus one small rule. They broke it. And ruined everything. As guilt and shame crashed in, their new sin-tainted natures urged them to cover the mess, avoid God, and blame others. They previously enjoyed fellowship with God every day, but they were unblemished then. For the first time, Adam and Eve felt the dread of broken friendship with their Creator. Will He want to see them again? How will He respond to their fig leaves? What kind of God could they expect to encounter on this far-from-perfect day? Can He fix guilt?

"When the cool evening breezes were blowing, the man and his wife heard the LORD God walking in the garden" (Genesis 3:8). Not wanting to find out, they hid. What did God say or do? His response may assist us when we fall and get dirty. He called. His familiar voice reverberated throughout the garden, "Where are you?" We can't overlook or underestimate this. **Before the day ended God called them, sought fellowship with them, just like every other day.**

Adam came out of hiding and fumbled his best pitch, "I heard you walking in the garden, so I hid. I was afraid because I was naked" (Genesis 3:10). In high school I joined a club requiring members to sell junk door-to-door. I despised unpacking random items on somebody's porch, only to have them turn me down. It was awkward and futile; I felt stupid and scared. Isn't that how guilt and shame feel? Burdened with junk, we approach God's door, trembling in our corduroy pants. Out mumbles a spiel way more lame than the one we mentally perfected. We hope He buys our pitiful goods to cover our dues, then brace for rejection.

Sin, guilt, and shame always lead somewhere; God wanted to know where it was leading them. He always seeks closeness with us and will do anything to bridge the gap. While Adam and Eve hid, God was approaching. He didn't stay home with the door shut and curtains closed, unavailable if they dared drop in. It's more about us opening our door to Him than knocking on His door. He made the first move, came searching, came calling. He's proactive, not reactive. **A word to the dirty and hiding—God longs for your friendship. He'd love to get together by the end of the day.**

Boundaries

God covered the bones in the valley with *skin*. The largest organ of the human body has major functions to fulfill. Simultaneously holding our internals in while keeping death-inducing elements out, it serves as a barrier. In the same way God desires separation, *but not us from Him!* Rather, us *from dirt*. While sin attempts to separate us from God, God can separate us from sin, guilt, and shame, casting them like garbage into a dumpster on the other side of the world. This makes room for Him. When we feel distant from God because of sin, and don't know how to approach Him dirty, it's good to remember that He's able to separate our dirt from us. We don't have to experience perpetual distance. Fear keeps many from enjoying God, but perfect love casts out fear. Debt breeds distance; "paid" breeds nearness.

When God yells "Stay out!"—He's not talking to *you*.

What did Adam and Eve experience by the end of history's worst day? God the Judge *and* the Merciful, who desires fellowship with humans after they fall. Whose love exceeds sin, guilt, and shame. Yes, they received consequences, but they also heard the promise of a coming Savior. He would be born one day as a human, and at great personal sacrifice would accomplish the enemy's utter defeat and their complete redemption. We get it backward when we feel the need to get cleaned up to meet God.

We come.

We "come clean."
He cleans us and makes us presentable.[110]

> **Point:** Friend, *where are you?* God is asking.
> Does guilt usually sound livid, silent, condescending? other?
> **Ponder:** When a person you really love feels uncomfortable around you because they hurt you, what would you be willing to do to restore fellowship?
> Does God respond to guilt more like Clyde or the hired hand?
> Hebrews 10 addresses how guilty souls approach God in worship.
> **Prayer:** "God craves fellowship with those hounded by guilt and holds the power to free them from it." Do you wish things with God could be like before, and all the guilt could go away? Knock on His door, talk honestly. After all, He first knocked on your door! (Matthew 11:28-30)
> **Practical:** Clean something while "actively listening" for God.
> **Playlist:** *Grace Flows Down* by Christy Nockles
> **Pocket:**

---

110 Dedication: In memory of Clyde Hoaglund. I'm glad we made everything right.

44: The Sting Means It's Working

> *You will not reject **a broken and repentant heart**, O God (Psalm 51:17).*

While preferring dirt piles or bikes, I'd occasionally grab the flat-black skateboard leaning against the garage wall. One day the lonely board whispered my name. Like Charlie Brown with the football, I heeded the call, determined to conquer. I practiced balancing and turning until something momentous happened. It kicked out. As my elbow felt a life-changing impact from the blacktop, my brain messaged me: "Keith, you're never doing this again." Angrily, I taught that dumb thing how to fly, then ran to mommy crying. I knew she could make it better.

I've never skateboarded since. The pain wasn't worth the fleeting pleasure. Sin whispers our name, promises a good time, convinces us we're in control; then we slip, fall, and get hurt. And live with regret. *There are so many better things, why did I choose that? Wish I never got on it.* While my consequences subsided by bedtime, imagine the heartbreak Adam and Eve faced! *Why did we eat that stupid fruit, or listen to that serpent? We ruined everything. Look what we've done to God, the garden, the animals. Our kids will never experience this perfect paradise. Wish we could go back.*

The conversation between God, Adam, and Eve was difficult and direct, but far healthier than silent avoidance. He called them to account and levied discipline, **but even the hard words of God are better than those of a fearful, guilty conscience.** "Who told you that you were naked? Have you eaten from the tree whose fruit I commanded you not to eat" (Genesis 3:11)? God pinpoints the cause of much human error, and thus a starting point of confession. *Who were you listening to? Whose words did you elevate over Mine?*

Mankind suffers from listening to ungodly influences and dismissing God's words. When King David wallowed in guilt and depression, he wrote, "Doing something for you, bringing something to you—that's not what you're after. Being religious, acting pious—that's not what you're asking for. You've opened my ears so I can listen" (Psalm 40:6 MSG). **While we're busy fixing and hiding, God wants us to listen.**

"What have you done" (Genesis 3:13)? God continued. He invited them to own their misdeeds. Confession acknowledges guilt when God pronounces "Guilty," then acknowledges Jesus, heaven's solution to guilt. Even in judgment He's merciful. Their far-from-perfect "confessions" ranked a higher quality than the rags they concocted. We hope religious sacrifices hide our dirt; God prefers we reveal our dirt and ask *Him* to clean us. "He who covers his sins will not prosper, but whoever confesses and forsakes them will have mercy" (Proverbs 28:13 NKJV).

After David committed adultery and covered it with murder, he wrote an agonizing confession, then said, "You do not desire a sacrifice, or I would offer one. The sacrifice you desire is a broken spirit. You will not reject a broken and repentant heart, O God" (Psalm 51:16-17). The only acceptable sacrifice we can offer is a heart soft enough to break over sin. Ironically, God bids us to *forsake* religious sacrifices so we can hear what He's saying and fall on His mercy. The Bible says,

> *The sacrifices under that system were repeated again and again, year after year, but they could never provide perfect cleansing for those who came to worship. If they could have provided perfect cleansing, the sacrifices would have stopped, for the worshipers would have been purified once for all time, and their feelings of guilt would have disappeared. But instead, those sacrifices actually reminded them of their sins year after year (Hebrews 10:1-3).*

God doesn't want us incessantly hounded by past sins.

The Godly Response to Guilt

All twelve disciples denied the Lord, but only the responses of Peter and Judas are recorded. Peter, deeply regretful, wept like a baby, then repented and returned to Jesus. Judas felt equally bad, but his sorrow led to despair-induced suicide. Regret is not enough. Tears accomplish nothing unless mixed with repentance. Sorrow guides some to freedom and others astray; it all depends on which sorrow is chosen—*worldly* or *godly*.

Paul vigorously challenged a church tolerating sins that made unbelievers blush. His convicting words, saturated in prayerful agony, *hurt*.[111] **But hurting Jesus and those around us *should* hurt.** *The grace of hurt*, if received, paves the way for *the grace of health*. While some prefer lambasting believers than helping them recover, Paul avoided condescension or condemnation. As with any confrontation, he didn't know how they would respond, but hoped they would choose godly sorrow. They did, and he wrote back:

> *When [Titus] told us...how sorry you are for what happened...I was filled with joy! I am not sorry that I sent that severe letter to you, though I was sorry at first, for I know it was painful to you for a little while. Now I am glad I sent it, not because it hurt you, but because the pain caused you to repent and change your ways. It was the kind of sorrow God wants his people to have, so you were not harmed by us in any way. For the kind of sorrow God wants us to experience leads us away from sin and results in salvation. There's no regret for that kind of sorrow. But worldly sorrow, which lacks repentance, results in spiritual death. Just see what this godly sorrow produced in you! Such earnestness, such concern to clear yourselves, such indignation, such alarm, such longing to see me, such zeal, and such a readiness to punish wrong. You showed that you have done everything necessary to make things right. (2 Corinthians 7:7-11)*

Pain jolted this church to the core. Godly sorrow urged them to slam the door on their sinful lifestyles and open their hearts to God's correction, and grace. When the dust settled, godly character emerged, and they experienced a freedom from guilt so powerful Paul called it salvation. This depicts how God wants us to respond to guilt. Worldly sorrow sees no recovery from guilt's grip; it only locks us in guilt, depression, shame. However, godly sorrow incorporates repentance, which produces godly fruit and often makes its owners better than they were before their fall. All because they took it seriously enough to change.

While God doesn't wink at sin, He also doesn't want failure to

---

111 Used in John 21:17 when Jesus' question *hurt* Peter.

defeat His children. When sin brings consequences, God extends grace to deal with and live under them, for He can redeem them. Paul wrote, "Dear brothers and sisters, if another believer is overcome by some sin, you who are godly should gently and humbly help that person back onto the right path. And be careful not to fall into the same temptation yourself" (Galatians 6:1). The Message reads, "If someone falls into sin, forgivingly restore him, saving your critical comments for yourself. You might be needing forgiveness before the day's out." **Paul encourages us to restore believers who fall, to extend the soap of grace to the dirty.**

Sometimes soap gets in the eyes and makes tears.[112]

Point: What about sin hurts most: Getting caught? Breaking God's heart? Hurting another? What does God desire for those who fall?
Ponder: How is discipline healthy? (Psalm 119:67, 71, 75; Hebrews 12:1-12)
Prayer: Read David's confessions (Psalms 32, 40, 51). Confess (to God and/or someone trustworthy) your sin, your need for mercy, the words you heeded, and God's words you dismissed. Confess that Jesus is Lord, even over guilt!
Practical: Godly sorrow adds repentance to regret. Pain caused me to abandon the skateboard for good. What's one way of taking things seriously enough to change?
Do you know someone who failed? Pray for them and those they hurt. Pray God's purposes to prevail. Resolve to interact in a spirit of restoration, not condemnation or condescension.
Playlist: *Purify My Heart* by Vineyard
Arise My Soul by Twila Paris
Pocket:

---

[112] Dedication: Mom. So glad you're my mom! Thanks for letting me come to you with anything!

45: Clothes by Jehovah

*Skin formed to **cover** their bodies (Ezekiel 37:8).*

The older I got in school, the more I cared about the names on my clothes. Purchases from The County Seat in the mall, not The Big N at the southside plaza, contributed to a confidence in knowing my clothing was acceptable. My Win Streaks were replaced with Nikes and those following me down the hallway read Levi's, not Country Kids. We willingly pay extra for quality and style. Or to avoid shame.

New clothes are great; so is new skin. How wonderfully God wraps little ones in the softest, purest baby suit! Ezekiel witnessed something similar—the multitude of skeletons attired in fresh, clean skin! God turned brokenness into beauty and splashed vibrant shades of melanin over them. In the transformation of houses, this is the stage of appealing hues and materials like paint, siding, wooden logs, marble pillars, stone. The bland becomes beautiful with color.

Isaiah painted with this brush, "To all who mourn, he will give a crown of beauty for ashes, a joyous blessing instead of mourning, festive praise instead of despair" (Isaiah 61:3). Ashes are fire's devastating remains, and some trials are like a fiery furnace or pressure cooker. The ancients, in times of such sorrow or failure, demonstrated their humility, grief, and shame by rubbing ashes on their skin. They didn't pretend to be happy, whole, or holy. Neither their lives nor their souls resembled beauty. Discarding adornment to display brokenness, they hoped God would see their lowly state and mercifully raise them up again.

Isaiah encouraged the people wearing ashes that God could give them new wardrobes, transform lowliness into loveliness, and replace sorrow with a smile. Have you witnessed the charred ruins from a house fire later become an attractive residence? More importantly, have you seen faces weathered by the wilderness transformed into portraits of wholeness? Those wearing guilt, regret, shame, and depression arrayed in a supernatural peace and joy more radiant than natural outward beauty? **The most attractive Christians once wore ashes. Then God clothed them.**

Made by GOD

Adam and Eve suffered for their disobedience, but God extended hope. Addressing the devil, He said, "I'm declaring war between you and the Woman, between your offspring and hers. He'll wound your head, you'll wound his heel" (Genesis 3:15 MSG). Wrapped in there is God's first promise to send a Savior who would take a big hit but destroy the enemy and rescue humanity in the process. His sacrifice would forever blanket the world's guilt and shame. There in the garden God offered a sacrifice: "God made clothing from animal skins for Adam and his wife" (Genesis 3:21). They never read an obituary in *The Garden Gazette* or stumbled over a carcass. This animal was the first to taste death. They must have been mortified to see it lay there, never to live again, so its skin could cover *their* sin. **In contrast to their cheap costumes, God presented them with expensive, presentable clothing.**

Adam and Eve shifted blame, as if knowing there was no chance of standing on their own. God also shifted blame: first onto an innocent animal, then later onto His innocent Son who bore the punishment of the world's sins once and for all. Humbly abandoning their best efforts, they allowed the offended Himself to clothe them. He did the same for His people in the valley. Their guilt, sin, and shame were completely covered in fresh, undefiled skin. The labels on their new wardrobe read, "Made by God." **Now *that's* a brand name to be proud of, sure to make those who stand before Him acceptable!**

Downcast Soul, Look Up

God confronts our errors, but also comforts us with His saving cure. In the book of Numbers (21:4-9) the nation's sins relegated them to the desert, then the desert surfaced more impurities, and they maligned God and Moses. Venomous snakes keeping cool under the desert sand emerged to bite the people, who rightly discerned the divine correction and humbled themselves. At God's direction Moses attached a bronze serpent to a pole. If anyone got bit, simply looking at it administered healing. **God mercifully provided an answer for failure, but it required faith.**

When sin bites, we instinctively look downward in shame. God's remedy required them to look upward in hope, trusting His immeasurable supplies of grace. This healing through forgiveness was extended to everyone and didn't require chores, religion, or money. Some looked in faith to a pole and praised the God of salvation! Surely some concocted "better" ideas, arrogantly rejecting God's solution. These died needlessly under the shadow of the answer.

Jesus' death on the cross is likened to that raised serpent. "As Moses lifted up the bronze snake on a pole in the wilderness, so [Jesus] must be lifted up, so that everyone who believes in him will have eternal life" (John 3:14-15). God had those bitten by snakes look to a snake. He beckons us bitten by sin to gaze upon His Son who, though perfectly pure, became sin. In other words, *all our* wrongdoing transferred on Him to bear. "He personally carried our sins in his body on the cross so that we can be dead to sin and live for what is right. By his wounds you are healed" (1 Peter 2:24). When He died, our sins died too. When He rose, He left them to rot in the grave!

Arrested

The first semester of my senior year at college was physically depleting and spiritually uncomfortable. I felt distant, sinful, weak; my soul a thistled wasteland. God was deeply pruning my pride, motives, will, and character. I was gettin' a trimmin.' Christ was being formed in my life through the forging process. All I knew to do was desperately cling to His words and wait for His help. Ironically, I felt stronger in weakness than in strength. Attending a college that thrived on expressive worship, I felt deficient. One chapel found me completely empty. Singing hurt my throat. I had no offering, couldn't "compete" with those around me. I simply raised weary hands, wishing I had something better to give God. Instead, He ministered to me in my weariness and loved me.

During this trial I got arrested…by artwork. While descending the stairs to the mailroom, a small picture on the bulletin board seized me. For several minutes I stared, oblivious to those trying to pass. Somehow this artist perfectly illustrated the condition of my soul. Dirty jeans and guilty conscience. Furrowed brow and buckled legs. One hand grasped a hammer, the other a nail. Behind me a Man in purest white held my dead weight with massive, scarred hands; His head bowed graciously. Blood flowed from His feet, giving life to beautiful lilies. **A Savior of utmost strength embraced dirty ol' me and covered me in love.**

Just as I was.[113]

> **Point:** What has the wilderness stolen? Does joy seem impossible? I tearfully write to you who lost a loved one or something irreplaceable. This book was written so you'd know God still colors barren landscapes.
> **Ponder:** Personalize Isaiah 61.
> **Prayer:** Borrowed prayer: "Lord, change the place or change me." God changes circumstances and hearts.
> **Practical:** Have you insisted on your own clothes, or believed you were too dirty? Don't die under the shadow of the answer. By faith look up and let God clothe you.
> **Playlist:** *Before the Throne of God Above* by Selah
> *God You Are* by We are Messengers
> **Pocket:**

---

113 "Forgiven." Thomas Blackshear II.
　　Dedication: Jeff Francis, great friend, lover of God's Word, restorer of marriages. *www.FCCHR.org*

46: All Hail the Dirtfighter!

> ***Wash me clean*** *from my guilt. (Psalm 51:2)*

Putting my Bible degree to good use, I got a job cleaning filthy, oily machines. The products usually worked great, but occasionally they didn't, no matter how much I used or how hard I scrubbed. In those cases, I was given one instruction: see Clint, a quiet man in the back of the shop. I'd explain my predicament and he'd concoct a secret brew. His solvent erased *every* stain I applied it to, no matter how ugly or persistent. Coworkers said the machines hadn't looked that good in years. **The blood of Jesus is powerful solvent!** When applied by humbly calling His name in faith, it removes *every* stain of shame, sin, or guilt. A young man on the streets of Rhode Island prayed to receive Christ. While walking away, he beamed, "I feel like a shower just went off in my heart!" We all need a sin-deleting shower!

An Older Brother and a Lawyer

I watched from the back of a crowded courtroom as a visibly rattled man anticipated judgment. In walked a smiling gentleman who put his arm around him and whispered. Tension dissolved into peace. A few minutes later the advocate addressed the intimidating judge for him. The Bible says, "I am writing this to you so that you will not sin. But if anyone does sin, we have an Advocate who pleads our case before the Father. He is Jesus Christ, the one who is truly righteous" (I John 2:2). This is for sinful saints, not perfect ones. **Imagine standing before God, but before spewing nonsense, Jesus pleads for you, presenting His nail scars as payment!**

Remember my door-to-door sales nightmare? I did what many kids do when facing challenges—asked an older sibling for help. Thankfully, Terry drove so I no longer needed to lug the goods on my bike. He offered several pointers and stood beside me. His presence eased the situation. **Wouldn't that make all the difference when trying to make things right with God—an older brother to stand beside us and live the experience with us?**

So how do guilty souls approach God in worship? In a word: Jesus. "You have come to Jesus, the one who mediates the new covenant between God and people, and to the sprinkled blood, which speaks of forgiveness instead of crying out for vengeance" (Hebrews 12:24). He washed our guilt, covered our shame, and not only stands *with* us, but *for* us. His sacrifice makes us presentable *and* opens the way to God's presence. He alone is the perfect Mediator between a holy God and sinful humans.[114]

> *Since we have a great High Priest who has entered heaven, Jesus the Son of God, let us hold firmly to what we believe. This High Priest of ours understands our weaknesses, for he faced all of the same testings we do, yet he did not sin. So let us come boldly to the throne of our gracious God. There we will receive his mercy, and we will find grace to help us when we need it most (Hebrews 4:14-16).*

This boldness "removes the fear and anxiety which characterize man's relation to God. It comes as the result of the ground of guilt being set aside and manifests itself in undoubting confidence in prayer."[115] Because of Jesus we may approach, confident in God's acceptance. *That's grace!*

Shut Up!

When the conscience properly alerts of right and wrong, we don't always need preachers or parents to spotlight errors. The conscience does that, then God's Spirit points to Jesus who washes our souls. Once clean, however, the conscience can repeat our violations, insisting there's more to do. We continue feeling guilty, ashamed, fearful, distant, indebted. Look at the injunctions God extends to Christians:

---

114 I Timothy 2:5
115 *The Complete Word Study New Testament.* Spiros Zodhiates. World Bible Publishers. 1991. (933)

> *How much more shall the blood of Christ…**cleanse your conscience** from dead works to serve the living God (Hebrews 9:14 NKJV italics mine).*
>
> *We can boldly enter heaven's Most Holy Place because of the blood of Jesus.* ***For our guilty consciences have been sprinkled with Christ's blood to make us clean*** *(Hebrews 10:19, 22 italics mine).*

When Jesus cleans, it's so thorough it even scrubs the conscience, allowing the guilty to approach God guilt-free. **Our heavenly Dad permits us to yell "Shut Up!" to every voice testifying of guilty deeds He's forgiven.** Whether the devil, a church member, or your conscience, you don't have to accept it. Jesus erased the dirt and made you presentable. "'No weapon formed against you shall prosper, and every tongue which rises against you in judgment you shall condemn. This is the heritage of the servants of the Lord, and their righteousness is from Me,' says the Lord" (Isaiah 54:17). When beckoned by guilt and fear to run away, God invites us over to talk.

Most lawyers wouldn't knowingly accept the case of someone guilty of serious offense, but for some reason Jesus took mine. When the verdict sentenced me to death, He willingly accepted the death penalty—but God raised Him from the dead! Defeating sin and death, He lives forever, and so do I. Now He sits at God's right hand and pleads on my behalf. "He has brought you into his own presence, and you are holy and blameless as you stand before him without a single fault (Colossians 1:21)." **There's room at God's throne for backpacks of guilt.**

Exit Strategy

Those declared innocent leave the courtroom lighter than air. *How do I know I've been forgiven?* You'll praise God, love Christ more, and desire to live a pure life. If sin led to a desert, desert led to sin, or you just wonder if you're too dirty, you can emerge with new skin. You don't have to crawl out, looking like you've been wallowin' in the hog pen. You can walk out (skip, run, dance) sporting new apparel made by God Himself.

Guilt whets our appetite for forgiveness; shame makes us thirsty for acceptance. God's graces provide both. "To the praise of the glory of His grace, by which He made us accepted in the Beloved. In Him we have redemption through His blood, the forgiveness of sins, according to the riches of His grace which He made to abound toward us..." (Ephesians 1:6-7 NKJV). **For our dual problems of guilt and shame, God offers cleaning grace for guilt and covering grace for shame.** Many who received the grace of forgiveness from sin need to receive the grace of acceptance from shame. "What I felt most was a glob of unworthiness...I could not tie down to any concrete sins I was guilty of. What I needed more than pardon was a sense that God accepted me...affirmed me, and would never let go of me even if he was not too...impressed with what he had on his hands."[116]

If this resonates, stick around.[117]

> **Point:** Have you discovered and applied the solvent of grace? Don't use useless "cleaners."
> **Ponder:** Is your conscience voicing guilt God has forgiven?
> **Prayer:** Thank Jesus for serving as your mediator.
> **Practical:**
> **Playlist:** *Clean* by Natalie Grant
> *Boldly I Approach* by Rend Collective
> **Pocket:**

---

116 Smedes, 80.
117 Dedication: Terry McEntire. I'm honored to have a brother and friend like you!

47: Graces Supremas

> *Sin...doesn't have a chance in competition
> with **the aggressive forgiveness
> we call grace**. When it's sin versus grace,
> **grace wins hands down.**
> Grace, because God is putting everything
> together again through the Messiah,
> invites us into life (Romans 5:20-21 MSG).*

A friend asked, "What is God putting on your heart?" Though unintended for public consumption I share my reply, believing someone will identify.

Regarding your question, which is a wonderful, probing question—my answer could also be described as "What is the Lord taking off your heart?" A month ago I asked friends: how would you define shame? My book has been on standstill, and I was hoping to get that one last piece of the puzzle needed to finish the section about guilt, shame, regret. While hoping for a definition or greater understanding about shame, God was perfectly orchestrating everything so I could experience healing from shame. He's so wise and gracious!

God revealed chronic shame that sits in the center of me. It gets stirred up multiple times a day, previously undetected, and sometimes on the heels of good things. For example, a friend comes to mind, which brings joy. Followed by "I could never be the man of God he is." And it leaves me feeling this nagging never-enoughness. My "ideal" self condescendingly looks down on the real me.

My shame is mostly tied to a deep seated (auto correct changed it to *seared*, which may be appropriate as well) belief that I'm not smart enough. It's heavy, clouds my thinking, steals my joy, holds me back, holds me down. There's always a gap between who/where we are, and the ideal us. This is good when it positively challenges us but can also tell us demeaning things. I'm learning, or relearning, to receive God's accepting grace. Ephesians 1:6; Psalm 34:5; Joshua 5:9. I've been accepted, gaps and all, in the present, because I'm united with the One He loves!

I always thought I needed fixed, usually accomplished by some kind of work. I'm realizing I need healing, which is the fruit of amazing grace. I'm thankful for a considerate God, who is more interested in my heart than my book. Who wants to give us more than definitions and statements. He wants us to experience, live and breathe grace.

I think few people are who they want to be, even those we assume have it all together. The version in the mirror falls below the standard in the mind. This is most palpable on the heels of failure or while disoriented in a wilderness. "The 'dark night of the soul' is no spiritual tourist attraction. I recommend it to nobody. But if you…land there and feel the full weight of shame…God may find you, and when he does, he will bring grace with him."[118]

Bland seasons offer little to be proud of. **Even when all is well, I dare say most humans, including those "right with God," harbor shame, deep down feeling they don't measure up.** Few remain unscathed from shame's tyranny. Here's my friend's response. Remember, this is correspondence from two middle-aged Christian ministers.

I really appreciate this. I've read your message many times and say with all honesty I can relate. In fact, your writing helped to put into words my own feelings—but which I had a hard time clarifying in my mind or expressing. I constantly struggle with my perception of my ideal self and am hammered down by how I don't live up to it. My response is often to try to do good works—sacrifices to God, so to speak—to make up for my shortcomings. There had rarely been a day when I feel that I have done "enough."

And those feelings weaken my spirit, steal my joy, and lead to all sorts of self-doubts. But I thank God I've been aware of this "disease" for a while and just 2 weeks ago was able to take a week off, be by myself, fast, and meet with God and talk about all this with Him, pray, cried often. It was a very good time for me.

He also showed me there are some things I've never repented of and that has hindered my prayers. (I knew this already—knew that deep down I'd never fully surrendered some things—particularly a love for the world, and a desire

---

118 Smedes, 131.

for affirmation from the world.)

I'm in a better place. Like you, I was touched afresh by how much the Father loves me. I always had trouble accepting that—thinking someday I will when I'm a better person. I know I'll have further such struggles, but I think I've internalized the truth which will help me fight those battles.

The Shame Space

Shame is a weird shape, and incredibly elusive. It's difficult to define or pin down. Is it subjective or objective? A feeling, emotion, or fact? Is it deserved or undeserved? What about the shards of shame unjustly piercing the innocent? The Bible illustrates shame by:

Barrenness—the inability to produce anything good.

Nakedness—the disgrace of exposure; the fear of rejection if people see the real us.

Leprous—incurably diseased, don't fit in.

"Shame is about our very *selves*—not...some bad thing we *did* or *said* but...what we *are*. It tells us...we *are* unworthy. Shame...is the painful feeling of being a flawed human..."[119] The revelation of our fallenness reveals the vastness between our image and the One whose image we bear. When the tension challenges us to let grace mold us into the image of Christ, that's healthy. **The world combats shame with pride, which is equally unhealthy, because pride goes before a fall.**

But a fall can go before humility (healthy shame).

And God dispenses grace to the humble.

Shame often hides in:

Numbers—grades, weight, rank, dollars, age. We spend gobs of life improving some measurement, but achievements hoped to eliminate shame usually do not. They simply raise the bar, so even successes die prematurely under the shadow of the next shame-cast deficit.

Lingo—*better, more, should, never.* "Wish I enjoyed devotions more. I should volunteer, and diet. Will I ever be a better dad? I'll never be as good as..."

Vague, self-demeaning feelings—hundreds of afflictions underscore *I don't measure up.* Maybe someday, just not today. I'm

---

119 Smedes, 6.

too far behind. "We can't escape the constant humiliation; shame is written across our faces" (Psalm 44:15). Multitudes settle into the space between "I'm too bad" and "just not good enough."

Fallen, but not from Grace

If I said, "God wants you feeling ashamed," would that confirm your suspicions? Check this out. While the bones lie scattered in a foreign valley, God spoke to their disgraced, overrun homeland, "I am furious that you have suffered shame before the surrounding nations" (Ezekiel 36:6).

God was *furious*? Why?

Something dear to Him suffered shame unnecessarily.

If this is how He felt about shamed *land*, He must feel infinitely more for shamed *people*! Shame is one of the weightiest sorrows humans bear yet, "It was our sorrows that weighed him down" (Isaiah 53:4). **Jesus carried every sin, along with every ton and ounce of shame, so we don't have to.** He never lugged anything to the cross He intended for us to keep lifting.

When laden with undeserved shame, God gets angry, not happy. He desires to make free, not make fun. Grace trumps disgrace, so even in times of humiliation or failure, we need not fear rejection. Clothed in undeserved favor, we have permission to shed all futile attempts (dead works) of being more acceptable to God. His acceptance frees us. Toxic shame tells me I'm insufficient funds, not enough. Grace doesn't necessarily acclaim I am enough, but that Jesus is more than enough, and I'm linked to Him. I'm acceptable to God because I'm clothed in the righteousness of Jesus. He's got me covered! **I don't always have what it takes,** *but* **I always have Who it takes, and He always has what it takes.**

I'm OK with that.

Grace is Beast

Guilt and shame seek concealment. When fear steers from God, His love invites me to a safe place of honest confession. The One who offered the costliest sacrifice simply bids my heart to break over sin. His unearned favor called grace clothes my nakedness, forgives my dirt, and unashamedly welcomes me. I stop vaguely hoping my good is good enough and start believing His arsenal of mighty graces are more than enough. I usually think of grace as sweet and kind, which it is. **I'm also learning God's graces are a force to be reckoned with—weapons of mass destruction against sin, fear, guilt, and shame!** "Where sin abounded, grace abounded much more" (Romans 5:20 NKJV). One pastor says, "For every mudpuddle of sin, there's an ocean full of grace."

Saving grace means I'm no longer guilty. Cleansing grace means I'm no longer dirty. Accepting grace means I'm no longer shamed. Freeing grace means I'm no longer enslaved. Sanctifying grace means He can change me. Keeping grace means I forever belong to Jesus. In Him I'm acceptable, so I don't fear rejection. In Him I'm righteous, so I don't fear punishment. "Mercy triumphs over judgment" (James 2:13 NKJV).

Grace disses disgrace, overturns the tables of religion-demanding sacrifices, and evicts the hired hand who told us God no longer wants us around. Grace cleans dirt, forgives sin, wrecks guilt, raises the fallen, clothes the shamed. **Amazing grace, how beastly the sound to my enemies. How sweet the sound to me.** "We praise God for the glorious grace he has poured out on us who belong to his dear Son" (Ephesians 1:6).

Yes, amen!

"When we are bone tired of our struggle to be worthy…to earn the approval of everyone…we are ready for grace. When we have given up all hope of ever being an acceptable human being, we may hear…the ultimate reassurance: we are accepted, accepted by grace."[120]

He clothes the lilies of the valley with rich splendor. How much more He clothes the bones in the valley with new skin![121]

---

120 Smedes, 109.
121 Dedication: In memory of Aunt Virginia Scriven, who embodied gracious strength.

Point: Do you resonate with the raw conversation? (Nagging never-enoughness. Hammered down by not living up to my ideal self. Good works to make up for shortcomings. Rarely feel I've done "enough." Someday God will love me when I'm better.)
What's God putting on or taking off your heart?
Ponder how to bridge where you are and where you want to be without shame.
Pride boasts about self. Grace boasts about Jesus. (Jeremiah 9:23-24. Galatians 6:14).
Prayer: Grace is a force to be reckoned with, and it's available! God gets furious when you unnecessarily carry shame. (Hebrews 4:16)
Practical: My shame is tied to a deep seated (deep-seared) belief that I'm...
Keep a shame log. Identify it in numbers, lingo, or vague feelings of chronic dissatisfaction about self.
Playlist: *Grace Like Rain* by Todd Agnew
Pocket:

PART 7:
The Restorer *sparks life* in broken pieces who feel *uninflated* or *unspiritual*.

Come, O breath, from the four winds!
Breathe into these dead bodies so they may live again.
Breath came into their bodies.
They all came to life (Ezekiel 37:9-10).

I will put My Spirit in you (Ezekiel 37:14).

The putting together
of the outward is
never the total goal of restoration.
It's also meant to impact
the interior, the spiritual, the invisible.
This requires the movement of God.

Dry things are highly combustible.
Sometimes the only thing needed
to reignite a fire is wind.
Don't just be alive. LIVE!

When Jesus' disciples were deflated,
He came close
and breathed on them.

John's story is a great example of how
The Restorer infuses life
into the uninflated or unspiritual.

48: Well, Light a Match and Call me a Doldrum

*They still had **no breath** in them (Ezekiel 37:8).*

My junior high basketball strategies consisted of quick midrange shots or passing the ball like hot potato. At youth group one Friday, rare confidence triggered a radical move. I drove. While "soaring" for a layup, my defender jumped too, as did the competitor chasing from behind. The sandwiching knocked the wind out of me. I didn't hurt, just had no air. I gasped desperately until breath returned. To this day I prefer an outside shot. Sometimes life gets knocked out of us, and we need resuscitated.

A '70s movie tells the true story of a teenager circumnavigating the globe by his sailboat, *The Dove*. Not surprisingly, Robin encountered storms and surprises, but on one occasion he lit his craft on fire. This obstacle apparently ranked worst. Ironically, it wasn't violent winds or mountainous waves. Quite the contrary. There was *no* wind, *no* waves, *no* movement, for twenty-two days! He was crossing the Doldrums, a region known for dreaded calm. Sail-driven vessels may sit for weeks or flounder from shifting breezes. No wonder the term speaks metaphorically for listless seasons. What happened to Robin? *A new wind* sparked hope in the sailor, who quenched the fire and continued his mission.

Stagnancy is killer. We may weather terrible storms and wear hard-fought scars, only to quit during periods of prolonged inactivity. This is common, especially for middle-aged men. Maybe that's why many check out, abort their mission, or self-destruct. Wind is vital. It invisibly relocates air masses of differing temperatures and ushers in new seasons. In a word, it's *movement*.

The people in Ezekiel's vision experienced years in the Doldrums. They needed more than a new job and better zip code. **They needed God to move *in* them.** Restoration addresses more than the outward, the material, the visible. It impacts the interior, the spiritual, the invisible. A phenomenal process of restoration already occurred, but God had miraculous work to do inside them. His vision was greater than rebuilding their external lives, as if to display them in a museum.

He wanted to fill them with life, with Himself!

Jesus used the analogy of wind: "The wind blows where it wishes, and you hear the sound of it, but cannot tell where it comes from and where it goes. So is everyone who is born of the Spirit" (John 3:8 NKJV). Like wind flowing from high pressure to low, God's heaven-sent breezes mysteriously blow into the lowest places where souls sit listlessly.[122]

God Will Meet You **There**

It's every writer's nightmare. I lost a significant chunk of material (right after saving it in two locations). I told myself everything was fine, but every search eroded hope. Frantic, I ran my hands through my hair (couldn't find that either), collapsed on the kitchen floor, and sobbed. There was no way to replicate the lost work. I urged friends to pray. Some gave suggestions, but I just wanted a professional to make it magically appear. One moment I stood with deep peace; the next I slumped in despair. Faith for full recovery competed with confusion for my next step. All momentum vanished, making it a double loss. The book and I entered the Doldrums.

Melissa encouraged me: "Whether you have to redo it, or it's recovered, God will meet you *there*." Such powerful truth. I clung to her words and told her she should write the book. A friend heard my dilemma and solicited the expertise of a fellow employee with a perfect record in data recovery. They worked for an hour, but every avenue proved futile until "If that doesn't work, we can try…" was no longer uttered. I thanked them for tackling my problem as if their own. Disappointed, they apologized, and directed me to the program's support line.

The young lady on the phone worked another hour when I recognized a lost file. "That's it!" I exclaimed, trying not to celebrate prematurely. After thanking her and ending the call, I made a dreadful discovery—many "recovered" files were empty when I opened them. My best three days of writing remained lost. What a roller coaster!

The next day felt claustrophobic, so I escaped to a park. I walked, wrestled with loss, and prayed for a miracle. And just plain hurt. Light rain increased, heralding this would not be a passing shower. I affirmed what I knew to be true and recounted God's faithfulness. Did God want me to rewrite from this place of loss? I wondered how others

---

122 Isaiah 57:15.

cope with losses much greater than mine. With nothing more to pray and nowhere to hide from the rain, I headed home.

I decided to attempt every recovery suggestion—trying this, trying that—until an alert recommended updating my program. That glimmer of hope proved to be another dead end, but it triggered a shot-in-the-dark idea. *What if I plug my external hard drive into a different laptop?* Five minutes later everything was found! After saving it everywhere, I bounded down the stairs and flailed like a madman. Melissa and Rachel celebrated with me like a scene out of Luke 15. A new wind blew. This miracle recovered the lost work *and the lost parts of me!* **God not only worked for me, He breathed life into me. I could function again.** It felt like being born again.

Even if the work didn't recover, Melissa is right. God would've met me *there*. He's able to restore *us*, even when losses are not. My story includes these too. Testimonies of the miraculous can encourage, but to the miracle-less in the waste place, they can hurt. Maybe you felt that after reading the last paragraph. *Good for you. Glad you got an answer.* All I know is my situation felt impossible. God can redeem pain, suffering, and loss. Most importantly, He can restore the interior, spiritual dimensions of *us*.

Paul went through such a difficult trial it felt like death strangling him. He recounts the situation and the outcome:

> *We were burdened beyond measure...so that we despaired even of life. Yes, we had the sentence of death in ourselves, that we should not trust in ourselves but in God who raises the dead, who delivered us from so great a death, and does deliver us; in whom we trust that He will still deliver us (2 Corinthians 1:8-10 NKJV).*

He didn't need someone who could just provide, direct, heal, or forgive. As great as those are, his situation demanded a God who could meet him *there* and raise dead things to life.[123]

---

123 Dedication: Lucinda Legters and Zip Cragg, for tackling my problem like it was yours!

Point: What's more challenging: stagnation or storms?
Are you experiencing the Doldrums?
Ponder: Wind is invisible, mysterious, and can rise any moment. Just like God's Spirit!
Prayer: What does your situation require God to be? He will meet you *there*.
Practical: Buy a sailboat and tackle the Doldrums!
Playlist: *Shattered* by Bianca
Pocket:

49: Highly Combustible

Come, O breath, from the four winds! (Ezekiel 37:9).

My brother Greg, following a lengthy, boring recovery, decided to clean his yard. He raked oodles of leaves into piles and burned them. That evening he quenched the fire and collapsed into bed. While resting the next day, exhausted from overdoing it, something phenomenal was happening outside. *Wind.* Hot, strong, summer wind. This might not sound unusual, but it consistently blew across those piles, incubating the inside. Light smoke wisped until a few leaves reignited. Flames multiplied, eventually engulfing pine trees, and endangering his home. Thankfully, a neighbor alerted Greg, who sprang into action and diverted the fire.

Ezekiel had been speaking *to the bones*, and heaven's words wrought heaven's transformations. Now God instructed the prophet to speak *to the winds* on behalf of the bones. He also spoke to the mountains of their homeland, telling them to prepare for their homecoming![124] While restoring *you*, God might be speaking to others *about you*. God sent Aaron to Moses at the same time as the burning bush commission.[125] **We have no idea what heavenly communications occur regarding us!** He may be preparing places for your arrival, people for your benefit, or wind for new life. Who is God talking to about you?

Life and Death

An anonymous songwriter chose the splendor of life as his theme. Psalm 104 is a resounding celebration of creation, praising the Author of heaven's starry curtains and the forest's ravines. Storks, rocks, olive oil, mountain goats, cedar trees, and humans find their way into the anthem. "O LORD, what a variety of things you have made! In wisdom you have made them all. The earth is full of your creatures" (verse 24). The writer connects life to God Himself. "They all depend on you… You open your hand to feed them, and they are richly satisfied. But if you turn away from them, they panic. When you take away their breath,

---

124 Ezekiel 36:8-15.
125 Exodus 4:14.

they die and turn again to the dust" (excerpts from verses 27-29).

In God's meticulous care of creation, He notices those who die, even small birds worth half a penny.[126] He's also aware when the living *figuratively* die. The song continues, "When you give them your breath, life is created, and you renew the face of the earth" (verse 30). **God's breath is the difference between life and death.** Take a deep, cleansing breath, compliments of your Creator. "I will sing to the LORD as long as I live. I will praise my God to my last breath" (verse 33)!

Has your fire gone out? Your soul dried out? Hardly ideal conditions, but only one thing is missing. Just one. Wind. Wind blowing on those dry, burned-out leaves created fire. **After all, dry things are highly combustible.** What if God blows over your barren landscape and lights a fire like never before? It's possible because the wind of His Spirit is the only necessary ingredient. Wind is God's work. Let's position our sails.

Make Room

Jesus gives life. "'The first *man*, Adam, *became a living soul* (an individual); the last Adam (Christ) became a life-giving spirit [restoring the dead to life]" (1 Cor. 15:45 AMP). That last statement bears repeating. Christ, the life-giving spirit, restores the dead to life. I know you want a story. A heartbroken leader named Jairus begged Jesus to heal his dying daughter. When Jesus agrees to come to his house, crowds follow, many no doubt interested in a good show. One woman, harboring a major issue of her own, reached toward Jesus, certain that touching Him could make her well. She was right. Healing power flew out of Jesus into her ailing body. "She could feel the change and knew her plague was over and done with" (Mark 5:29 MSG). He ministered to her soul as well, affirming her as a loved daughter of God.

As great as this was, it must've been havoc for Jairus to wait. Sure enough, the delay brought news. *Don't bother the Teacher. She didn't make it.* They were afraid of bothering the Master, but He wasn't bothered at all. Jesus immediately encouraged the dad. Words of life countered those of despair and death. In fact, Jesus reiterated His promise to see her. Many already gathered to weep, but Jesus didn't come to mourn. He came to revive. "Make room," He said, evicting everybody except the parents and three disciples (Matthew 9:24 NKJV).

---

126 Matthew 10:29.

With the faithless commotion locked outside, the family led Him to the lifeless body. The giver of life held her hand, then said, "Little girl, I say to you, arise" (Mark 5:41 ESV). Breath-giving *and* breathtaking! He restored life to her body, much like the winds invaded the bodies in the valley. **Jesus ruthlessly relegated the noisy, mocking voices outside before He could speak life into something dead on the inside.** We must do likewise with the unbelieving chatter and worldly noise dominating our airwaves. Jesus doesn't compete with noise. If we silence the distractions and oust the voices, the Life-Giver may revive some things!

Going for unforgettable I told Michele, publishing agent at Equip, "I'm writing a book for dead people." After her shocked laugh I explained myself before she considered me a hair-brained psycho. *This book is for all who breathe oxygen but have no life—the broken, shattered, listless, and lifeless.* I have sought God to instill hope and truth, to remind you He cares about dead things, and has the power to revive. **Like the dead bones and the young daughter, may you hear the life-giver say, "Son, daughter, Rise!"**[127]

Point: God is the wind-whisperer.
Ponder God talking to others about you.
Prayer: Whisper the chapter's last sentence as though God is speaking it to you.
What makes you weep? Ask Jesus what He wants to do about it.
Practical: What noises, distractions, or faithless messages need silenced?
Playlist: *Gratitude* by Brandon Lake
Secret Place by Phil Wickham
Pocket:

---

[127] Dedication: Greg McEntire, brother, friend, and fun-guy. You're gifted for divine purposes!

50: God's Got Fresh Breath

> *Breath came into their bodies. They all came to life (Ezekiel 37:10).*

I previously referred to a "purpose weekend" when God reiterated my call to preach. Not something I asked for or earned, just His design. Finding confidence from this fresh certainty, I availed myself to local pastors as a simple but definitive step. In the orchestration of God, a friend already scheduled me to speak the next weekend.[128] I felt rusty. It had been a long time.

I woke abruptly at 2:00 Monday morning. Realizing my mind was too engaged for sleep, I prayed about the upcoming message. If ever God "downloaded" a sermon to me, it was that one. But God was doing more than giving a message. Having been in a long, dry season that left me feeling worthless and useless, to hear God's voice again, to have His Spirit move *in me*, felt like being resuscitated. At the end of that precious hour, with tears soaking my pillow, I looked up and whispered, **"I feel like I'm being restored."** My Restorer was breathing life into me!

It was a long-awaited wind gently blowing across my soul. God hadn't forgotten; wasn't done. My heart beat again. Sprouts of green pushed through the winter snow. "I will cause you to rise again," God told the people. He must have meant it for me too. I previously loathed my life, hoping it would end soon. But I was rising into a new day and season, glad to be alive! I reiterated daily, "I don't want to live. I want to be ALIVE!" Restoration is often long, but there are golden occasions along the way. One of mine happened early one February morning—when God commanded a wind to blow.

Start Your Engines

Engines don't always run. Sometimes they need a battery or gas, but sometimes they need rebuilt. Ever watch mechanics wrestle with lifeless motors? They investigate, experiment, think. Many a wrench

---

128 God had been talking to someone about me!

has flown in the process. The climax occurs when the key turns and the accelerator pumps fuel through the veins. (Can you tell I'm not a mechanic?) The engine cranks as everyone mutters *come on* under their breath. If that doesn't work, they keep trying. Eventually the victorious roar to life prompts hoopin' and hollerin,' sometimes during the wee hours of the night. The atmosphere is vibrant where old, worn-out things revive.

That's what God does, minus the throwing-tools-in-frustration part. As mechanics resuscitate dead engines, the Master Mechanic breathes newness into dead lives. A former coworker said his heart surgery made him feel like a new man. We chatted a few minutes before he hopped in his truck and drove off. He's ninety. I walked away smiling.

In the beginning it was said, "God formed the man from the dust of the ground. He breathed the breath of life into the man's nostrils, and the man became a living person" (Genesis 2:7). My study Bible explains,

> *The body is a lifeless shell until God brings it alive with his 'breath of life.' When God removes his life-giving breath, our bodies once again return to dust. Our life and worth, therefore, come from God's Spirit. Many boast of their achievements and abilities as though they were the originator of their own strengths. Others feel worthless because their abilities do not stand out. In reality, our worth comes not from our achievements but from the God of the universe, who chooses to give us the mysterious and miraculous gift of life. Value life, as he does.*[129]

How powerful, precious, supernatural, sacred—this gift called life! When it gets knocked out of us, we need God to revive it. Jesus' death knocked the wind out of His disciples. Traumatized, terrified, uncertain, their quality of life eroded. Jesus slipped in, showed His scars, and settled their hearts. What He did next is powerful. **He came super close to His deflated men, "breathed on them and said, 'Receive the Holy Spirit'" (John 20:22).** Jesus doesn't extinguish

---

129 *Life Application Study Bible.* Tyndale. 2004. (8)

people gasping for air. He resuscitates them.

Oh Honey!

We earlier relayed a story of heroic faith when Jonathan, King Saul's son, confronted an army with one weapon and one sidekick. And God. These three routed the enemy, but a massive plot twist unfolds. By day's end, Jonathan almost died. By his dad![130] Rewind a sec. When Saul noticed Jonathan's invasion, he flippantly ordered an edict for his army: no victory, no food. This distressed the men incredibly. Saul expected great results from them but did nothing for them. They were to plow ahead without intake, to produce like machines without oil. The story repeatedly connects the army's fatigue to the foolish command.

The route led them through a wooded area with beautiful, abundant honey. This would be like a fountain freely dispensing ice-cold Coke or caffeine-laden coffee (or whatever your preference) to get you through the afternoon madness. The soldiers pass by, fearing the king's wrath. Except one. "Jonathan had not heard his father's command, and he dipped the end of his stick into a piece of honeycomb and ate the honey." Notice the result. "He felt refreshed" (1 Samuel 14:29).

It literally raised his sagging eyebrows. "Refreshed" can be stated "his eyes brightened." It awakened worn-down senses. Now, Jonathan didn't pull up a chair and go hog-wild at the all-you-can-eat honey bar, but the bit of honey rejuvenated him for the rest of the day's battle. He was a sharp contrast to the others. His countenance beamed; their eyes were half-mast. He was energized with a second wind; they inched along, their first wind littered a way's back. To their credit, they forced their rival backward three hard-fought miles.

Honey is depicted as a means of nourishment, satisfaction, and sweetness.[131] The promised land was described as flowing with milk and honey. Smith's Bible Dictionary reports the prominence of bees there, so even rocks and trees in wilderness places dripped with honey. Solomon wrote, "Kind words are like honey—sweet to the soul and healthy for the body" (Proverbs 16:24). **God's kind words are like the honey that revived Jonathan's decimated soul.** His voice, or those He speaks through, can raise dead things. Jesus said, "The Spirit gives life;

---

130 1 Samuel 14:24-46.
131 Deuteronomy 32:13. Psalm 81:16.

the flesh profits nothing. The words I speak to you are spirit and they are life" (John 6:63).

A missionary recounted a seven-month spiritual drought—bronze heavens, fruitless toil, half-dead workers. One day he climbed a hill, desperate. As he cried out in prayer, the Restorer breathed life into him, renewing his vigor. He hurried home shouting, "God is back! God is back!" New life flowed into their hearts and catapulted a new season of ministry. Dead is awful, feels so final. No amount of planning or striving raises the dead, but God can. He had a message for the bones, "I will open your graves of exile and cause you to rise again" (Ezekiel 37:12). When Ezekiel spoke it, wind rushed from every direction![132]

Point: If foolish words deflated you, find some kind words.
Ponder: I don't want to be alive. I want to LIVE!
Has God put someone on your heart? Maybe He's speaking to you about someone undergoing restoration.
Prayer: "I lie in the dust; revive me by your word" (Psalm 119:25).
Practical: Take a deep, cleansing breath. Have a spoonful of honey.
Playlist: *You Raise Me Up* by Selah
Presence (My Heart's Desire) by Newsboys
Pocket:

---

[132] Dedication: Tim McKeever. You gently but persistently nudged me back to preaching.

51: *Who's* Moving In?

> *I will put **My Spirit in you**, and you will
> live again (Ezekiel 37:14).*

The annual ministry convention felt stuffy. Maybe it reflected my stagnation more than a corporate one. An unusual thought popped in my head (which is not unusual). Ever seen those massive fans? *Air movers*, as they're marketed. I envisioned several above the stage, blowing across the congregation. Just as strong gusts in a weather system evict oppressive humidity, leaving behind light, healthy air, the robust movement would dispel languid air and invigorate our bodies. **I also longed for it to blow out sluggishness, doubt, sadness, and spiritual poverty, replacing them with exhilarating doses of praise, joy, faith, and oomph!** We need the Spirit to change the atmosphere in our hearts, homes, churches, and ministries. No wonder believers throughout the ages penned songs imploring God to breathe on them.

The winds of God impart physical and emotional life, like turning on a light after a dark night. Things that had been there all along are seen as if for the first time. A new day replaces "another day." Vigor swallows mere existence. But the wind of God does more. It exhales life deep into our spiritual realms, where the Spirit tends, teaches, and transforms. These heart miracles point to God, and those receiving them experience Him more fully. He told the bones, "I will put breath into you, and you will come to life. Then you will know that I am the LORD. I will put My Spirit in you, and you will live again. Then you will know that I the LORD have spoken, and I have done what I said" (Ezekiel 37:6, 14).

Some emerge from life's barren wastelands with better bodies, esteem, careers, and relationships. Some beat addictions. We rightly celebrate their inspirational, life-changing progress. It's unfortunate, however, *if they never let God breathe in them.* Uninterested in spiritual wind, they just wanted their bones reattached. This equates to restoring the exterior of a car while ignoring the seized engine or building a beautiful house that will never become a home.

Engine Swap

God cares about the "engines" (hearts, minds) in His people. He wants them running good and strong, powered by godly motivations. Prior to their season in the valley, the dry bones hardly resembled God. The chapter preceding Ezekiel's vision revealed His plan for a spiritual engine swap:

> *I will give you a new heart and put a new spirit within you; I will take the heart of stone out of your flesh and give you a heart of flesh. I will put My Spirit within you and cause you to walk in My statutes (Ezekiel 36:26-27 NKJV).*

God's Spirit is limitless, so there's no limit to what He can accomplish in the heart. Yesterday's limitations don't decide today. God's prevailing winds eject the dust, crust, dead, and dry, making way for the new. Ezekiel 36 reveals how God's winds changed His people. They became:
- Secure in their own place.
- Vitally connected to God, not distant from Him.
- Free from soul-polluting sources.
- Fruitful. God's increase melted the shame of inadequacy and barrenness.
- Sensitive to their sin.
- Restored—honoring God who revived them.

What a difference! **The spiritually empty experienced the Spirit's filling.** His presence dynamically changed their heart! The third sentence of Scripture provides our first glimpse of God's Spirit. "The earth was formless and empty, and darkness covered the deep waters. And the Spirit of God was hovering over the surface of the waters" (Genesis 1:2). What was He doing? Noticing chaos, emptiness, and darkness; seeking to bring order, presence, and light. He maintains this desire still. Though not the extent of His ministry, the principle of "the law of first mention" highlights its importance. Is this not the work of God to the scattered bones? His Spirit noticed them, reassembled them, reignited them, and moved in.

Jesus' ministry resembles that of the Spirit. "God anointed Jesus of Nazareth with the Holy Spirit and with power. Then Jesus went around doing good and healing all who were oppressed by the devil, for God was with him" (Acts 10:38). **God's Spirit still hovers over broken lives!** Over those in confusion, to bring wellness. Over the wreckage from sin and injustice, to work good. Over those in darkness, to shine. Over empty, depleted souls, *to fill with Himself.*

I lost all wind during writing, ironically during the part about wind! After feeling dead for some time, I had to do something about it. I pulled to the side of the road and paced next to a pond, encouraging myself and praying for words of life. I wasn't hopeless because I had God. I prayed for Him to move and trusted His timing. It felt good to audibly pour out my heart to a God I knew was listening. After ten minutes a strong, distinct wind started blowing! I praised God for the invigorating wind my body felt, confident He would breathe into my spirit too.[133]

> **Point:** God's Spirit works phenomenally in us.
> **Ponder** God's Spirit hovering over you, moving inside you. Read Ezekiel 36.
> **Prayer:** Are you "empty?" Invite God in.
> **Practical:** Take a walk into the wind or sit in front of a fan.
> **Playlist:** *Rushing Wind* by Keith Green
> **Pocket:**

---

[133] Dedication: Joyce Moore, "living" proof that God revives!

52: The "Son of Thunder" Saga
Episode 1—#1

*I will take out your **stony, stubborn heart** (Ezekiel 36:26).*

One of the most poignant demonstrations of this infusing, transforming God-wind is found in the life of a man named John. He and his brother James left their career when Jesus called. Maybe an explosive nature earned their nickname *Sons of Thunder* by their Teacher. Toward the end of Jesus' earthly ministry, after announcing His approaching death, a trio of surprising events unfold. All include John. When I think of John, I envision tenderness, perception, and *glue*. He caught on quick, and stuck close to Jesus. Many scholars rank him as Jesus' best friend and fondest confidant. Sometimes Jesus whispered secrets only reaching his ears, which drove Peter nuts. But other traits beat inside John. Tenderness might not have been his leading characteristic yet.

"His disciples began arguing about which of them was the greatest" (Luke 9:46). There's a lot wrong here. Isn't "who's the best?" an ironic question when hanging around Jesus? Instead of focusing on His greatness, they debated over their own. And the timing was crude. Jesus just forecasted His imminent violent death. Sure, they felt bad, but as quick as they got alone, they argued about being best. Their big heads couldn't comprehend Jesus' words.

These guys walked and talked with Jesus for years. Heard Him pray, preach, and call. Saw Him heal, forgive, love. No doubt Thunder John engaged in this argument. My guess is Peter initiated, but John quickly joined! The story reads as if all participated. Wrangling for rank. Pining for position. Comparing credentials. Belittling others to better themselves. Boasting about their loyalty, theology, and ministry. Whatever was considered a measurement of greatness, they wielded it. These were the ones who would soon be leading His Church. Things looked grim for Jesus' worldwide mission! Those closest to Him hardly resembled Him.

They were argumentative, arrogant, and insensitive[134] to the Lord.[135]

> **Point:** Those closest to Jesus can be
> —spiritually arrogant.
> —argumentative with each other.
> —insensitive to Him.
> **Ponder** Jesus' response in Luke 9:47-48.
> **Prayer:** Confess pride, argumentativeness, or insensitivity.
> **Practical:** Embrace humility.
> **Playlist:** *Revive Us, Oh Lord* by Carman
> **Pocket:**

---

134 A synonym for *insensitive* is *stonyhearted*, a characteristic the Spirit addressed in God's people (Ezekiel 36:26).
135 Dedication: Tim Kangas. You've made a career of walking humbly with God. I admire you greatly.

53: The "Son of Thunder" Saga
Episode 2—He Didn't Smell Like Us

> *Master, we saw someone using your name to cast out demons, but* **we told him to stop because he isn't in our group** *(Luke 9:49).*

When the disciples argued about the greatest in their little circle, Jesus corrected their pride. John didn't seem to be listening. He eagerly recounts an incident with some unknown minister who apparently threatened their ambitions. *I am best, most important* lends easily to *we are best, most important.* This is corporate pride, an exclusive spirit. "*Our* ministry, *our* church, *our* denomination is the real thing. If you want anything to do with Jesus, you must belong to *us*, look like *us*, think like *us*, smell like *us*."

What's funny is the disciples encountered an evil spirit and couldn't do anything, but this guy could! And they argued about *their* greatness? They did what many have done—told him to stop. He had a legit ministry of deliverance and those closest to Jesus forbid him! Out of a divisive spirit, they mandated him to close his doors. John expects Jesus to pat him on the back. "Phew! Thank you. We certainly don't want some guy out there setting people free. Well done!"

Imagine if they befriended and blessed him, saw him as partner rather than competitor? **The further we go from day one with Jesus, the greater the danger of forgetting we were invited by sheer grace alone.** Take Peter. After meeting Jesus, he bowed, knowing he didn't deserve the presence of such greatness. Fast-forward a few years and he's exalting himself. Paul addressed blatant divisiveness in a church he started:

> *I appeal to you…by the authority of our Lord Jesus Christ, to live in harmony with each other. Let there be no divisions in the church. Rather, be of one mind, united in thought and purpose. For some…have told me about your quarrels. Has Christ been divided into factions? Was I, Paul, crucified for you (1 Corinthians 1:10-13)?*

Their Sunday School classes might've been "The Paulites," "The Apollos Group," "Peter's Leaders." The *really* spiritual called themselves "The True Jesus Followers." Paul didn't speak as a heady pastor, but under God's authority, as if to say, "Jesus says, 'Stop the pride-driven divisions!'" Spiritual pride is insidiously real but doesn't make sense. It's a misnomer. *Spiritual* and *Pride* are rivals. One ousts the other. To be proud of one's spirituality is to forget who blessed us with every spiritual blessing.[136] **When we forget grace, pride fills the vacuum.** Exclusivity often follows.

A Wedding Exclusive

There *is* a God-ordained exclusivity, and a man-made version. John exhibited the latter. Is God's good news inclusive or exclusive? Let me humbly offer my answer: *both*. **The gospel is *inclusive* because it's available to *all*, extended to *whoever*.** "Whoever calls on the name of the Lord shall be saved" (Romans 10:13 NKJV). "Whoever comes to Me I will never drive away" (John 6:37 NIV). If you're a whoever, you're invited.

The gospel is *exclusive* because it requires action. There's a condition. To be saved "Mr. Whoever" *must call on Jesus*. Mrs. Whoever won't be driven away *if* she humbly comes to Jesus. Invitations are wonderful, but not enough. The recipient must respond, show up, and meet any requirements in order to enjoy all the host prepared. Jesus highlighted this inclusive-exclusive message with a story likening God to a king whose son is getting married.[137]

The king invited certain guests, but they refused or ignored it. They were too busy or uninterested to mail their RSVP. It angered some and insulted others. That boggles me. How do you feel insulted by an invitation to a royal wedding? It gets worse. Some beat and killed the couriers. The king rightly punished them, then printed thousands of new invites. "Now go out to the street corners and invite everyone you see. So the servants brought in everyone they could find, good and bad alike, and the banquet hall was filled with guests" (Matthew 22:9-10). He invited *everyone,* regardless of position, prosperity, or pedigree. That's inclusive! Some accepted. Others didn't. The choice was theirs.

As the king mingled with the guests, someone caught his attention.

---

136 Ephesians 1:3.
137 Matthew 22:1-14.

Imagine everyone in coordinated, beautiful attire except one man in a ripped T-shirt and frayed jeans. And clip-on tie. "'Friend, how is it that you are here without wedding clothes?' But the man had no reply. Then the king said to his aides, 'Bind his hands and feet and throw him into outer darkness, where there will be weeping and gnashing of teeth'" (Matthew 22:12-13). He threw him out, even though he was invited. That's exclusive!

What just happened? *Kicked out 'cause he didn't have certain clothes?* We cry "foul!" He shouldn't be punished so severely for something so trivial. God's "narrow-mindedness" grates our thinking, offends our pride. Especially to western anti-discriminatory culture touting *everything is accepted, no one is excluded,* this is a dealbreaker, the turnoff proving God a farce. We shouldn't be told anyone's sincere religion falls short or so-and-so's lifestyle is wrong. The harsh reality: many will be excluded.[138] **However, they will be excluded *because of their doing*, not God's.**

Declaring truth may offend people, but speaking false "good news" offends Jesus, which I will not do. The gospel is doubly exclusive because it establishes Jesus as God's only way of salvation and requires action on our part. "I am the way, the truth and the life. No one comes to the Father except through Me" (John 14:6). "There is one mediator between God and men, the Man Christ Jesus" (1 Timothy 2:5). "For there is no other name under heaven given among men whereby we must be saved" (Acts 4:12).

It's inconceivable to stare at Jesus' bloodied body on the cross and conclude, *I'm decent enough.* If another way to be reconciled with God existed, don't you think He would've done it? As if Jesus, nailed to rugged wood, thought, *This is really kind of unnecessary. After all, people can get to God a bunch of other ways if they want.* He agonized in prayer the previous night, asking if there was another way to save us without the cross. The following day proves there wasn't. "I do not treat the grace of God as meaningless. For if keeping the law could make us right with God, then there was no need for Christ to die" (Galatians 2:21). This version is worthwhile:

> *I tried keeping rules and working my head off to please God, and it didn't work. So I quit being a "law*

---

138 Matthew 7:21-23. Ephesians 5:5-6. Revelation 21:8.

> man" so that I could be God's man. Christ's life showed me how and enabled me to do it. I identified myself completely with him. I have been crucified with Christ. My ego is no longer central. It is no longer important that I appear righteous before you or have your good opinion, and I am no longer driven to impress God. Christ lives in me. The life you see me living is not 'mine,' but it is lived by faith in [Jesus], who loved me and gave himself for me...If a living relationship with God could come by rule-keeping, then Christ died unnecessarily (Galatians 2:19-21 MSG).

If your spirituality points to *your* ability, the gospel of Jesus likely offends you. Or appeals to you! **To understand the gospel is to be offended. Or liberated.**

More to the Story

We could label the king a harsh despot, but it is *his* kingdom, *his* son's wedding, and *his* party! He can invite whoever and require whatever he wants. Requiring specific attire for admission is exclusive, but even that was gracious. The story runs deeper. In that culture guests customarily received special wardrobes by the family for the big day. So it's not that the man was too poor to afford acceptable clothes; he just considered his good enough.

The king wanted him there, wanted to be friends, and *even provided the necessary garments*. Do not feel bad for him! **He ignored the king's requirement, refused what he offered.** His refusal seriously insulted the king and landed him outside. When confronted, he stood speechless, without excuse. Those brashly speaking a big line about calling God to account someday are desperately unrealistic. *We* will be the questioned that fateful day.

Think of it—the king invited everybody, required certain clothing, and then offered the clothing! Law-abiding citizens and the riff-raff alike needed the garments. All were welcome to stay who humbly received them. **The good and bad were all invited because of the covering.** Nobody strutted around that dining hall, arrogantly telling how much they paid for tickets or where they purchased their clothes. All were equally dressed in royal attire, speaking only of how undeserving to be invited, the grace of the good king, and the glory of the groom.

Nobody else stood out; all eyes were on him.

If you resonate with *I'll never be good enough; I'm too dirty*, the *inclusive* message of the gospel is for *you*! Every whoever is invited by God Himself! If notions such as *I'm good enough, I'm better than so-and-so, God accepts me as I am* coddle you, the *exclusive* message of the gospel is for *you*! **God never accepts anyone as they are.** He *invites* us as we are, but *only accepts* those who trust in Jesus, who are clothed in His righteousness.[139] To be accepted by God, we first accept Jesus. This is freely extended to all but humbly received by whoever calls on Him. "To all who believed him and accepted him, he gave the right to become children of God" (John 1:12).

People receiving God's salvation are made new by grace. It is to enter a fresh, exhilarating relationship with God. Some forget and become harsh toward unbelievers or other believers. **How could the well-dressed guests at the banquet scoff at those outside in dirty clothes when the king extended the same invitation and attire to them?** How could Jesus' disciples, so unfit to be chosen, become so critical and exclusive about another disciple just because he wasn't in their group? Man's harsh exclusivity tells people God doesn't want them. God's gracious exclusivity tells people He wants them, but they must respond.

These first two conversations with Jesus revealed a spirit in His disciples that was argumentative, egotistical, divisive, and exclusive.

But wait, there's more.[140]

---

139 Ephesians 1:6-7.
140 Dedication: Roy Miller. You wisely and eagerly connect the body of Christ and strengthen pastors. *www.thebetterplace.org*

Point: You're invited to heaven! Don't forget to respond!
Ponder Jesus' response in Luke 9:50.
Is the gospel inclusive, exclusive, or both?
Prayer: Do I harbor an exclusive spirit?
Practical: Be willing to value or work with Christians from different denominations. They may offer a unique contribution.
Playlist: *My Victory* by Crowder
Pocket:

54: The "Son of Thunder" Saga
Episode 3—Pyromaniacs for Jesus

> *As the time drew near for him to ascend to heaven, Jesus resolutely set out for Jerusalem. He sent messengers ahead to a Samaritan village to prepare for his arrival. But the people… did not welcome Jesus because he was on his way to Jerusalem. When James and John saw this, they said, "Lord, should we call down fire from heaven to burn them up, as Elijah did?" But Jesus turned and rebuked them, and said, "**You do not know what manner of spirit you are of. For [I have] not come to destroy people's lives, but to save them**" (Luke 9:51-56 NLT/NKJV).*

Determined to complete His Father's mission, Jesus heads toward Jerusalem—to die. Some disciples go ahead to arrange logistics like lodging and food. When they announce to a certain town that Jesus is coming, the community gets excited. They want him to stay, but are informed there will be no news teams, events, or pictures with Jesus. They probably won't even know His arrival or departure. Disappointed and offended, the town treats Him like an outcast.

It was so bad the Thunder-Boys offer to punish these scoundrels who dared to disrespect their Teacher. Maybe Elijah was their hero, or they had devotions in 2 Kings 1, but whatever the prompt, they asked permission to pray like Elijah, who called down fire on a pair of generals and their armies centuries before. "They rejected you! Let's ask God to burn 'em like toast! James will begin and I'll close. Isn't it exciting to partner with God and see Him work!"

This is actually respectable faith. They sincerely believed their prayer might initiate heaven-sent fire. (Their love still needed some work.) John didn't consider Samaritans worth much anyway. The world would be better without these half-breed outcasts. Jews labeled them too Gentile. Gentiles hated them for being too Jewish. They were stuck-in-the-middle untouchables who rarely ventured from their 'hood, and rarely hosted visitors. Except Jesus.

He traveled their roads and conversed with them. No wonder His visits were breaths of fresh air. Jesus revealed God's love *for them*, who wanted *them* to be His people. He taught and healed, and even made a successful evangelist out of a sketchy woman. He was likely the only religious teacher who cared. Conversely, the disciples viewed Samaritans as scum, and presumed God would eagerly grant their prayers to burn the ungrateful outsiders to a crisp.

This didn't start as face-to-face conversation, but it ended that way. They were probably walking down the road, Jesus leading, when their suggestion incurred a swift, unforeseen reaction. The first two episodes netted patient correction. This time a vehement volcano erupted inside Jesus, resulting in a severe upbraiding. It equates to doing something so naughty in public you receive the full brunt of parental discipline on the spot. This wasn't, "Oh Johnny, that's not nice. Tell Sam you're sorry. We'll talk later and get ice cream." **Their recommendation proved a serious, intolerable affront to the character and ministry of Jesus.**

He is literally en route to sacrifice His life for the world, even the Samaritans, and His right-hand men are ready to annihilate them. Interestingly, Jesus was more upset about His disciples' behavior than that of the Samaritans. The spirit in James and John diametrically opposed the One inside Jesus. Technological devices have an internal operating system causing them to function as they do. It controls them. Likewise, we have an internal operating system determining what we can or can't do, or will or won't do. Jesus reprimanded His disciples' spirit of destruction. It was utterly unacceptable.[141]

Point: Is there a group of people you wish would go away?
Ponder what offends Jesus most.
Prayer: That the people you wish would go away will experience God's love. (Galatians 5:6)
That God's people would experience and demonstrate God's love.
Practical: Would you be willing to show kindness to the people you wish would go away?
Playlist: *Create in Me a Clean Heart* by Keith Green
Pocket:

---

141 Dedication: Adrian Despres. Author of *Christian Man Laws* and *Four Chairs*. All kinds of fish have gathered into your nets! Book this speaker (*ForgeForward.org*) and thank me later.

55: The "Son of Thunder" Saga
Episode 4—Feelin' the Love

> *I will give you a **new heart**, and I will put a **new spirit** in you (Ezekiel 36:26).*

The spiritual atmosphere inside Jesus reverberates the resonant tones of salvation. *I want to save him, deliver her, rescue them. I am for them. I died so they can truly live.* When Jesus launched His ministry, He quoted,

> *The Spirit of the LORD is upon Me, for He has anointed me to bring Good News to the poor. He has sent me to proclaim that captives will be released, that the blind will see, that the oppressed will be set free, and that the time of the LORD's favor has come (Luke 4:18-19).*

The Spirit in Jesus moved Him to save humanity from their varied forms of brokenness, but those carrying on His ministry were argumentative, proud, divisive, and even destructive. Unrighteousness doesn't produce righteousness. Hatred doesn't obliterate hate. We don't overcome darkness with darkness or positively influence the world with negativity. "The anger of man does not produce the righteousness of God" (James 1:20 ESV).

This is highly convicting. How often do I harbor a spirit of destruction instead of salvation? How often has my heart pulsed vengeance, retaliation, and ill-will against those who don't believe like me, or adamantly criticize God and His Word? How often has my operating system violated that of Christ? "Don't grieve God. Don't break his heart. His Holy Spirit, moving and breathing in you, is the most intimate part of your life, making you fit for himself. Don't take such a gift for granted" (Ephesians 4:30 MSG).

True Love

We find ourselves in the great conundrum of balancing truth and love. Emphasizing love alone (often incorrectly defined as acceptance or niceness) erodes truth and undermines Jesus' death. **If I'm not right with God, *please* don't coddle me and say everything is ok.** That feels like love, but isn't. Things are *not* ok. I've offended God. Tell me Jesus can forgive and transform me! Some things merit warning, correction, even in-your-face rebuke. If your toddler migrates toward the road, does love let him continue? Absolutely not! You will alert him and take appropriate action. If he persists, you will ratchet up the efforts because your love wants to protect him from harm. True love requires truth.

Emphasizing truth alone drains grace from the gospel and treats people harshly. It resembles the leaders of Jesus' day—so dogmatic, religious, principled, so near to God yet so little like Him. They had no caring bone for anyone they labeled a sinner. Their religion didn't leave room for ministry. It merely placed them on a pedestal where they could look down on the heathen below.

Resemblance

No wonder Jesus breathed on His disciples after His resurrection and said, "Receive the Holy Spirit." No wonder He instructed His followers to wait until vested with His Spirit. He couldn't have His protégés operating from a nature of fighting, strutting, division, or calling down fire on any unwelcoming town. Things would get messy quickly. Ministry would hardly resemble His and behavior would contradict the One who commissioned them. Ironically, Jesus di ask God to send fire—not on the heads of Samaritans, but into the hearts of His disciples! A holy fire to refine, not a hellish fire to destroy. If I seek destructive fire on others, I need heaven's fire. **Sometimes God's people need "to get saved."** Saved from ungodly motivations and lifestyles. Saved from a critical, proud, destructive, or unbelieving spirit.

I heard a story about Napoleon Bonaparte questioning a lawbreaker's name. An undetectable muffle slipped through the man's lips. The inquiry became a demand. The silent reply sounded like *Naholeah*. "What did you say? Tell me your name!" Finally came an intelligible answer: "Napoleon." The furious commander retorted,

"Then change your ways or change your name!"[142] His irreputable lifestyle wasn't worthy of his reputable name. Anyone wearing the label *Christian* may do well to examine what needs changing so the name of Christ is not discredited.

Return to Samaria

Shortly after Jesus returned to heaven the disciples received His Spirit.[143] They began operating from His internal operating system, and their lifestyles and ministries more closely reflected His. As a result, the good news spread like wildfire, just like He promised. "But you shall receive power when the Holy Spirit comes upon you, and you shall be my witnesses in Jerusalem, Judea, Samaria and the ends of the earth" (Acts 1:8). They started in Jerusalem, then to the region of Judea. Notice the next place on God's heart—*Samaria!*

Things turned volatile in Jerusalem and Judea. Christianity created a disturbance, and retaliatory forces sought to squelch the movement. Persecution pushed believers to surrounding areas, but they went with the good news of Jesus on their lips.

> *Philip, for example, went to the city of Samaria and told the people there about the Messiah. Crowds listened intently to Philip because they were eager to hear the message and see the miraculous signs he did. Many evil spirits were cast out, screaming as they left their victims. And many who had been paralyzed or lame were healed. So there was great joy in that city (Acts 8:5-8).*

That reflects God's heart for the Samaritans! To bless their town and fill it with joy. Notice their receptivity. **Not long ago they rejected Jesus. Now they received Him eagerly.** If John had his way, they wouldn't have had this second opportunity. News reached the Church headquarters, which commissioned two leaders to superintend this dynamic ministry: Peter and—you guessed it—John. Previously he suggested nuking them. But a new wind blew into him.

---

142 I can't verify its historicity, but the point is solid.
143 Acts 2.

God rewired him.

A nature of destruction was replaced with the Spirit who inhales and exhales salvation. The love of God compelled John to come alongside them. They were no longer half-breed mutts but fellow heirs of God's kingdom! The scum were sons and daughters of the King. They were not hated by God, but cherished. Even when they rejected His Son, He still desired to rescue them. Jesus felt that all along. John eventually got there. **Places like Samaria only hear about salvation when Christians experience a salvation transforming their spirit.**

John's ministry extended many years to many people. Love exuded from this former son of thunder. You hear it in his letters. Terms of endearment grace the pages. Far from being a wishy-washy, sappy message, it's counter-balanced with hard-hitting truth. Truth coexists perfectly with love and frees those who embrace it. Love rejoices in the truth. Truth rejoices in love. No wonder John wrote,

> *[Jesus] became flesh and dwelt among us, and we beheld His glory, the glory as of the only begotten of the Father, full of grace and truth. And of His fullness we have all received, and grace for grace. For the law was given through Moses, but grace and truth through Jesus Christ (John 1:14,16-17 NKJV).*

Well said from the man who became known as "the apostle of love." Jesus wanted to move in Samaria. He wants to move in *every* life in *every* neighborhood of *every* people group, even those I don't care much about. He also wants to move in every heart of His own, including mine, so His Spirit infuses us—and whatever came out of Him comes out of us. Can God breathe new spiritual life into dead bones?

A desolate valley, an empty tomb, an upper room, and a place called Samaria all testify, "Yes! He can!" So does a man once resembling thunder.[144]

---

144 Dedication: Charlie Marquis, lover of "the ends of the earth." Author *Mudrunner*. Co-host *Fuel for the Harvest* podcast. Let him fuel your group! www.CharlieMarquis.org

Point: How would you describe the spirit, or nature, of most Christians? What about yours?
Are you a Christian in need of "saving"?
Ponder: Is there a danger of being so near to God, yet so little like Him?
What "spirits" did David mention in Psalm 51:10-17?
Prayer: God's fire replaced John's spirit of destruction with salvation. Do you need heaven's fire to touch your heart?
Practical: Read *I John* in light of the transformation God produced in John.
Playlist: *Mighty to Save* by Hillsong United
Pocket:

56: The Parable of the Pallet

I've developed a love for pallet wood over the years. First, it's free! But more than price, I love their stories. Pallets are tough, designed to assist items in transit. They're more interested in being gashed or splintered than letting their cargo take the hit. They get stapled, nailed, drilled, dropped, burdened, picked up, and thrown around, which they do with a smile because that's why they're made!

Their silent pride brims as a family receives their package in perfect condition. They're not expecting credit or attention—they've simply done their job, transporting parts to shops, copiers to offices, and supplies to warehouses. They hear rain against the roof, the whirring of tires against pavement, and exhaust from the diesels. And they love it. Sometimes they cross international boundaries. Their strength equipped them for this, yet their demeanor whispers comfort to the frightened loads they serve. You think I'm crazy? Go ask them! Oh, the stories they tell.

And then...

Customers gather the shipment's packaging and glance at the pallet.

"You want it?"

"Nah."

"Ok, throw it behind the barn."

Weeks turn into months and sometimes years. It has a lot of life left, but no purpose. Its lifespan exceeded its season of usefulness, so it leans against a barn and dies.

Until someone wakes the sleeping beauty.

"Ooh! I need this! Can I have it?"

They wrestle it from dirt and vines and load it. The pallet has no idea where it's going but doesn't care. It's brought into a shop full of tools, stains, screws, and saws. I love the word *reclaimed*. Someone saw its value and re-claimed its worth and purpose. The skilled craftsman begins transforming it into a unique creation.

You may be leaning behind the barn, considering yourself useless, worthless, weathered. and forgotten. Someday, The Restorer will come around the corner and claim you for purposes only His eyes can see. He will bring you home, clean you up, whisper life.

And you will rise again.[145]

---

[145] Dedication: Jason Richardson. I met you around a guitar and reclaimed wood! Thanks for helping many discover and pursue their purposes.

PART 8:
The Restorer *springs faith* under broken pieces once *unable* to stand.

*They all came to life and stood up on their feet **(Ezekiel 37:10)**.*

To the tangled, insecure, weak, and waning,
God wants to:
—put you back together,
—tether you to the immovable,
—strengthen your faith,
—and make you as firm as bedrock.

The Restorer uses many instruments
to perform these tasks,
but personally takes the lead
to oversee and accomplish them.

57: Blueprints
Part 1—Untangling Fish

> *He will **restore** you (I Peter 5:10).*

After God breathed into the bodies, they didn't lie in the dirt or bemoan their past. They rose to their feet!

A Fish Tale

One of Rachel's first obsessions was fish—decorations, toys, movies, bedding, and the mobile hanging in her room. The brightly colored circling fish mesmerized her. One day it fell, leaving a glob of strangled fish. Anyone with guts to tackle it quickly conceded. I'm not exaggerating. This thing was pure havoc. At a New Year's Eve party, Melissa's cousin Pam volunteered to detangle the nightmare. (Must have been a real humdinger of a party.) We warned her of the perilous undertaking, to no avail. While engaged in conversation, she meticulously, patiently, painstakingly restored order to the chaos. Three hours later it was finished! Rachel was elated. We were grateful. It performed according to its function because someone put it back together.

Peter, a man well acquainted with The Restorer, lists four purposes He desires for those face down in the dirt. "In his kindness God called you to share in his eternal glory by means of Christ Jesus. So after you have suffered a little while, he will restore, support and strengthen you, and he will place you on a firm foundation" (1 Peter 5:10). God goes to work on behalf of those wrecked by seasons of havoc, suffering, and struggle. **He uses many instruments to accomplish them, but He personally oversees the process.** This fish story describes the first one—restoration. Some versions prefer *complete* or *perfect*.

Joining two definitions, to restore "is to put a thing in its appropriate position…in order to equip it for future service."[146] Notice the dual functions. The first is to put something together or fix something broken, like *reassembling* the bones or fishermen *mending* nets. It's

---

146 Zodhiates, 904; *Wiersbe's Expository Outlines on the New Testament.* Warren W. Wiersbe. Victor. 1992. (756)

the family *aligning* hundreds of puzzle pieces until they replicate the box, the physical therapist *rehabilitating* a body, and the pastor gently *rebuilding* the broken fragments of a man. It's God magnificently *building* worlds from scratch.[147]

Let's make it personal. It's Him *forming you* in your mother's womb—intimately, profoundly, mysteriously fitting everything in its proper order at the right time. A baby's development in the womb is so precise, utterly genius. Down to the last detail, nothing is left to chance. **If your life falls and shatters, He who put you together in the first place knows how to realign your broken pieces.** The same work of God in creating is what He does when His creation breaks.

Added to building or repairing is equipping. It's put in order…to accomplish something. The bones were reassembled…so the people could live again. The nets were mended…to catch fish. The puzzle was assembled for the family's enjoyment. Every session of therapy enables the body to move better. The broken man is rebuilt to fulfill his purposes. When The Restorer rebuilds a life so it functions as planned, in that sense it is complete, perfect, or restored.

So Unoriginal

This doesn't guarantee life will be exactly as before. That every loss, relationship, dream, body, mind, or plan will be restored to original. A perfect example is Joni Eareckson Tada. A vigorous teenager, she dove into shallow water and hit bottom, making her a quadriplegic. Her free life became severely confined. A girl so full of ability broke into a thousand pieces. Her mind longed to ride horses full speed but her body was imprisoned to a rotisserie apparatus. Her hands longed to paint beautiful pictures but were incapable. The losses Joni experienced are incomprehensible.

During this season she heard the gospel and gave her life to God. Joni believed the One who saved her soul could restore her body. She even told friends she'd be walking next time they saw her. But the healing never came. She eventually concluded—*Maybe God wants to use me in my wheelchair.* He has. Though she's never functioned as before, God arranged her broken pieces in a way only He could do so she could accomplish purposes only she could do.

That chair has refined Joni into the likeness of Jesus and opened

---

147 Hebrews 11:3.

countless opportunities, allowing her to minister to millions worldwide. She's a sought-after speaker, whose words, forged in adversity, flow from joy and grace. She loves God and trusts Him with her life. I believe it's appropriate to say her latter glory exceeds her former.

God's promise is spoken in a future tense following a "little while" of suffering. "Suffering not only helps the believer grow, but it also equips him for future service."[148] Does it happen in someone's lifetime or in the realms of glory? My simple answer: God doesn't put Himself in a box. In heaven's glory—absolutely; in this life— to some extent.

> *Now may the God of peace who brought up our Lord Jesus from the dead, that great Shepherd of the sheep... make you complete in every good work to do His will, working in you what is well-pleasing in His sight, through Jesus Christ, to whom be glory forever and ever. Amen. (Hebrews 13:20-21)*[149]

Point: What are the dual purposes of restoration?
Ponder: God *personally* supervises the restoration process. (Philippians 1:6)
Restoration doesn't always mimic the original. What if God rearranges the pieces to accomplish other purposes?
Prayer: Maybe God wants to use *this* for His purposes. Trust Him.
Practical: Watch a time-lapse video of a baby's development in the womb.
Playlist: *All Things New* by Big Daddy Weave
Pocket:

---

148 *Spirit-Filled Life Bible.* Jack W. Hayford, General Ed. Thomas Nelson. 1991. (1884-5)
149 Dedication: Pam Shilling. Anyone brave enough to tackle that fiasco deserves recognition!

58: Blueprints
Part 2—Well Done Stakes

> He will...**support** you (I Peter 5:10).

My brother Greg, our friends Carl and Pete, and I ventured on an overnight off-road excursion over Easter break of my high school freshman year. We first pitched camp in a beautiful spot nestled among the Pennsylvania pines near a creek. Feeling proud of our forethought, we were free to enjoy the sun's warmth and the picturesque trails. We had a blast, but our lack of camping experience started to show during dinner. The thought of flame-broiled burgers proved idealistic. The single tiny pot made it an extensive process. We eventually retired to our tents. It wasn't like home, but hey, we were rugged outdoorsman.

Sleep eluded us that endless night. I dozed off but woke to a rude feeling. We were not only cold, but wet. The tent's mid-section laid on our bodies under the weight of snow! Two tent stakes were missing, but we assumed it would be fine since it was seventy degrees when we set it up! The mean white intrusion dashed our breakfast plans for bacon and eggs, so we settled for cereal in milk slush. Mmm. Cold, wet, tired, and hungry, we headed home. Future campers, note—*every* tent stake matters!

And check the weather forecast.

Mr. Babyfaith

Our tent needed stakes to keep it from collapsing or blowing away. Likewise, our faith needs stakes in solid ground. This is what Peter (from the Bible, not my camping buddy) meant by "support." It's God's second desire for those who suffer. It's the word Jesus used when commissioning Peter to *strengthen* his brethren.[150] Heavy winds can take us far away. Rugs gets pulled, catapulting us into a flailing freefall. **We need secured, tethered, tied to something immovable.**

This happened at age fifteen during a family crisis. Solid ground

---

150 Luke 22:32.

unexpectedly gave way. My childhood faith, which I had all but cashed in, proved insufficient to hold me steady. Trials often incite a desire to cling to something solid, to find higher ground. Otherwise, we blow wherever the wind takes us, which is often not a good place. This is precisely when many with a small or infant faith turn from it completely. It was perhaps a faith that blamed God, considered Him uncaring or incapable, or was simply unprepared for trials.

Many accusations have been leveled against God, when the reason lies in weak faith that can't hold in a storm. God was not suspect, insufficient, or imperfect; my faith was. Trials are dynamic, pushing toward or pulling away from God. Thankfully, while uprooted, I ran to God in my longing for steadiness. I found anchors in prayer, pastors, the Bible, and godly friends. No longer *have-to* or *should*, I needed and craved them. That's when I asked God to save me. In His grace, He did. My faith grew three sizes that day. When the dust settled, my life miraculously fused with God. I found Someone to whom I could stake my tent. There began *my* track record of God's faithfulness. Third-grade faith became tenth-grade faith. It was maturing, and it was mine. *Support* means:

> *to fix something so that it stands upright and immovable; to support a vine by a stake and an aging man by a stick. It presupposes that the Christians who are to be strengthened are under assault and in danger of becoming uncertain or slothful in their faith or walk. The effect or aim of strengthening is the impregnability of Christian faith despite the troubles which have to be endured.*[151]

We need support to combat the unsteadiness of doubt and confusion. Sometimes faith resembles the sapling's infant roots. It can't weather ferocious winds alone, so a wise groundskeeper tethers it to a strong tree or stake. God longs to shore up doubting hearts with certainty. We echo the cry, "I do believe, but help me overcome my unbelief" (Mark 9:24)! God is way more gracious to doubters than we assume; far less inclined to pitch us out. However, He's not soft on doubt.

---

151 *Theological Dictionary of the New Testament, Vol. 7.* Gerhard Kittel, Editor. Eerdmans. 1974. (653-6)

It rightly merits warning and correction because it's so dangerous. It immobilizes us and blocks untold blessings. It can be the first slip backward. Doubt is like having two contrasting minds. The result is like a boat adrift at sea. **Jesus ministers to disciples with wavering faith. His aim is to secure them.** Thomas the disciple struggled with doubt. Maybe Jesus planned His second post-resurrection visit to the hiding disciples expressly for his sake.

Here are six stakes to support your faith:
- **Worship of God.** Connects you to the greatness of an everlasting God, the unshakeable Rock. Read a psalm. Grab a hymnal. Play a faith-building song. Worship may not include singing at all, but a posture like kneeling, laying prostrate, or raising hands.
- **Words of God.** Connects you to eternal truth, which nurtures and stabilizes faith. Find a devotional, book, or video. Learn about God's promises. Memorize a verse. Marinade in Scripture. There's a consistent relationship throughout the Bible between life and God's words.
- **Wisdom of the godly.** Connects you to mature believers who impart faith and encouragement. They help you up or keep you from falling. They may be your support system until you can stand again. Shy on faith? Borrow someone's.
- **Wings of love.** Far from being childish lyrics, "Jesus Loves Me" has great holding power. A man inspected the charred damage of a brutal fire. When he kicked an unidentifiable ashen lump, little yellow chicks emerged, chirping like crazy! How did they survive? Upon investigation the black lump was their mother. Her sacrificial umbrella of love kept her little ones alive through the fire. Like the mother hen hiding her little ones under her wing, the immovable love of God holds firm through the storm. That's why it's so vital to tether to it when all else shakes in the wind. Find a quiet place and whisper "God loves me!" Or shout it!
- **Wall of faith.** Ephesians 6 employs the imagery of military gear to illustrate the equipment God gives His kids to overcome attacks and threats. One piece is the shield, constructed of solid faith. I liken it to a filter. When doubts, unbelief, and fears fly like destructive arrows at our minds, this shield of faith deflects them and protects us. They are unable to penetrate the faith filter. Be careful. There's also a shield of *un*belief. This negative filter keeps arrows of love, encouragement, and joy from penetrating the heart. I've done this when depressed. Compliments were internally

refused. Scriptures snuffed. Encouragement didn't benefit because I clung to despair. My obstinance was a disservice to them, myself, my Lord, and my family. Two rungs helped me climb out of a specific time of depression. *How is this affecting my family?* This is strangely revolutionary because turmoil can blind us to everybody else. The second: *I'll someday regret that I allowed depression to ruin this season.*

- **Works of the past.** God has an impressive track record. Remember what He's done. It will serve you well. Count your blessings. The psalmists often recollected God's prior deeds to strengthen their faith for the present.

In case you lose one, let me pitch in a freebie.

- **Winds of joy.** "*Don't be dejected and sad, for the joy of the Lord is your strength*" (Nehemiah 8:10)!

Let's stake our faith to the immovable.[152]

> **Point:** Are storms blowing you from God or breeding doubt? God desires to tether you!
> **Ponder** Luke 24. Notice doubt contrasted with belief. In a nutshell, doubt stands frozen while faith runs confidently.
> Would you rather *feel* God's presence or *know* it? One is based on emotion, so we strive for it. The other is based on promise, so we believe it.
> **Prayer:** Rely on the promise of His presence.
> **Practical:** Which stake is most helpful? Tether to at least one to increase your faith.
> **Playlist:** *Praise the Lord* by Russ Taff or Selah
> **Pocket:**

---

152 Dedication: Ben Pratt. You're strong. May your strength strengthen many.

59: Blueprints
Part 3—It'll Make a Mime Talk

> He will...**strengthen** you (I Peter 5:10).

Our team had been in India nearly three weeks. On the final day of ministry, we were weary. Our hearts craved home more than performing mimes at the massive open-air market. I was sick from contaminated water and had no desire to be there. The thought of standing in ninety-five-degree heat felt monumental, let alone playing the part of Satan in our cardinal skit. After we drew a crowd using a crazy drama, I pulled our leader aside and begged him to cover for me. Mick advised me to try, and if needed, would fill in next time. Nothing about me liked his answer.

I made it through but reached physical poverty level. Our leaders guided us to another part of the market and rallied an audience. I asked Mick for help and received the same dreadful reply. I looked forward to lying down, but we just kept going. I finally quit asking. Altogether we ministered in eight places across the sandy grounds. People came for fresh vegetables and fruits and got the gospel too! Many for the first time.

Of all the villages traversed and all the days conducting ministry, this one reached the most. Approximately one thousand people saw the good news depicted by five exhausted laborers. One of my all-time treasured pictures was snapped in that market.[153] On our ride home we thanked God for strengthening such weak vessels to extend His kingdom. A familiar verse rang true, "My grace is sufficient for you, for My strength is made perfect in weakness" (2 Corinthians 12:9 NKJV).

God's third restorative intention is strengthening struggling believers. Peter's pen strokes this word's single usage in the New Testament. It may best be understood by its antonyms: sickly, weary, powerless, destitute, inner poverty, impotence. When the believers were teetering from weariness, Peter sent a letter to steady them. It's easy to compartmentalize our makeup, but our physical, mental, and spiritual components intertwine. An exhausted body easily leads to

---

153 Check it out at *www.keithmc.org*

an exhausted spiritual life. Financial poverty can trigger emotional collapse. Jesus told Peter his spirit was willing to pray but hampered because his flesh was weak.

I visited a sick friend in South Africa. Closed curtains made him barely visible on his bed of suffering. He was in rough shape, unable to perform even the smallest task. We prayed. By the time our team departed for a mission to the north, he led with energy, humor, and enthusiasm.

Wisdom is another source of strength. After signing with Equip Publishing, I drowned in an insurance fiasco. The nightmare lingered, robbing vast amounts of time and mental energy, and threatening us financially. The saga drained me because I didn't know how to proceed. I asked friends to pray three specific things and requested practical pointers. Their advice strengthened me with courage, clarity, and confidence, and hastened closure to the situation.[154]

Point: God desires to strengthen the weak and weary.
Ponder: What strength do you need? Physical, wisdom, spiritual, emotional, financial, all the above?
Prayer: Personalize this for you or a struggling loved one: "He gives power to *the weak* [substitute a name] and strength to *the powerless* [a name]" (Isaiah 40:29).
Practical: Do a workout.
Playlist: *Power of Your Love* by Darlene Zschech
I Feel Jesus by Carman
Pocket:

---

[154] One request was for an *ally* at the insurance company. When I called *Allie* answered! God also honored the other two requests!
Dedication: Mick Veach. Your love for Jesus is unstoppable! Things happen when this guy speaks! *www.ForgeForward.org* (Don't bother asking him to perform your mime role for you!)

60: Blueprints
Part 4—Hard Rock

> *He will…place you on a **firm foundation** (I Peter 5:10).*

Judas betrayed Jesus and Peter denied him. What about the other ten? Each pledged loyalty to the death, and each abandoned Him. How did Andrew cope? How did Matthew face sorrow's restless nights? How did Bartholomew process failure's heavy turmoil? Amazingly, Jesus *pre-planned* to restore these who failed Him. Before "run away, save yourself" entered their minds during Jesus' arrest, **He already took measures so they could rise from the graves of regret into the graces of renewal.** God isn't surprised by our errors, so He doesn't react flippantly. He intended to lift His fallen ones long before they fell.

What solution did Jesus arrange to restore the other disciples?

The answer, so characteristic of Jesus, is surprising:

Peter.

The guy who crumbled? Yes. This restored disciple would make them strong in God's grace. Like Ezekiel, Peter wrote to struggling exiles to solidify their faith. "My purpose in writing is to encourage you and assure you that what you are experiencing is truly part of God's grace for you. Stand firm in this grace" (1 Peter 5:12). He took Jesus' assignment to shepherd the people seriously, reminding them:

God chose you.

Struggles are natural.

Suffering refines faith and love for Jesus.

Live humbly under God and watch for the devil's tricks.

At the end of his letter, he reveals God's blueprints for struggling servants. May these four elements of God's restorative graces encourage you to not give up. Let Him do this work. After suffering, God may use you in unlikely ways to help others. Jesus still fashions stones into bedrock.

Strengthened to Strong

After the relative "little while," God restores the broken, supports the floundering, and strengthens the weary. But that's not all. He settles—makes firm like a foundation. I've wondered why this isn't listed first. Don't you start with the foundation? It seems backward. However, if something is broken, you first gather the pieces and make them usable (restore), then make sure it's stable (support) and strong (strengthen), and *then* fasten or cement into place (make firm).

God isn't just setting you on a firm foundation. Your life becomes a firm foundation! You've encountered people made steadfast by persevering through suffering and standing against headwinds. They're the ones you seek when you're shaken. Their words and demeanor are solid, upon which you can rest. These are the great crowd of witnesses in the hall of faith, of whom it was said, "Their weakness was turned to strength. They became strong in battle" (Hebrews 11:34). Peter said, "You are coming to Christ, who is the living cornerstone of God's temple…and you are living stones that God is building into his spiritual temple" (1 Peter 2:4-5). Christ is the cornerstone and everyone gets plumbed into place based on Him. He makes those built *on* this foundation a sturdy part *of* the foundation!

"Be strong and immovable" (1 Corinthians 15:58). He's making you firm bedrock. The previous work is God strengthening you. This is **God making you strong.** Your life is cemented to the immovable Rock of Christ. Cement requires the right mixture with the right amount of time. It can't be hurried or delayed, but once set it becomes permanent. You can walk on it or drive cars over it. It's going nowhere! God wants permanent living stones on which He can build other living stones.

After writing the previous paragraph, I had to stew in it more. It ignited praise, which turned to thanksgiving for the bedrock saints God placed in my life. Some for a moment, others for a lifetime. All of them weathered difficult storms and faced confusing battles. **They could've given up, crumbled down, cashed in, or checked out. Instead, they stood.** Maybe not always with courage, joy, or stamina, but the standing made them strong.

I don't hear much whining, bitterness, or complaint from their lips or see doubt, faltering, or panic in their steps. Their lives are sure because they remain on a secure foundation, confirming Jesus' words: "Anyone who listens to my teaching and follows it is wise, like a person who builds a house on solid rock. Though the rain comes in torrents and the floodwaters rise and the winds beat against that house, it won't collapse because it is built on bedrock" (Matthew 7:24-25).

The strengthened become strong.[155]

> **Point:** Keep standing! (See Ephesians 6:10-18)
> **Ponder:** Wow! Psalm 18 combines all four themes. If weak or shaken, this P18 vitamin supports good faith health. So good it's found in two places! Where's the other?
> Read *I Peter*. What encouragement and strength can you glean?
> **Prayer:** Thank God for your bedrock saints.
> **Practical:** Thank or encourage a bedrock saint.
> **Playlist:** *Steadfast* by Maverick City
> *Where There is Faith* by 4Him
> **Pocket:**

---

[155] Dedication: In memory of Mary Corey, one of my favorite *bedrock saints*.

PART 9:
The Restorer *spearheads* kingdom movements through once-broken pieces now made *useful*.

They…stood up on their feet—a great army (Ezekiel 37:10).

The Restorer uses those who endure
seasons of brokenness
to fill vital roles in fulfilling
Jesus' mission.

The advancement of God's kingdom owes much
to the untold masses who once thought
they were broken beyond repair.

61: Special Forces

*They all came to life and stood up on their feet—a **great army** (Ezekiel 37:10).*

For our summer kid's program, we purchased a complete curriculum kit, as many churches do. The theme was fun. The stage rocked. The lessons well-done. But I questioned the videos. "The kids probably think they're stupid," I confided in Melissa after the first night. "You have to use them now. They'll expect it," she wisely advised. Against my personal tastes, I consented.

Melissa was right. The kids anticipated each night's video. More importantly, those videos opened opportunities to teach the children, some who had no understanding of Jesus. Of all my children's ministry memories, the dialogue following those movies ranks at the top. I shudder to think I nearly trashed them because they didn't meet *my* preferences. It's mind-blowing who God uses in His Kingdom army. Why would God use *them*? Where could He use *me*? How could He use *us*?

What an exhilarating transformation Ezekiel witnessed! Those bones were *dead*, but rose again—blessed, smiling, grateful, alive! The prophet lends one observation of the standing masses: they resembled a great army. An army is a community banded together under a commander for a shared commission. Let's start with the community of soldiers. Who's included?

*God Can Use **Them**?*

The Bible shares unusual war stories and unlikely war heroes. An anonymous woman with a massive stone, killer aim, and the law of gravity saved her city from a madman. Another woman downed a nasty commander with her cool wit, warm milk, and tool know-how. Let's just say something got spiked. Gideon, lowest rank in his tribe (at least in his mind), rose to position of warrior-general. Every step he took the odds were against him. Really against him. He routed a vicious army four hundred times bigger using items perfect for a tiki party. **Well, God won the battle, but chose to do it with smallness.** We would've overlooked many of God's "soldiers" or "instruments" as useless, unfit, or unclean: a donkey, a fisherman, a prostitute, a demonic madman, a widow, a bush, a stone, a star. God insists on choosing, calling, and using *less-thans*.

God taught Peter a lesson in a vision during devotions one afternoon. After being instructed to eat non-kosher, he resisted firmly. He never ate unclean things and wouldn't contaminate himself now. God unearthed a deeply held, religiously-generated value in Peter, and wanted to replace it. Peter classified a group of people as inherently dirty. *God is for certain people. Others are outside. I'm OK with this, and so is God.* This belief so solidified in Peter the Spirit repeated the order two more times before announcing, "What God has cleansed, no longer consider unholy" (Acts 10:15 NASB). God restructured Peter's belief system, which had immediate and lasting ramifications.

God Can Use **Me?**

Sometimes that's how we label others; sometimes that's how we see ourselves. Those in wastelands naturally question whether God could use unclean, damaged vehicles like them. **If Jesus can enlist saliva as an agent of grace, He can use humans created in His image.** To piggyback on the Spirit's revelation to Peter, God may say, "Rise up! I want to use you for my glory!" You may retort, "I'm too unclean!" To which God replies, "What I have cleansed, no longer consider unclean."

God thrives on enlisting the ordinary and the least likely to accomplish historic feats. We feel the burden to be qualified when God comes a calling, but He consistently chooses the unqualified on purpose. In fact, it appears disqualification *is the qualification* in a try-to-figure-GOD-out kind of way. As one meme says, "When God called you, He factored in your stupidity!" Maybe that's why Paul bragged about weaknesses and impediments, not strengths and accomplishments.

God Can Use **Us?**

In 2003 I experienced a church service unlike any other. Many gathered from Argentina's nearby urban neighborhoods to praise God. To this upstate New Yorker, the Sunday evening felt more like June than March, but who was I to complain? We sang old hymns and new choruses, then enjoyed an array of special music. This is when it became so indelibly unique. A youth choir vibrantly sang a modern favorite as the congregation clapped. We feasted on peace as a quiet, middle-aged man played his flute. A trio of teens gave their electric guitars a hefty workout as they cranked a Christian rock song. Smiling senior women harmonized a cappella with a classic hymn.

Each special was extremely different and meaningful, but I never saw a disapproving glare or heard a whispering complaint. When the sermon concluded, the senior ladies bowed in solemn prayer next to the teenagers loudly crying out to God. **It's the greatest modeling of loving Christ and one another, despite vast differences, I've ever witnessed.** The piano, the electric guitar, the clapping hands, the flute, the vocal cords...all had a place. My focus is not worship styles or musical instruments, but God's favorite instruments—individuals created in His image, saved by His grace, serving by His Spirit. Add them together and you have a phenomenal organization called the Church.

It's like one body with many parts. Hands serve differently than ears. The spleen shouldn't disqualify itself by thinking *I'm not feet, so I don't belong*. If your spleen tries to mimic feet, I don't know what will happen but I'm sure it won't work! Neither should the spleen say, "Hey, elbow! Yeah, I'm talking to both of ya. You can't (whatever a spleen does) so you don't belong to God or the rest of us." I like my elbows. I don't want to trade them for spleens. All who believe in Christ are part of His "body." *You're* a part. *I'm* a part. *We're* a part. **You may be a little toe, a lung, a lip, or the liver. No matter what, you and I, and we together, can glorify God and benefit others.**[156]

> **Point:** Do you consider yourself or others in the "uncrowd"? Too undone, unclean, unfit, or unqualified?
> **Ponder** what "part of the body" you think God created you to be. Do you wish you were something different?
> What's the most surprising thing you've seen God use?
> **Prayer:** For your church.
> **Practical:** Thank God for your weaknesses and impediments. Expect others to have them too!
> **Playlist:** *The Army of the Lord* by Harvest
> **Pocket:**

---

156 Dedication: Caleb "Biz" Bislow, one of the Kingdom's elite special forces. Author of *Dangerous*. Founder of <u>www.unusualsoldiers.org</u>

62: The Shepherd Wears Flannel

*Day after day **more men joined David** until he had a great army, like the army of God (I Chronicles 12:22).*

I can show you the spot. I was retrieving a basketball from the stage in our church gymnasium when the new youth pastor arrived. He didn't see me, but that distant interaction dramatically affected this floundering thirteen-year-old. I saw a big, bearded man sporting boots, jeans, red flannel jacket, and warm smile. Pastor Jeff looked like a friendly lumberjack as he shook hands with the circling teenagers. He stood strong, confident, happy. Everything I was not. God brought me a shepherd, and with him, stability and hope.

School of Kings

David lived in limbo ten years after God told him he'd be the next king. That uncomfortable season groomed a godly man into a powerful king. It was not wasted time, though sometimes he just tried staying alive. Many nights he questioned if he'd see the sunrise, let alone the throne. Maybe you were called to some special work. Maybe someone close to God spoke words sounding the bell of your divine purposes. Maybe a need gripped your heart during an unusual time of prayer, after which you told your closest friends, "God just spoke to me!" God electrified your soul, then went silent, like He forgot, misspoke, or retracted the offer because you blew it.

This appears the norm as much as the exception in Bible stories. **Patience is imperative because we won't receive everything from God if we can't wait or persist.** Not everything comes via live stream or drive-through. "The LORD is good to those who wait for Him, to the soul who seeks Him" (Lamentations 3:25 NKJV). Delay doesn't imply expiration. I offer no blanket statement here. It would be easy to say, "Your breakthrough is around the corner!" Perhaps it is. I pray it will be for many. While I can't predict every situation, I know God's call for you right now is at least to trust and remain faithful.

Sometimes God only says *what not to do*.[157] David didn't always have clear direction for his next step. One time he tried aligning with a foreign leader but quickly realized it was a mistake. When it morphed into a life-threatening scenario, he pretended to be a drooling lunatic. The king's reply is hilarious, "Must you bring me this madman? We already have enough of them around here" (1 Samuel 21:14)! He escaped to a cave, where the broken tones of Psalm 142 were likely penned.[158]

Army of Misfits

We don't know how long David resided in this cave alone, but powerful things happened there. His family came. How welcoming that reunion must have been! Then hundreds of men showed up and offered to help David! At the proper time, God provided the future king with an army. Mind you, they were a most unusual army—not exactly prime candidates. Most generals would've dismissed them, but David received them. **Their only defining characteristic? Not one had it all together.**

"Then others began coming—men who were in trouble or in debt or who were just discontented—until David was the captain of about 400 men" (1 Samuel 22:2). The Message is raw: "All who were down on their luck came around—losers and vagrants and misfits of all sorts." Some were broken in a million pieces or had gotten in trouble. Others a bankrupted mess, longing to get on their feet again. Others had crusty souls embittered by disappointment, injustice, and failure. The sweetness of life had long passed. Not one perfect person came. Only those in need of restoration. David apparently took them in, built them up, and gave them purpose and community.

A king needs an army. Broken lives need a king.

Making News

A short time later, while watching the news, they heard about a nearby town targeted by the Philistines, of whom Goliath the giant hailed. Whom teen-aged David gave a thorough beat-down. These bullies were snatching their friends' lunch money. Holy anger triggered David, who asked God if he should do something. Now that's the

---

157 Acts 16:6-7.
158 This one-minute read tells the state of his soul.

way to watch the news! Detecting *yes*, he gathered his ragtag band, who were not exactly a well-oiled, fearless fighting machine. They countered, "We're afraid...here. We certainly don't want to go... fight the whole Philistine army" (1 Samuel 23:3)! *We're nervous in our living room watching TV. We don't wanna go to the epicenter of trouble!* **They were wimpy. Their leader was a victorious fighter.** His bravery sufficed for all of them; his courage could carry them.

He knew they had issues. They didn't ring with confidence or consider themselves capable of greatness. I love David's approach to their vulnerability. He didn't squawk like a chicken in their faces or lather the guilt. Knowing they were spiritually illiterate he revealed his secret—closeness to God. Though he already heard God he asked again, and in so doing taught his army to pray.

God instructed them to go, then promised His presence and victory. They reluctantly launched their inaugural mission trip and ended up liberating a town and replenishing its food supply! They must have been stoked! *That was awesome! God used us!* Ironically, most townsfolk didn't appreciate their heroism, but two hundred men showed their gratitude by enlisting in his army. None of them had it all together either, but their band of imperfect soldiers now numbered six hundred!

As I write, I sense God stirring. I think about another general—a one-of-a-kind descendent of King David, before whom every world leader will buckle their knees. **He too is raising an army from many who are in trouble, in debt, and unhappy with life.** All have issues; not one has it all together. He takes them in and builds them up. The unworthy belong. The unqualified learn. Those blinded by their own issues awaken to God's workings around them. The insignificant become the catalyst for others to join.

Jesus is assembling an unusual army and commissioning it to a massive assignment. His bravery transforms fear. His knowledge illumines ignorance. His passion ignites for harvest. His community provides space. Like a weak teenager with a strong leader, He is what we aren't. He has what we lack.[159]

---

[159] Dedication: Dwight Robertson, life-long lover of Jesus' mission. Book this passionate speaker! *www.ForgeForward.org*

Point: Are you in trouble, indebted, or discontented? Do you need a strong "leader"?

Ponder Matthew 28:18-20. Is it time to enlist or re-enlist in Jesus' mission? You don't have to have it all together. Jesus does. You don't have to be perfect. Jesus is.

Prayer: "Lord, include me in your army. Build me. Teach me. Spend time with me. Activate me. Go with me." (Isaiah 6:8)

Practical: Do you need a good leader? Ask God to help you find one.

Playlist: *Do Something* by Matthew West
More Than Conquerors or *Revival Anthem* by Rend Collective

Pocket:

63: Marching Orders

Therefore go…and be sure of this: ***I am with you always,*** *even to the end of the age (Matthew 28:19-20).*

Pastor Jeff cared for us teenaged sheep. He pulled us in, put up with our stupidity, and encouraged us. But he also pushed us—sometimes literally. He apparently didn't want wimpy youth in his group. He certainly pushed us spiritually, wanting us to get hold of God. I remember him mention a verse that "blew his mind," and it made me look it up, although I never found it. We wore his spit as he pounded the keyboard and shouted, "Be bold! Be strong! For the Lord your God is with you!" We learned to sit toward the back.

He called us to an all-night prayer and praise rally. Wow did God work miracles that night! There was something else Jeff pushed us to—mission. He served as the local high school football chaplain, met us Tuesdays before school to pray for unsaved friends, and sent us into our city to share our faith. **I not only needed a shepherd to pull me in, but I needed one to push me out.** Like David with his army. Like Jesus with His Church.

The Loathsome Foursome

There's a story of four guys united by skin disease. Sounds like an exciting group, doesn't it? They were barely alive, just like their city. An invading army cut off their resources, leaving them extremely desperate. People traded silver for a cup of donkey poo. Mothers cooked their children for sustenance. Brutal times. These four lived alone, their contagious condition further isolating them. It was the worst of times to depend on charity.

One evening they decided to sell themselves to the enemy for some vittles. I love their no-nonsense approach: "Why should we sit here waiting to die? We will starve if we stay here…we will starve if we go back [in the city]. So we might as well…surrender. If they let us live, so much the better. But if they kill us, we would have died anyway" (2 Kings 7:3-4). Off they go at twilight, likely to their end. Figuratively they were dead, but God had other plans. He was about to make *them* an army!

Before we continue this epic story, how useful, powerful, strategic, or noteworthy would you rate this "army"? I think .5 out of 100 is fair. Yet God did something utterly extraordinary as they neared enemy headquarters. "The Lord had caused the army to hear the clatter of speeding chariots and the galloping of horses and the sounds of a great army approaching" (2 Kings 7:6). Their enemy panicked and abandoned camp! Horses, food, and money free for the taking. Not bad when you're expecting sinister eulogies.

The dumbfounded men enjoyed their first all-you-can-eat buffet, capped with wine and relaxation. For entertainment they deposit armloads of gold and silver in the first bank of dirt. It's the greatest day ever. After a while they muse, *I know we're awesome, but this would be more fun with a bunch of people!*[160] There was so much provision they felt guilty. "This is not right. This is a day of good news, and we aren't sharing it with anyone" (2 Kings 7:9)! *While we party like animals, our country is at death's door.* They head into the night to invite 'em to the bounty. By morning, the people rush out like it's California in the 1840s.

God invisibly accompanied them on their spontaneous trip and used them more than they could have imagined. Those decimated men simply walked, but God walked with them, and the enemy heard a mighty army! When Jesus commissioned the disciples, He promised His continuous presence. **Every mission step we take He steps with us. We never step alone.**

An interesting notation bears repeating. While concocting their plan they said, "We might as well surrender." *Surrender.* The unreserved offering of life to another. In this case, a no-good enemy. The history of God's people is laden with examples of those who surrendered to Him from their lowest place. With nothing to lose or offer they gave their lives to Him. This has been the turning point in many a story. These men abandoned themselves to ruthless villains, and I struggle surrendering to a merciful God? "I plead with you to give your bodies to God because of all he has done for you. Let them be a living and holy sacrifice—the kind he will find acceptable. This is truly the way to worship him" (Romans 12:1).

What else will God do with dead-end lives willingly surrendered to Him?[161]

---

160 I embellished a little.
161 Dedication: Jeff Bennett. Thanks for showing up at the right time!

Point: Jesus pulls in *and* pushes out!
Ponder the confidence in knowing God walks with you *every* step in mission.
"This is not right. This is a day of good news, and we aren't sharing it with anyone" (2 Kings 7:9)!
Prayer: Lord, raise up laborers for Your harvest! (Matthew 9:37-38)
Practical: Read, watch, or do something about Jesus' mission. (Example: *www.forgeforward.org* or their app)
To who or what will you surrender your life?
Playlist: *Control* by Tenth Avenue North.
Gracefully Broken by Matt Redman (feat. Tasha Cobbs Leonard)
Pocket:

Part 10:
The Restorer *specializes in rewarding* broken pieces who entrusted themselves to Him *unashamedly.*

Then you will know that I, the LORD, have spoken, and I have done what I said. Yes, the LORD has spoken (Ezekiel 37:14)!

Nobody likes the wilderness,
but those who remain with God through it
often emerge better.

Living streams flowing through waste places
transform the broken into the blessed.

From scattered bones to a standing army—
God is a powerful Restorer!

64: Bullheaded Blessings

> *Springs will gush forth in the wilderness,*
> *and streams will water the wasteland (Isaiah 35:6).*

My family was hired to transport a dog from Ohio to California. The southerly route linked us to Indy, Tulsa, and Albuquerque, as well as landmarks like The Arch, historic Route 66, and Cadillac Ranch. The continent sizzled that week, except for Venice Beach, which was sixty-five and drizzly. On a gorgeous Thursday morning we departed Grand Canyon's rim for California's ocean. The Mazda's digital display read 104 (degrees, not mph). Chuckling at the unusual sight, and anticipating its peak, I took a picture at 112. But it wasn't done. The rays of the sun finally climaxed at 120!

After periods of empty expanses, we descended into a massive valley and entered Bullhead City,[162] a bustling little casino city where Arizona greets Nevada and California. It brought an unexpected, welcome change of pace and scenery. Crossing the Colorado River mesmerized me. Amid the stony terrain and burning tentacles of the sun lay a luscious blue oasis adorned with palm trees and inviting sand. Families splashed in the refreshing waters as jet-skis shot their aqua tails high into the air. It was an incredible scene, one I could've cherished longer.

As the desert sun raged unmercifully, these blessed ones found a tantalizing river. This scene embodies the imagery captured by God's prophet Isaiah:

> *The wasteland will rejoice and blossom with spring crocuses. Yes, there will be an abundance of flowers and singing and joy! There the LORD will display his glory, the splendor of our God. With this news, strengthen those who have tired hands, and encourage those who have weak knees. Say to those with fearful hearts, "Be strong, and do not fear, for your God is coming to destroy your enemies.*

---

162 Don't ask your spouse if this is where their family originated.

> *He is coming to save you." And when he comes, he will open the eyes of the blind and unplug the ears of the deaf. The lame will leap like a deer, and those who cannot speak will sing for joy! Springs will gush forth in the wilderness, and streams will water the wasteland"* (excerpts from Isaiah 35:1-6).

What God did in parched wilderness places, He can do in our desolate seasons. The desert may surprise us with trees of beauty, springs of satisfaction, and the sound of saints getting closer to God. New vision, perspective, and blessings often emerge from barren ground, though rarely perceived at the time.

Nutrients

The dry bones were not exactly wonderful before their descent. Sure, they had stuff and a reputable religious veneer, but look what they *gained* in the valley—the Shepherd's presence and Ezekiel's ministry. Skilled hands reattaching scattered bones and adding muscles for God's purposes. Fresh graces covering their past, clothing them in dignity and honor. Holy wind reviving them and raising them to their feet. **They were better because of the wilderness.**

Many stories include a line like, "It was the worst season of my life. I didn't know if I'd make it. But I wouldn't trade it because God showed me this and did that." Countless jewels hide in the desert, like those sparkling blue waters I witnessed. Some treasures are only found in the hidden waters of wasteland places. Many need these nutrients, but they're often only brought to them in the lives of those who endured the desert.

> *How precious is your unfailing love, O God! All humanity finds shelter in the shadow of your wings. They are filled with food from your house, and you allow them to drink from the river of your delicacies. For you are the one who gives and sustains life. Pour out your love on those who love you; give justice to those with honest hearts* (Psalm 36:8-10).

"It is in the quiet crucible of your personal, private sufferings that your noblest dreams are born and God's greatest gifts are given in compensation for what you've been through."[163]

> **Point:** The desert can be a place of blessing.
> **Ponder:** "You don't understand now what I am doing, but someday you will" (John 13:7). If you question what good can come out of your circumstances, Jesus' statement gives perspective and hope.
> **Prayer:** "You have allowed me to suffer much hardship, but you will restore me to life again and lift me up from the depths of the earth" (Psalm 71:20).
> **Practical:** Enjoy a stream.
> **Playlist:** *Graves into Gardens* by Elevation
> *Desert Rose* by White Heart.
> **Pocket:**

---

163 *How Great Thou Art DVD*. Wintley Phipps. Gaither Music. 2007. Dedication: Tim Heyer, your friendship is a joy! Let's meet in Albuquerque sometime!

65: Restored to Greater

> *You will **restore me to even greater** honor*
> *and comfort me once again.*
> *Then I will praise you…because you*
> *are faithful to your promises*
> *(Psalm 71:21-22).*

I never imagined seeing these sights again. I was a million and nineteen miles from home recognizing trees, buildings, and roads. Four years ago, our mission team spent a weekend here in Gulu, Uganda. Only it's better, stronger. Maybe I am too. I had been through a desert since then. The sun rose dutifully at 6:00. Four of us ministers from western NY partnered with leaders in Africa to conduct a three-day conference for hundreds of pastors and leaders. *Who am I?* sent shivers of doubt through me, but three words rebutted this natural inclination—*God chose me*. I counseled myself: *Just enjoy. You'll never have this day again. Don't waste it with worry.* **I shoved my wrinkled insecurities in the hotel drawer and put on fresh joy and faith.**

After breakfast our team boarded the vans and soon said *farewell* to paved roads and *hello* to the signature orange dirt. Tidy plots housed thatch-roofed huts. Mango trees boasted their bounty. Children in bright uniforms waved. As we rounded a sweeping curve our host joked, "This is our Florida!" I've never seen anything like it. Hundreds of palm trees speckled the vast, lush countryside!

We turned down a little road passing industrious farmers, another school, and more smiling children. If not for four-wheel-drive, we might still be in the mud! The slightest resemblance of a trail slipped through grasses as tall as the van. I relished all this, yet curious what place out here could host our conference. Minutes later dual iron gates opened for us as jubilation permeated the atmosphere. The spacious school grounds, with its colorful buildings situated like a horseshoe, was perfect. The backdrop of serene, rolling hills greeted me with shalom. I felt *welcomed*. A line from a long-forgotten poem flooded my mind:

Oh, to be shut in with God!

After an intriguing conversation with the leaders, we entered the lively sanctuary. Our seats of honor in the front corner placed me next to an open window. The view outside and the celebration inside elicited inexpressible joy! As I flashbacked recent years, gratitude lifted to The Restorer. **I had considered my life a dead-end. Now I'm worshiping with hundreds of God's people in rural Africa!** After the opening we scattered to various break-out sessions. Roy wore his counselor hat and listened to individuals pour out their hearts. Mel bounded off with the pastors. Dan gathered with his favorites, the youth.

I stayed with the remaining adults. Just one problem—I don't speak Acholi and didn't have a translator. A few minutes later I met Pastor Daniel, and I knew we were in for a good time. We smiled, shook hands, and hugged. It's amazing how people from different cultures can bond immediately simply because they belong to Jesus! Together we spoke with unusual freedom the message deposited in my heart for these beautiful people. The seventy responded with shouting and clapping.

An hour later we concluded. The schedule said it was lunchtime and I didn't want to delay that. After consulting with the organizers, Pastor Daniel smiled, "We have another hour! Your audience wants you to keep going." I knew I had the best group. *What more do I have to say?* I thought as I agreed, confident in the Spirit's continued help. Daniel perceived my need for a refresh, so he handed me a bottle of water and encouraged me to sit while he led in a song.

God graced us another hour. Gleanings from study mingled with spontaneous illustrations from the African context. When I neared completion of a sentence, the next thought came with great clarity. I've never preached like this. The Spirit so clearly led that I was ministered to as much as anybody! That evening it took thirty minutes to record all those new insights. People were obviously praying, for it far surpassed my abilities. The eager, receptive hearts of the audience also played a key role.

As I floated to lunch, I mused: *That was the most fulfilling thing I've ever done in ministry!* The next day a pastor said, "That message was a historic day in my life." It moved me. During my dark nights, I doubted my usefulness in God's kingdom. I felt too far gone, too depleted, to ever have anything to give. I share this because it happened after I considered my life permanently dried up. **What a miracle that God restored my scattered bones and called me to such a rewarding assignment.** Again, I don't propose a formula or sell a guarantee. I don't know your future or the Lord's directives, but often the greater rewards occur after the darkest valleys.

The years after I felt worthless, useless, and hopeless have hosted my favorite vacations, richest laughter, and even this book. Not every day is glorious. Not every insecurity vanished. I'm not immune to depression, laziness, or selfishness. In some ways I feel less than before. Maybe that's how Jacob felt with his newly developed limp. Sometimes I miss aspects of the younger me I can't seem to recover. In other ways I'm hopeful God has made me better. Regardless, here's my observation—the wise and gracious Restorer rarely restores us to original.

But to greater.

I'll never forget those three days when God called me to a glorious task past the dotted palm trees. What if God's greatest days and assignments for you lie ahead? God makes good soldiers out of dry bones. Regardless of your past, a post exists for you. Everyone gets in on this. **Your restoration may result in a historic day for someone else.**

"Better Than New"

Maybe Mom said this after kissing a boo-boo. Or Dad after repairing a broken toy, a doctor following surgery, or a mechanic after lowering your vehicle to the ground. We spoke of Job's horrific struggles, but his story doesn't end there. The last chapter sharply contrasts the previous forty-one. **His testimony is ultimately one of restoration, not loss.** It's a bulwark of hope, proving the Almighty can reach His own in the lowest places and raise them higher than ever.

Job descended into the valley as gold. He emerged as pure gold. Notice how he grew in His experience with God: "'I had only heard about you before, but now I have seen you with my own eyes. I take back everything I said, and I sit in dust and ashes to show my repentance.' The LORD restored his fortunes. In fact, the LORD gave him twice as much as before! So the LORD blessed Job in the second half of his life even more than in the beginning" (Job 42: 5-6, 10, 12).

St. Augustine asked, "What is it, therefore, that goes on within the soul, since it takes greater delight if things that it loves are found or restored to it than if it had always possessed them? Everywhere a greater joy is preceded by a greater suffering."[164]

---

164 *Confessions*. Augustine of Hippo. 398 AD.
　　Dedication: Joseph Nsubuga and Daniel Olara, men of wisdom, encouragement, and power. What a privilege to partner with you in the Gospel.

Point: God's best may lie ahead. Expect His presence in your future.
Ponder: Have you considered Job's story as one of restoration?
Think of a time St. Augustine's remark proved true.
Prayer: Ask God to help you or another endure difficulty, that *the greater* may be experienced.
Practical: Make something better than new!
Fill in the blank: I don't want to waste this day with _____.

Playlist: *Restored* by Jeremy Camp
My Tribute by Andrae Crouch
Pocket:

66: Saving the Best for Last

> *Still, I know that God lives—*
> *the One who gives me back my life—*
> *and I'll see him (Job 19:25-26 MSG).*

Many stories in this book arose from mediocre seasons, difficult days, insignificant things, and despised places. Some are mine. Some the stories others lived. While sharing the common thread of brokenness, they also point to a Restorer competent and compassionate enough to put broken pieces back together! **I wrote from this hope-filled vision: many of the future's greatest masterpieces feel broken beyond repair tonight.** They just need to get through this trying season first.

40 hours, 40 days, or 40 years from now:
- **Some of the most infectious smiles** will be worn by those currently occupying a pit of depression or addiction.
- **Some of the most gracious ministers** presently wrestle with worthlessness, abandonment, or sin.
- **Some of the most influential leaders** feel stuck, insignificant, or lost.
- **Some of the most productive** are wandering around a wilderness.
- **Some of the most vibrant lives** currently wish theirs would end.
- **Some of the most fulfilled** are reeling from loss right now.
- **Some of the most God-like** lie completely broken in dark places tonight.
- Yes, some of the world's greatest lives will be those who have been picked back up.

In a one-time-only event, Jesus takes Peter, James, and John up a mountain, where they get an exclusive peek of His radiant divinity. "As the men watched, Jesus' appearance was transformed so that His face shone like the sun, and His clothes became as white as light" (Matthew 17:2). Suddenly Moses and Elijah appear! They affirm Jesus' identity as the Chosen One whose approaching death and subsequent resurrection will fulfill the salvation God promised in the Old Testament. By no means the main point of this experience, I'd like to focus on these two guests.

Moses. His powerful life detoured down some dead-end backroad, ruining any chances for significance. His calling seemed hijacked or canceled until God encountered him! One day, long after Moses took his last breath, he had one last earthly task, more special than anything he'd ever done. God personally selected him to minister to Jesus! This honorable occasion existed only because he stayed—let The Restorer put his broken pieces back together in His time. Though God used him tremendously, his best moment and greatest privilege was seeing Jesus face to face!

Then there's Elijah, so desperate, deflated, and depressed he wanted to die. He had no hope or peace for his future until God met him in a secret place and reactivated him. The pinnacle, however, had to be when the Father called him out of retirement to stand with His Son on a mountain.

What if God wants to restore you to greater things? While we don't know what life holds, someday all who persevere will stand triumphantly with Jesus in heaven! We will shout His praises, be embraced by His love, and thank Him for raising us up. And probably say, "I can't believe I get to do this!" All because a compassionate God still tells wilderness wanderers, "I am going to put breath into you and make you live again!" (Ezekiel 37:5)!

- The Restorer still *spies* wasteland valleys for broken lives!
- He still *sprouts hope* inside the hopeless!
- He still *speaks worth* over scattered bones!
- He still *spends time* connecting sinews!
- He still *spurs muscles* toward divine activity!
- He still *spreads new skin* over dirt, guilt, and shame!
- He still *sparks winds* into the Doldrums!
- He still *springs* us to our feet and *steadies*!
- He still *sends armies* of restored people to *spearhead* kingdom pursuits!
- He still *specializes* in rewarding those who stay with Him!

I've chosen to conclude where the vision does. Three times God tells Ezekiel about something powerful taking place during the process of restoration. The third time marks the grand finale, "Then you will know that I, the LORD, have spoken, and I have done what I said. Yes, the LORD has spoken!" Hope. Worth. Calling. Cleaning. Wind. Faith. Grace. Resuscitation. Sending. These things and more are performed *every day* in God's Restoration Shop! Those who experience them experience God Himself. And will know Him like never before.

May God put untold masses of broken pieces back together again!!![165]

> **Point:** Which of the ten "marks of restoration" resonates most?
> **Ponder:** Many future greats currently trudge a bewildering wilderness.
> **Prayer:** Lord, keep me till I see You face to face!
> **Practical:** Do something!
> **Playlist:** *I Can Only Imagine* by Mercy Me
> *There Will Be a Day* by Jeremy Camp
> *Eternity* by Brian Doerksen
> **Pocket:**

---

165 Dedication: *YOU,* dear reader! May the day you meet Jesus face-to-face be THE GREATEST EVER!

Bonus Features

Biblical Proportions

Equipped with Navigation

Bible quotes in *God's Restoration Shop* are followed by an "address" in parenthesis. This includes a name and two numbers separated by a colon. Think of it as a town name, street number, and house number. For example, (John 3:16) would be in the town of John, on Third Street, in house number 16. The name is the name of the book within the Bible and is the first thing to locate. The Bible consists of 66 individual books written by dozens of authors (under God's inspiration) over 1600 years. Its consistency and preservation showcase its unparalleled uniqueness.

A table of contents lists the books in order, starting with *Genesis*. If reading digitally, simply use the search option. It's OK if you can't pronounce the name or are unsure of its meaning. Sometimes it's the author's name, like *John* or *Ezekiel*. Sometimes it's the original recipients' name or location. For example, *Romans* was written to Christians in Rome; *1 and 2 Timothy* to a guy named Timothy. Sometimes it reflects the subject, like *Proverbs* or *Kings*. Occasionally there are sequels so a 1, 2, or 3 precedes the name. A dash refers to multiple chapters, such as John 3-4.

Once you've found the town (book), the first number is the chapter (street), typically in large or bold font. If looking for John 3:16, find the bold 3, then scroll down until you find verse 16 (house). You'll read, "For God so loved the world that he gave his one and only Son, that whoever believes in him will not perish but have eternal life" (John 3:16 NIV).

Three capitalized letters following the address refer to a particular version of the Bible. Don't stress over these. These are translations from the original languages of the Bible—Hebrew and Greek—into English. They have different purposes, such as readability, study, literal, or even modern vernacular. References without these letters default to the New Living Translation (NLT). I chose it because it reads easily, like a modern conversation or story. If you prefer another, use it!

I'm a visual learner. When a story mentions a house on a hill, a lame man invited to a king's table, or fire-grilled breakfast on a seashore, I envision, observe, and wonder why certain contents are noted. Hidden secrets and glorious insights are often embedded in minuscule details! When studying I often write on a fresh page: *Who. When. Where. Why.*

What. How. Then I fill in the blanks from the passage as best I can. I engage my imagination, as you will notice, but don't equate it with the authority of God's words. Especially with the story of Moses, I use creative license, as if an autobiography. Think of it as a novel based on a true story. **I don't bring the Bible to life or make it alive. It's already alive.** I just need to get into it and let it get into me.

When reading the Bible, arrive on the scene like a detective and look around. Immerse yourself, meet the people, ask questions, drink in the sights, and consult other passages. Grab your metal detector and discover the precious metals just below the surface. It's filled with wonder! A donkey talking to an obstinate prophet? A nation walking through a dry corridor couched by walls of water? The pinpoint second when the eyes of Jesus opened in a tomb? Awesome!

I love words and enjoy studying definitions of Hebrew and Greek words, especially when they employ word-pictures. I appreciate the father in *My Big Fat Greek Wedding,* who traces every word in the world to a Greek word. Rachel says he reminds her of me. My greatest fear is writing in an unworthy or untrue manner regarding the Bible. I don't claim to be an expert, but my desire is to glean from the Bible and share it in enjoyable, transferable, and practical ways.

Hope's List

The difference between hope and hopelessness often hinges on perspective or attitude. God's words, like medicine, infuse hope and health. Use as needed. Higher dosages are encouraged.

"Remember the word to Your servant, upon which You have caused me to hope. This is my comfort in my affliction, for Your word has given me life" (Psalm 119:49 NKJV).

"This I recall to my mind, therefore I have hope. Through the LORD's mercies we are not consumed. Because His compassions fail not. They are new every morning; great is Your faithfulness. 'The LORD is my portion,' says my soul. Therefore I hope in Him" (Lamentations 3:21-24 NKJV)!

"I pray that God, the source of hope, will fill you completely with joy and peace because you trust in him. Then you will overflow with confident hope through the power of the Holy Spirit" (Romans 15:13).

"I would have lost heart, unless I had believed that I would see the goodness of the LORD in the land of the living. Wait on the LORD; be of good courage, and He shall strengthen your heart; wait, I say, on the LORD" (Psalm 27:13-14 NKJV).

"So humble yourselves under the mighty power of God, and at the right time he will lift you up in honor. Give all your worries and cares to God, for he cares about you" (1 Peter 5:6-7).

"Because You have been my help, therefore in the shadow of Your wings I will rejoice. My soul follows close behind You; Your right hand upholds me" (Psalm 63:7-8 NKJV).

"Abraham believed in the God who brings the dead back to life and who creates new things out of nothing. Even when there was no reason for hope, Abraham kept hoping. Abraham never wavered in believing God's promise. In fact, his faith grew stronger, and in this he brought glory to God. He was fully convinced that God is able to do whatever he promises" (Romans 4:17-18, 20-21).

"Nevertheless we made our prayer to our God…" (Nehemiah 4:9 NKJV)

"The Scriptures give us hope and encouragement as we wait patiently for God's promises to be fulfilled" (Romans 15:4).

The Father's Blessing

This blessing is a compilation of Bible verses. Some things are true of everyone simply because we're all created in God's image. Others are true for those who have found peace with God through Jesus. Read this slowly, and often. Let it captivate, liberate, and overwhelm. Read it aloud. Ask Dad or Mom or someone you admire to read it over you. It will give a new picture of God the Father. Maybe a new picture of you, His treasure.

I have loved you with an everlasting love. With unfailing love I have drawn you to Myself. As the mountains surround Jerusalem, so the Lord surrounds you, both now and forever. The Lord Himself watches over you! The Lord stands beside you as your protective shade. The Lord keeps watch over you as you come and go, both now and forever. I am your shepherd. I am close beside you. Surely, My goodness and unfailing love will pursue you all the days of your life.

I am a shield around you…the One who holds your head high. I keep track of all your sorrows. I have collected all your tears in My bottle. I know everything about you. I know when you sit down or stand up. I go before you and follow you. I place my hand of blessing on your head. I made all the delicate, inner parts of your body and knit you together in your mother's womb. You are fearfully and wonderfully made! How precious are My thoughts about you. They cannot be numbered! They outnumber the grains of sand!

Don't say, "The Lord has deserted me; He has forgotten me." Never! Can a mother forget her nursing child? Can she feel no love for the child she has borne? But even if that were possible, I will not forget you! See, I have written your name on the palms of My hands. Don't be afraid! The Lord your God is living among you. I am a mighty Savior. I will take delight in you with gladness. With My love I will calm all your fears. I will rejoice over you with joyful songs. I reached down from heaven and rescued you; I drew you out of deep waters. I rescued you from your powerful enemies; I support you. I rescued you because I delight in you.

Even before I made the world, I loved you and chose you in Christ to be holy and without fault in My eyes. I decided in advance to adopt you into My own family by bringing you to Me through Jesus Christ. I am so rich in kindness and grace that I purchased your freedom with the blood of My Son and forgave your sins. I bought you with a high price and I will never fail you. I will never abandon you.

I am for you, not against you. Who dares accuse you when I have chosen you for My own? I Myself have given you right standing with Me. Who will condemn you? No one—for Christ Jesus died for you and was raised to life for you, and He is sitting in the place of honor at My right hand, pleading for you. Nothing can separate you from My love. But now, listen to the Lord who created you, the One who formed you: Do not be afraid, for I have ransomed you. I have called you by name; you are Mine! You have been chosen to know Me, believe in Me, and understand that I alone am God. I am slow to anger and filled with unfailing love and faithfulness. Now I honor you by anointing your head with oil; yes, I place My hand of blessing on your head, blessing you with every spiritual blessing.

Love,
Your Heavenly Dad

His-Story Lesson

God has ever desired to bless our planet, has sought relationship with people throughout every age. His rhythm has been to choose a man, a group, a nation—to know Him, live according to His ways, and reveal Him to others. Consider God's words to Abraham, "I will bless you… and you will be a blessing to others" (Genesis 12:2). Sometimes God's people lived this way, but much of their history records opposing notes. In such instances of habitual rebellion and sin, God warns, often through a messenger. When they persist, He disciplines, often through tragedy.

Following the glorious reigns of David and Solomon, the nation of Israel split (930 BC) into ten northern tribes, keeping the name "Israel," and two southern tribes called "Judah." For 200 years Israel veered from God until, in 722 BC, they fell prisoner to a notoriously merciless nation, Assyria—believed by many to have invented the earliest form of crucifixion. See 2 Kings 17. Judah remained, but would they follow God, or Israel's example?

In 627 BC God sent a prophet named Jeremiah to alert Judah of their rebellious ways. If they didn't heed correction, God prescribed their discipline, "You will be in Babylon for seventy years." Amazingly, in the next breath, He forecasted their restoration: "Then I will come and do for you all the good things I have promised, and I will bring you home again. For I know the plans I have for you…plans for good and not for disaster, to give you a future and a hope. In those days when you pray, I will listen. If you look for me wholeheartedly, you will find me. I will end your captivity and restore your fortunes. I will gather you out of the nations where I sent you and will bring you home again to your own land'" (Jeremiah 29:10-14).

Content with their sinful, yet religious, lifestyle, they rejected the message and mistreated the messenger. Time expired in 605 BC. As with Israel, correction came through a pagan nation. King Nebuchadnezzar invaded Jerusalem and trafficked the noblest, including Daniel, Shadrach, Meshach, and Abednego, more than 500 miles to Babylon (50 miles southeast of modern-day Baghdad, Iraq). Ezekiel was about eighteen when he watched his nation seriously unravel.

In 597 BC more were killed in a siege and 10,000 taken captive, including Ezekiel. Five years later, at age 30, God ordained him a minister to his fellow captives, who were hoping this would be a quick stint so they could return home. God instructed Ezekiel to tell them things would get worse. Way worse. Nebuchadnezzar besieged their homeland one more time in 586 BC, this time leveling Jerusalem, destroying the Temple, and killing or deporting most of the remaining population. Jeremiah witnessed this. (2 Kings 24-25. Jeremiah 39.) His book *Lamentations* records his heart-wrenching reaction. Many relocated to Egypt, forcing Jeremiah to go along, and those left behind suffered poverty and chaos in the ruins of their once-glorious nation.

This period is known as The Exile. God's people couldn't descend any lower. Psalm 137 reveals the embittered existence of those stuck in Babylon. No wonder they concluded, "We have become old, dry bones—all hope is gone. Our nation is finished" (Ezekiel 37:11). That the bones in the valley were *scattered* symbolized the nation's extensive scattering among various countries. But God wasn't finished. He promised to put them and their nation back together! Messages eventually turned from judgment to hope. In 539 BC Babylon fell under the command of Persian King Cyrus, setting the stage for at least the initial unfolding of God's promised restoration!

The figurative speech throughout Ezekiel's vision foretold actual events, though various interpretations abound. While some see references to the Messiah, the Holy Spirit, or end times, the purpose of this short lesson is to highlight three post-exilic periods, which may at least in part fulfill the rebuilding and rebirthing of the bones.

1. 538 BC. Cyrus established an edict allowing any captives to go home! Imagine the joyful stir this news evoked! Was this the rattling noise Ezekiel heard? Two years later 50,000 people returned, 70 years after the first deportation, just like Jeremiah predicted! By 516 BC the temple was rebuilt, 70 years after its destruction. (Ezra 1-6. Haggai.)

2. 458 BC. A second group of exiles returned under the direction of a priest named Ezra, who led them in spiritual renewal. Maybe this partially fulfills the life-giving winds Ezekiel saw enter the bodies? (Ezra 7-10.)

3. 445 BC. The bones rising as an army may allude to a third return of exiles, led by newly appointed governor, Nehemiah. God stirred his heart to rebuild the still-broken walls of Jerusalem and stirred the heart of Persian King Artaxerxes to support the project. Though facing discouragement, distraction, and outright opposition, they overcame everything by the good hand of God. Read *Nehemiah* for this fascinating historical account.

To people who regarded the land of their captivity as "graves," God said, "I will open your graves of exile and cause you to rise again. Then I will bring you back to the land of Israel. When this happens, O my people, you will know that I am the LORD (Ezekiel 37:12-13)." According to their own lingo, the miraculous return to their homeland was very much like being raised from the dead!

The point of all this—God literally restored the nation, just as He promised! And what is still to be fulfilled, will be.[166]

---

166 *Life Application Study Bible.* Tyndale. 2004.
The Jamieson, Fausset, and Brown Commentary. Zondervan. 1985.

Experiences!

What has God spoken to you or accomplished in you while reading *God's Restoration Shop*?

www.ingramcontent.com/pod-product-compliance
Lightning Source LLC
Chambersburg PA
CBHW060514080526
44586CB00012B/485